IMAGES
of America

ASHBY

ON THE COVER: Taken in the late 1890s, the cover photograph shows the Ashby Cornet Band. The band was organized in 1886 by a few gentlemen who gathered once or twice a week to practice. As more members joined the group, they gathered donations from clubs and individuals to purchase uniforms and instruments. By 1891, they were playing in various venues in Ashby and surrounding towns. The musicians shown in this photograph are, from left to right, (first row) John Piper, Curtis Huckins, Frank Huckins (behind bass drum), and Lester Parker; (second row) Fred Bernhardt, Walter Hardy, William Partridge, a Mr. Gorkey, Ed Walker, Bill Green, Robert Walker, and John Elliott. (Courtesy of Ashby Historical Society.)

IMAGES
of America

ASHBY

Ashby Historical Society

ARCADIA
PUBLISHING

ISBN 978-1-4671-2371-6

Published by Arcadia Publishing
Charleston, South Carolina

Printed in the United States of America

Library of Congress Control Number: 2014959564

For all general information, please contact Arcadia Publishing:
Telephone 843-853-2070
Fax 843-853-0044
E-mail sales@arcadiapublishing.com
For customer service and orders:
Toll-Free 1-888-313-2665

Visit us on the Internet at www.arcadiapublishing.com

Dedicated to Richard P. Catalini, Nancy S. Jakobowicz, and James A. Stacy

Contents

ACKNOWLEDGMENTS

The latest book of Ashby's colorful history is essentially pictorial in nature, reflecting life in Ashby prior to the 1950s. Captions noting interesting, pertinent, and factual information accompany each image, explaining the time, people, and place. Many residents, both current and former, offered photographs from their personal albums along with their memories and recollections of each one. Some townspeople and others talked about living and growing up in Ashby—activities, celebrations, or businesses that their parents and grandparents had. It would be difficult to name individuals who have helped in so many ways, so please know that your story is included here in this collection, and the book committee thanks you for your valuable contributions.

The Ashby Free Public Library offered valuable meeting space, while making archival materials readily available. Three members of the Townsend Historical Society Book Committee offered advice on organizing and assembling material, based on their experience of having recently published their own book. *A History of Ashby* by Ithamar E. Sawtelle, published in 1890, *The Official Journal—Ashby Bicentennial 1767–1967*, and *A History of the Town of Ashby 1890–2000* were referenced on a regular basis to support and authenticate materials when necessary. *A History of the Ashby Band 1867–1967* provided much otherwise unknown information so unique to Ashby. The Ashby Historical Society archives, housed in the Old Engine House, were especially helpful, reminding the committee of long-forgotten treasures to include in this book.

The idea for a vintage pictorial history of Ashby was presented to the historical society's board about 18 months ago. After discussing the work involved and the necessary people coming forward to help, the board decided to proceed. With the contributions and assistance of numerous people during a lengthy process of collecting materials and information, a small group of historical society members assembled to organize and prepare the manuscript for publication. Much of the legwork and continual scanning of images, plus keeping this project on track, can be attributed to some of the society's members. Thank you.

And a final thank-you goes to the people of Ashby, from our collective ancestors down to the present generation who have persevered through adversity and challenges and peace and prosperity to grant us the privilege of living here in our beautiful New England village of Ashby. May you reflect on happy, youthful memories as you browse through the pages of Ashby's history.

All photographs are courtesy of the Ashby Historical Society unless otherwise noted.

The Ashby Historical Society Book Committee includes Alan W. Pease, Florence Reynolds Bryan, Nancy L. Hargraves Catalini, and Catherine L. Catalini Foster.

INTRODUCTION

The town of Ashby was incorporated on March 5, 1767, comprising land from Lunenburg, Fitchburg, Townsend, and Ashburnham. Its 12,283 acres of hilly and diversified land are rocky, with numerous outcroppings of granite, including Mount Watatic, which has the highest elevation in town and resembles a dome-shaped wigwam (*witeauk* in Algonkian).

The first settlers included the families of James Colman, James Locke, and John Fitch, a noted citizen by virtue of his and his family's capture by Indians in the 1744 war with France.

Following incorporation as an official town, the first town meeting was held at the house of Peter Lawrence. Measures were soon taken to erect a house of worship, and it was completed enough to be occupied by 1771. To administer justice, the town built stocks and placed them upon the town common, where they served as a public disgrace for anyone who violated the "good order" that had been established. Thus the citizens of Ashby prospered and enjoyed the freedom to trade and govern themselves while still acknowledging their allegiance to the Crown. As soon as the British government resolved to put in force its measures of oppression, Ashby and other colonial towns became involved in the Revolutionary War. Ashby was largely represented at battles such as Bunker Hill, Ticonderoga, Saratoga, West Point, and Valley Forge.

Although many of the citizens of Ashby gave their lives for freedom, from 1800 to 1840, the population continued to grow due to the desire of people to own and farm their own land and create local industries. Local sawmills cut lumber for building homes, and there were tub and pail factories, blacksmiths, and stores along with other small industries, including a pipe organ manufacturer. In the 1790s, a significant clock-making industry began with two competing families, the Edwards and the Willards. It is estimated that over 1,000 tall case clocks were produced in Ashby. The gears of the clock movements were made entirely of wood. Many of these wooden-geared clocks survive in museums and homes around the United States.

The population of Ashby would not see a high level of population again until 1950. Historical reasons for the decrease of population were varied and impacted Ashby in different ways. For instance, in the 1860s, 118 men who served in the Civil War saw other parts of the country, and the Homestead Act was in effect, encouraging people to settle the West.

Although a railroad to Ashby was planned at one time, it never materialized, and thus Ashby had no fast and convenient way to ship its wares to other cities like Fitchburg or Boston. Industrialization like the textile mills in Lowell, Massachusetts, were a monetary draw for some of the citizens, and the mechanization of agriculture, the mainstay of Ashby, consolidated farms.

From 1900 to 1950, other changes occurred in Ashby. In 1906, Loveland's Mill received electricity and initially was able to provide up to six hours of power a day to the center of town. The automobile made Ashby accessible now that people had the ease, ability, and freedom to travel. In 1935, the Federal Home Loan Association offered loans to people who wished to buy their own homes. It was during this time that the last of Ashby's many mills closed, and the one-room classrooms were combined to become a centralized school system.

Today, one can still stand on the quaint town common in front of the 1809 meetinghouse and look over an area that has undergone little change in the past 170 years. Join us now as we journey through the photographs of a time in Ashby's past that still resonates with us today.

One

FAMILIES AND FARMS

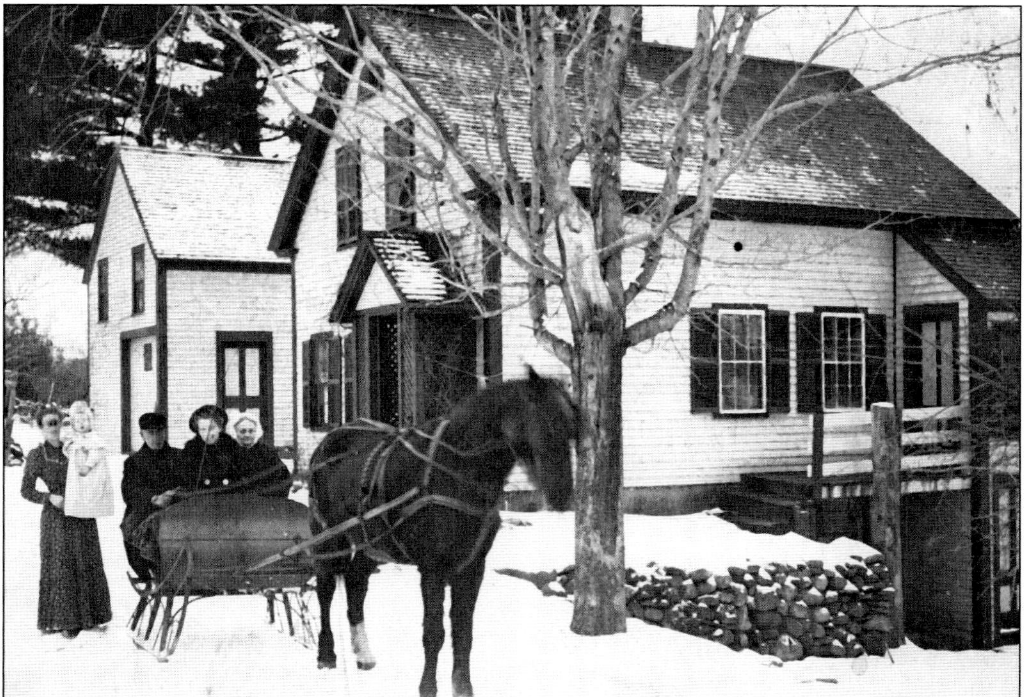

This house on Erickson Road was owned by the Wheeler family from 1858 until 1970. Here, one of the Wheeler women greets guests arriving in a sleigh about 1900. (Courtesy of Carol Bennett Lielasus.)

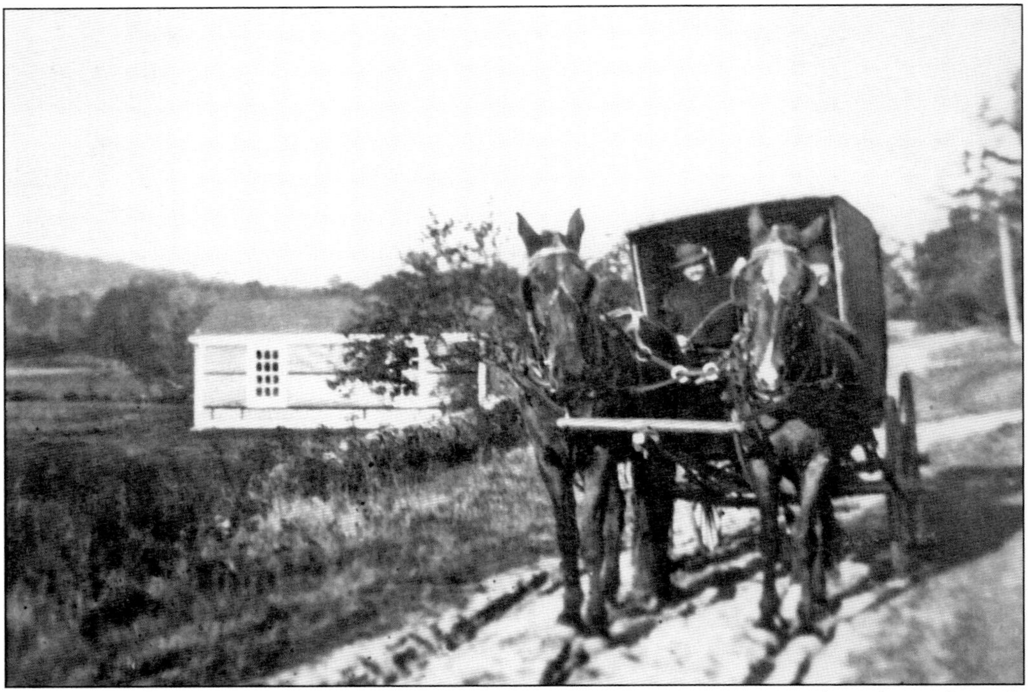

Here, Walter Bennett is driving his school hack, or bus, on Bennett Road in the early 20th century. Horse-drawn hacks delivered children from all parts of Ashby to the new Lyman School. (Courtesy of Carol Bennett Lielasus.)

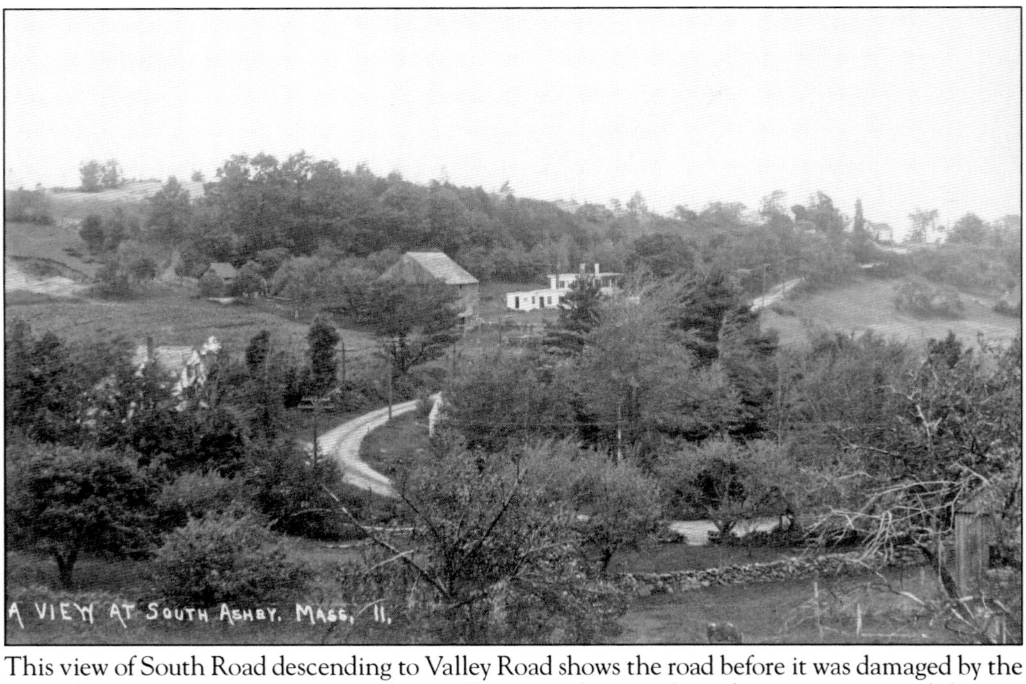

This view of South Road descending to Valley Road shows the road before it was damaged by the embankment giving way under it. The road has since been realigned to improve its stability.

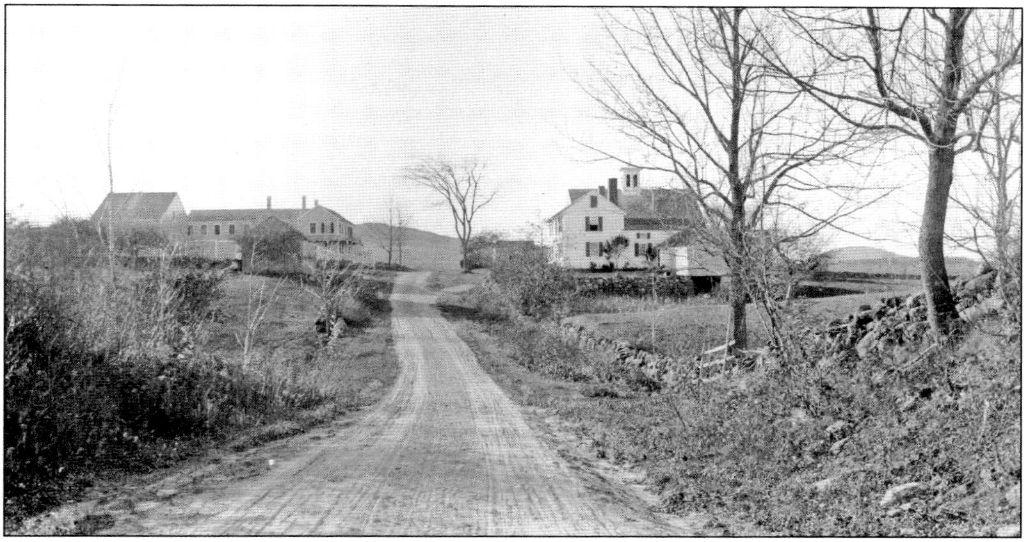

This view looks west along Piper Road, with the Woodside Inn on the left and what is now Michael Reggio's farm on the right. Much of the land in Ashby was cleared for agriculture at the time, creating views that are no longer available since the return of the forests. Mount Nemosett, now Blood Hill, can be seen in the distance at the center, and Mount Watatic is between the trees on the right.

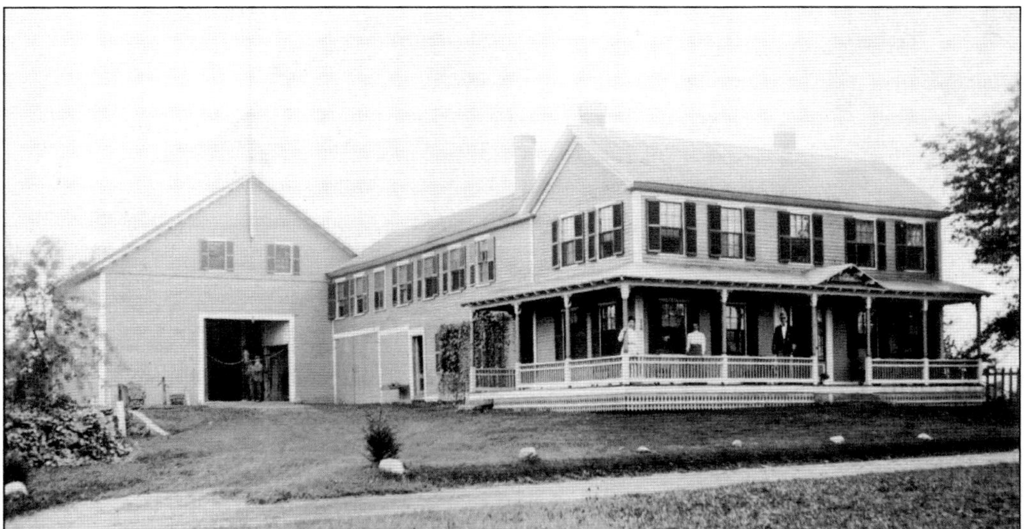

The Woodside Inn on Piper Road is one of several inns that catered to summer visitors from metropolitan areas in 1895. In the days before air-conditioning, those who could afford to went to the country to escape the heat of the cities.

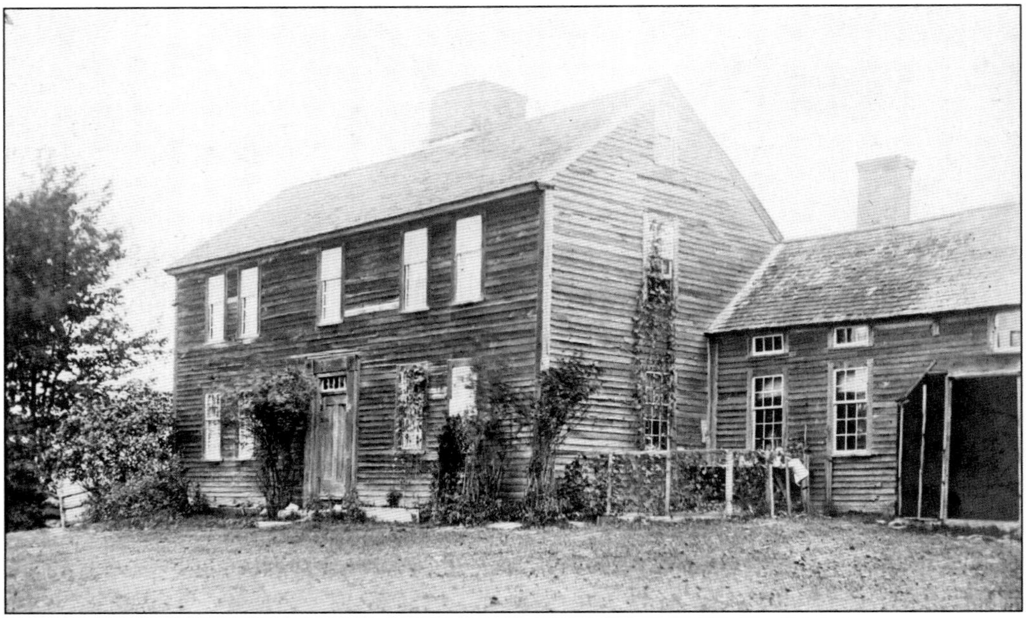

The oldest house in Ashby was photographed about 1900. It was built in 1764, three years before John Fitch's garrison was overrun by Algonkian Indians. The design is a classic center-entry Colonial with a large center chimney. It is notable that the house is not painted, but rather the clapboards are left raw. The lack of paint meant the clapboards would need to be replaced more frequently, and newly replaced clapboard is apparent just to the right of the second-story center window. (Courtesy of William and Katherine Stanwood.)

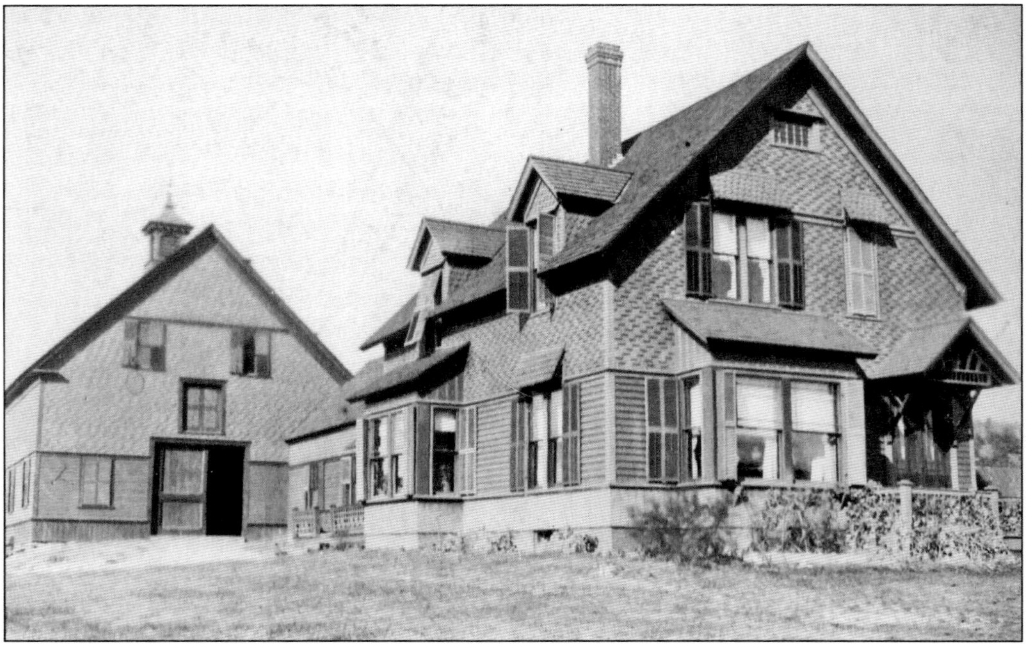

This Shingle Style home was built by Phillip and Katherine Piper in the mid-1880s on Piper Road. It was a successful chicken and produce farm through the 1930s. The home is now owned by Richard and Nancy Catalini. Nancy is a descendant of the Pipers. (Courtesy of Richard and Nancy Catalini.)

Here are John W. and Emeline Piper at their 53rd wedding anniversary, celebrated in 1899 at their son Philip's home. The furnishings and interior decoration show the increasing wealth and sophistication of the residents of the town as business ventures began to supplant agriculture as a source of income. (Courtesy of Richard and Nancy Catalini.)

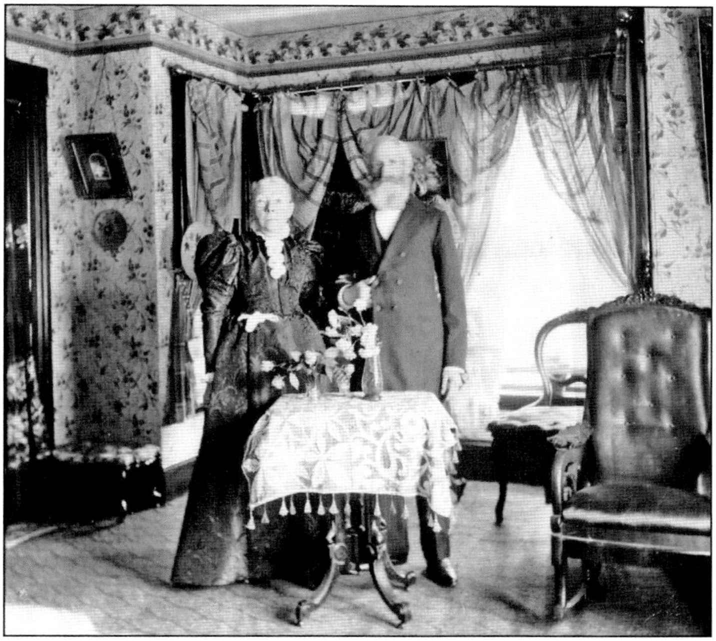

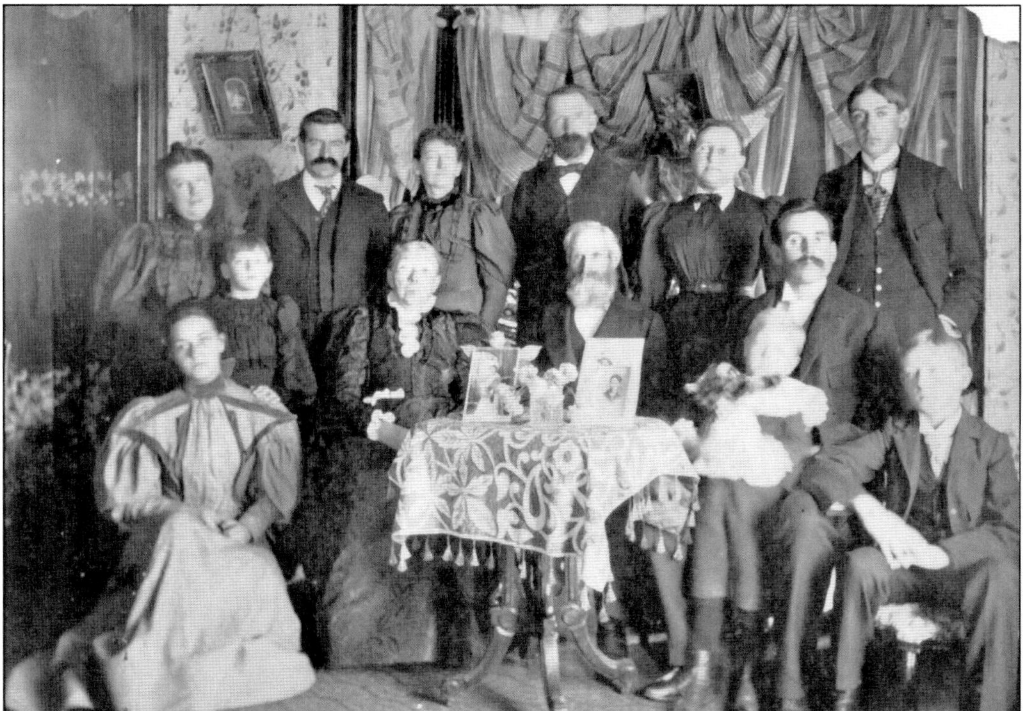

The family of John W. and Emeline Piper is gathered in their parlor. Pictured here are, from left to right, (first row) unidentified, Walter Piper, and Edward Piper; (second row) Cora Piper, Emeline Piper, John W. Piper, and unidentified; (third row) Katherine Piper, Philip Piper, Emily Piper, John A. Piper, Abbie Piper Curtis, and Philip Curtis. In the picture on the table is Florence Piper, a nursing student at Burbank Hospital. (Courtesy of Richard and Nancy Catalini.)

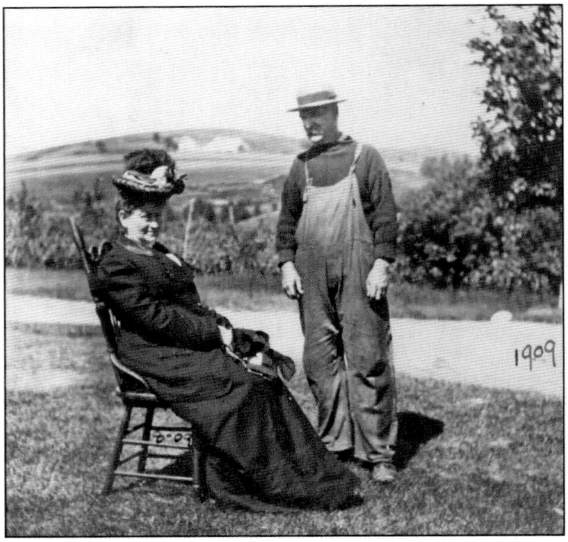

Emily and John A. Piper are pictured here on their front lawn in 1909. Emily appears ready to go to town, while John is dressed for another day of farming. (Courtesy of Richard and Nancy Catalini.)

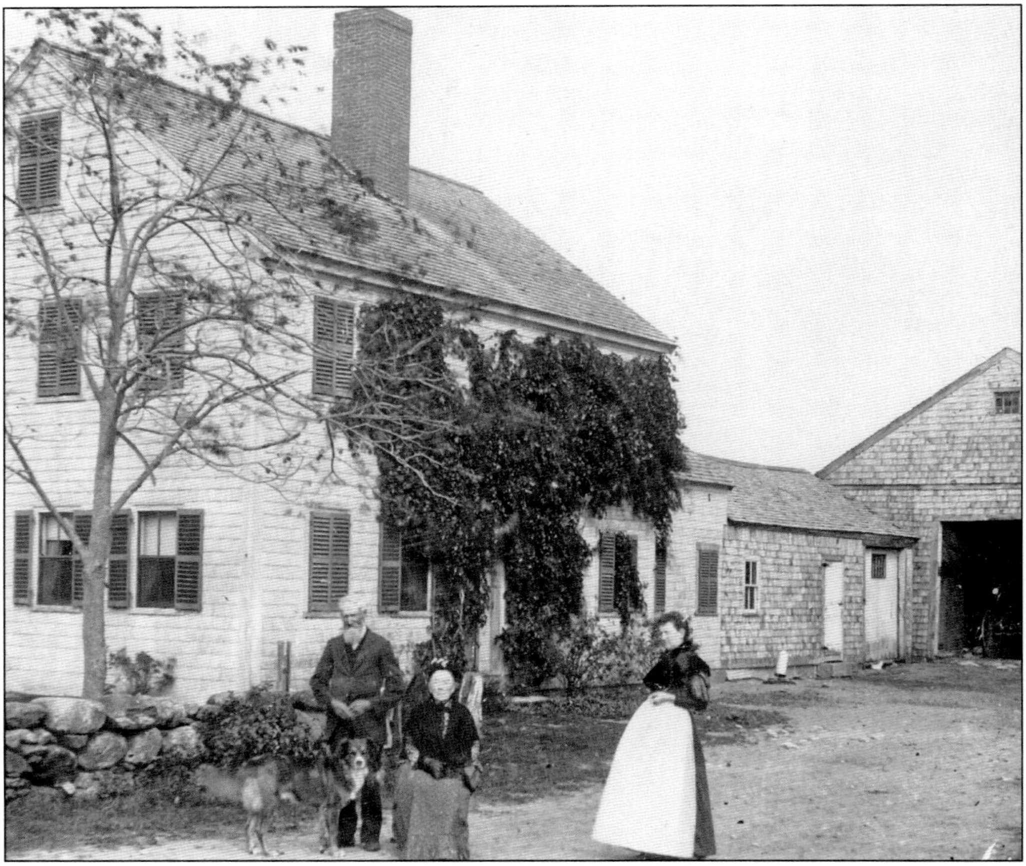

John W. Piper and his family are pictured here in front of their family home in 1896. The house with attached barns was built in the 18th century. It survived two major fires. The second fire, in 1920, destroyed the barns but spared the house when the wind direction changed. The neighbors arrived to help fight the fire and managed to empty the house of its contents in minutes. (Courtesy of Richard and Nancy Catalini.)

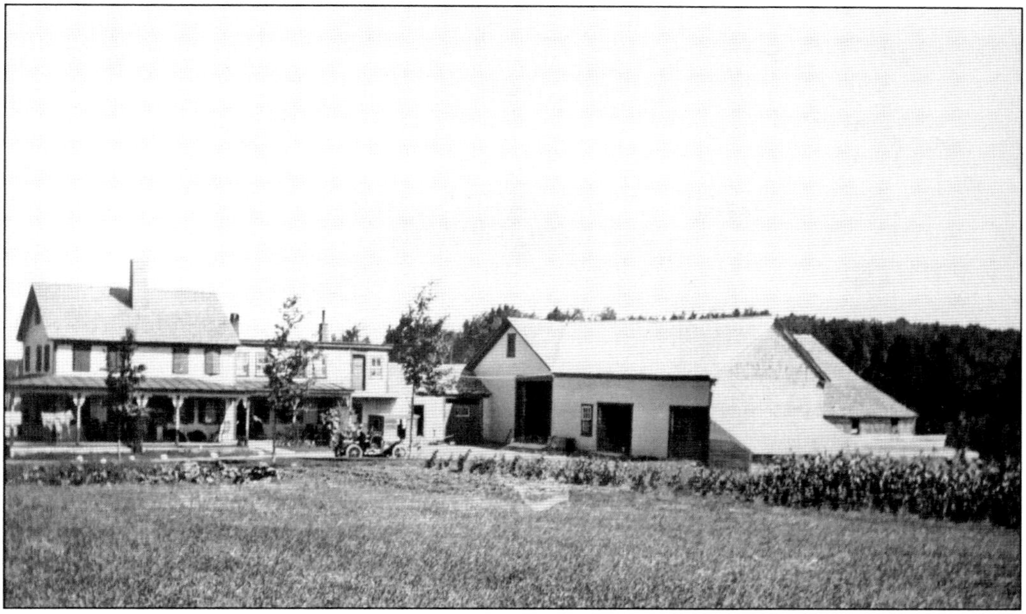

This is a summertime view of the John A. Piper homestead before the 1912 fire. In the drive are two automobiles. Charles Metchear, Piper's son-in-law, was one of the first Ashby residents to purchase an automobile. (Courtesy of Richard and Nancy Catalini.)

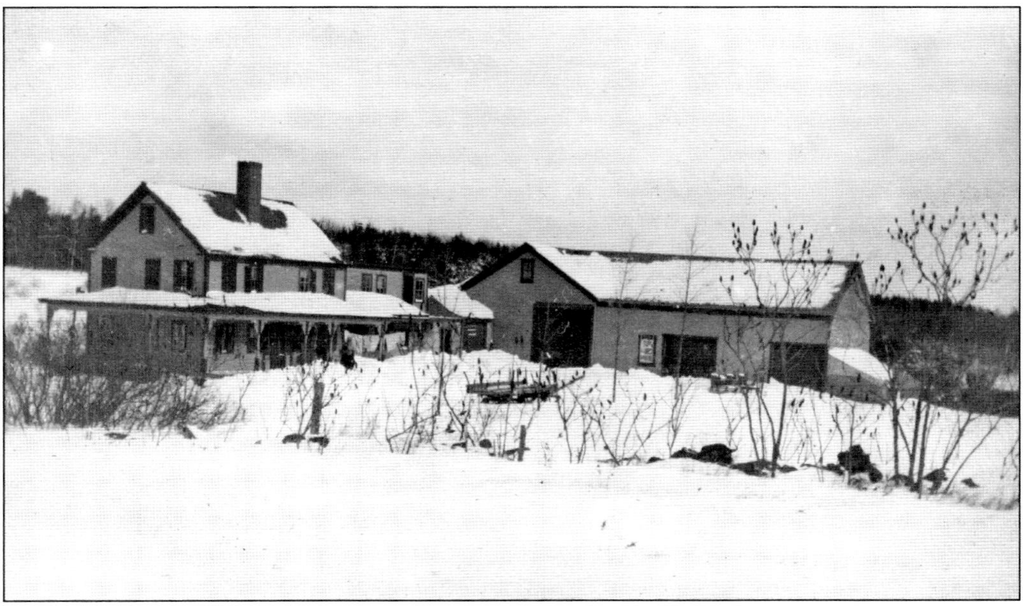

Pictured here in December 1909, the Piper homestead has a work sled and a sleigh in front of the barn ready to go. The sleigh was used to deliver milk and eggs to market in Ashby. The work sled was used to haul heavy loads such as timber across the snow. The lilac bushes along the stone wall are ancestral to those blooming there today. (Courtesy of Richard and Nancy Catalini.)

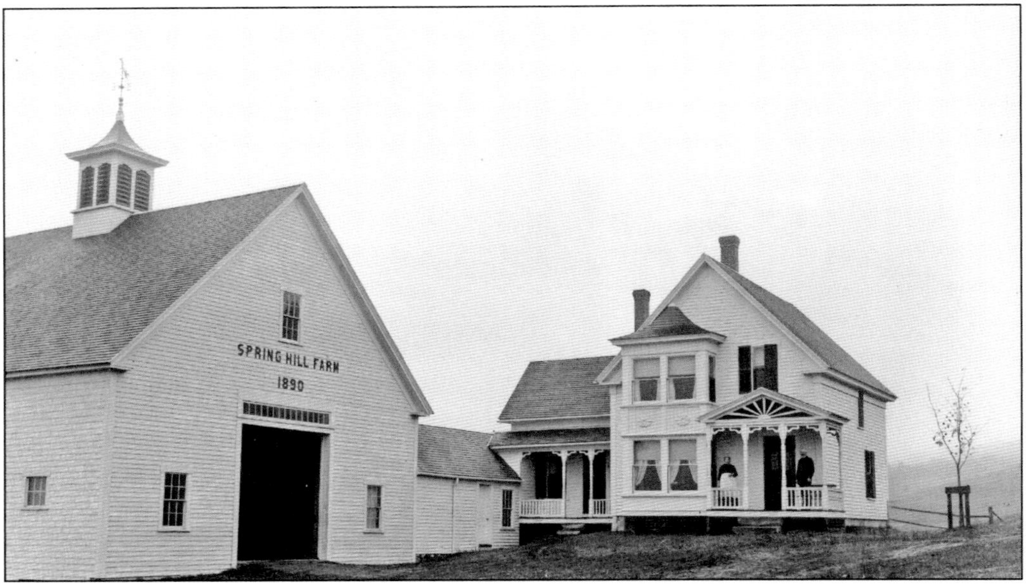

Spring Hill Farm, located at the top of Spring Hill Road, was representative of farms in Ashby that produced hay, potatoes, oats, dairy products, apples, and grapes for home use as well as to send to market in Fitchburg and Boston. This photograph shows the farm as it appeared about 1900.

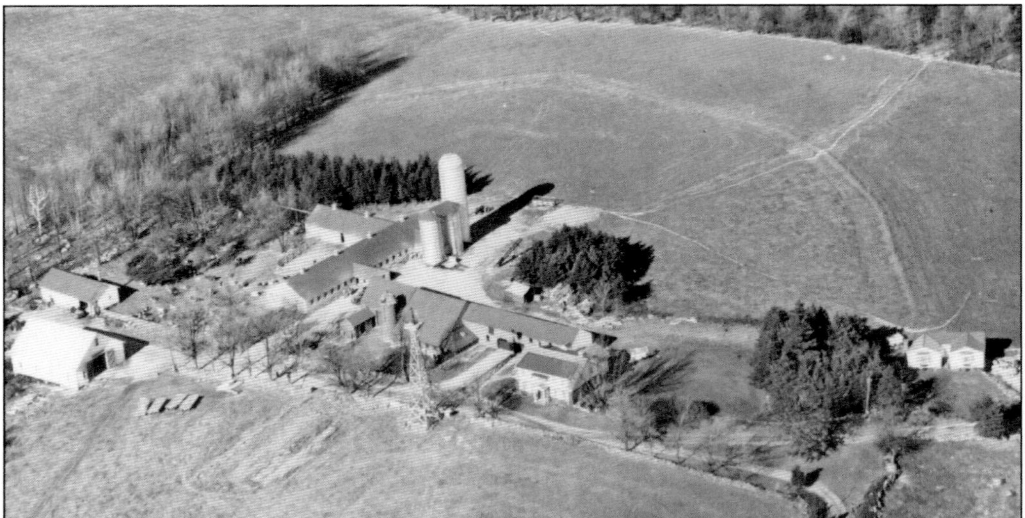
This is an aerial photograph of Jewell Hill Farm on Crocker Road in 1952. The farm of about 300 acres has been in the Crocker family since 1917. The Jewell Hill Farm was one of the more successful dairy farms in Ashby. The year this photograph was taken, the farm won the Green Pastures Award for the best dairy farm in Massachusetts. The farm ended dairy production in 1986, when the Department of Agriculture bought the herd as part of a national program to reduce milk production.

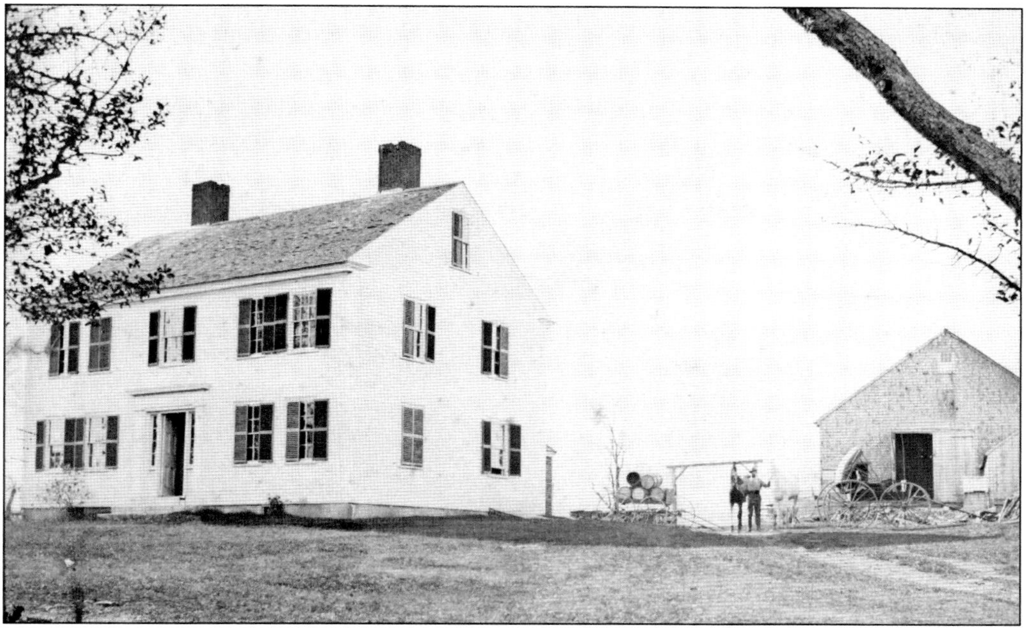

This farmhouse was built in 1835 by Jesse Foster's father. In 1841, the barn was struck by lightning and burned to the ground. The neighbors gathered together to build the new barn shown in this photograph. Jesse's father died later that year. Jesse noted that when his mother remarried several years later, the property was sold to "foreigners."

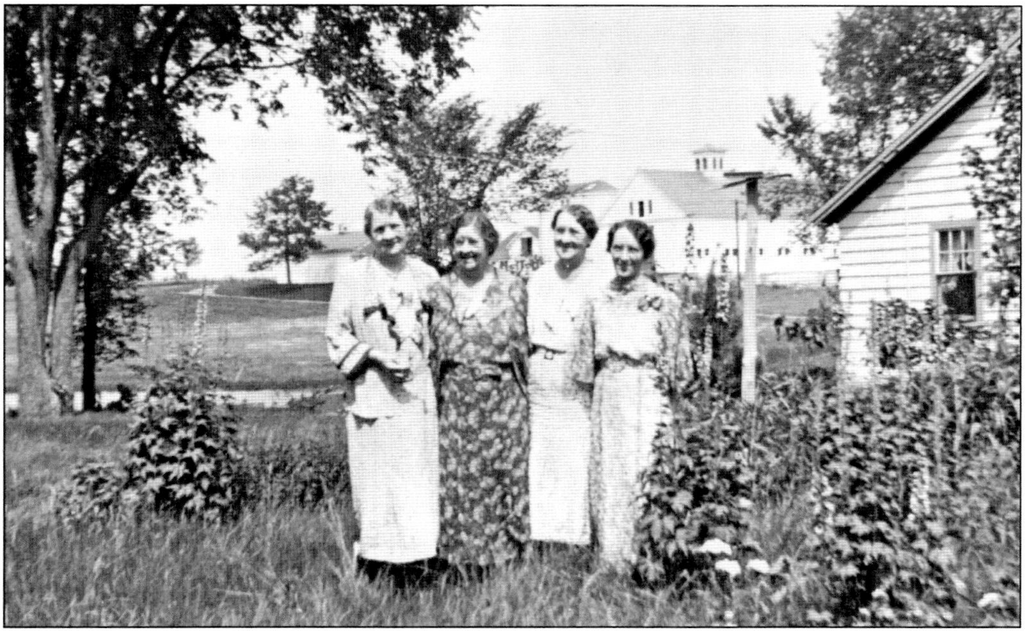

This photograph was taken at the home of Alfred and Lena (Sunbury) Holmes, parents of Irma Holmes Catalini, in the 1920s. The Ashby Stock Farm is in the background. From left to right, Ethel, Jennie, and Ida are visiting their sister Lena for a Sunbury family reunion. The sisters were four of the 12 children of Abigail Rolfe Sunbury. (Courtesy of Richard and Nancy Catalini.)

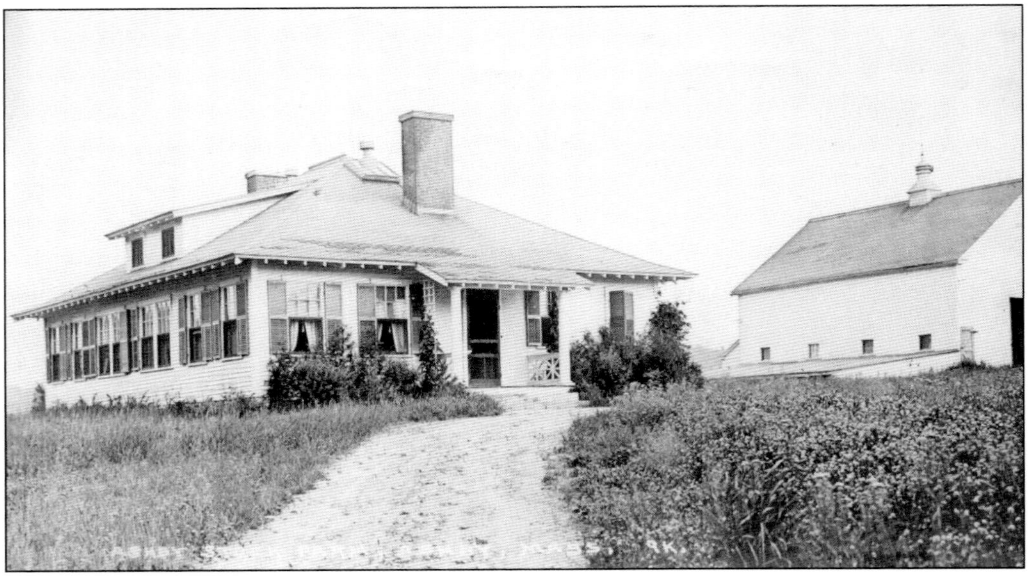

The Ashby Stock Farm was one of the major farms in the community. The house, which still can be seen, is built in the cottage or bungalow style popular in the early 20th century. It was built on the site of the Willard mansion, which burned to the ground in the late 1890s. (Courtesy of William and Katherine Stanwood.)

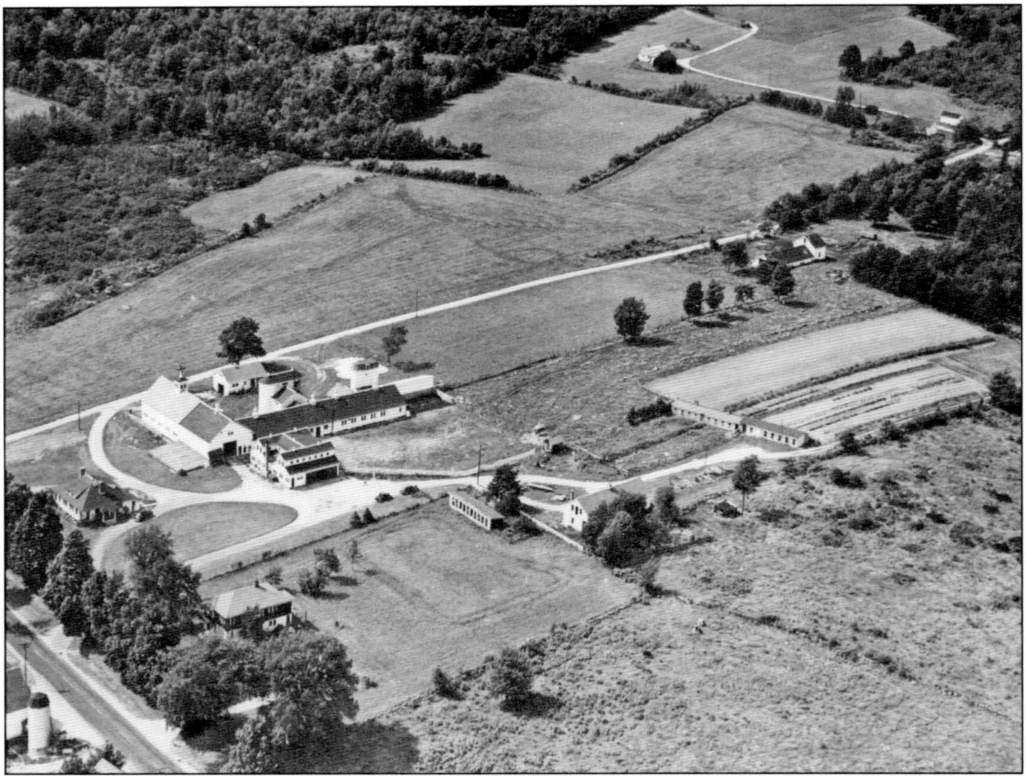

This aerial view of the Ashby Stock Farm from about 1940 shows its extensive operations. Although it was primarily a dairy farm, chickens and pigs were also raised for family consumption and outside sale. (Courtesy of Charles Parlee.)

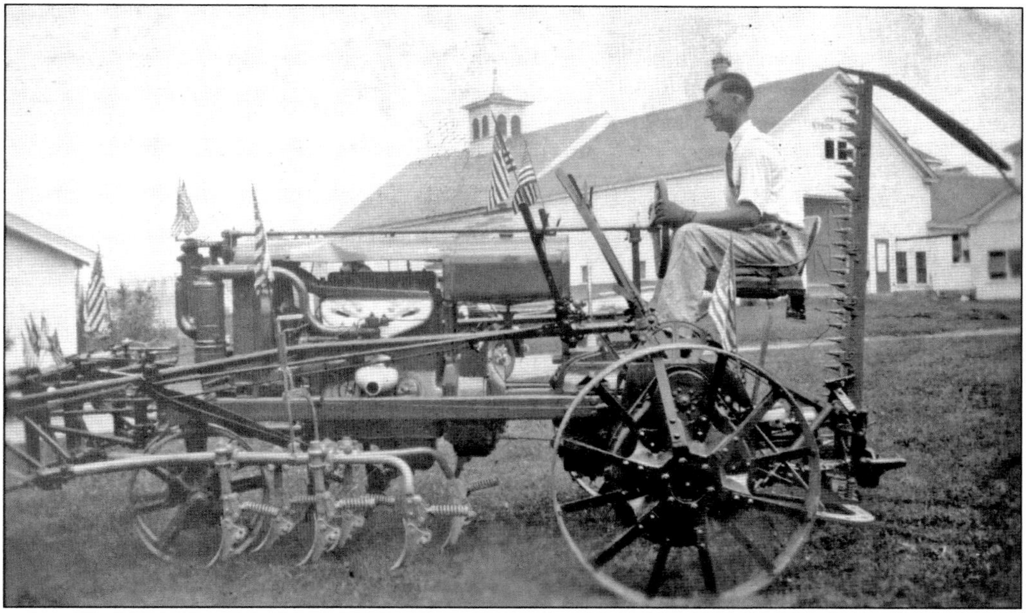

George Elliott Sr. is pictured here on a 1920s Farmall Regular tractor with cutter bar and cultivator at the Ashby Stock Farm. The 16-horsepower Regular combined a tricycle wheel pattern, high ground clearance, and interchangeable implements to become known as the tractor that replaced the horse on the farm. In this photograph, the tractor is fitted out with flags and appears to be headed to a parade. (Courtesy of Nancy Elliott Rogers.)

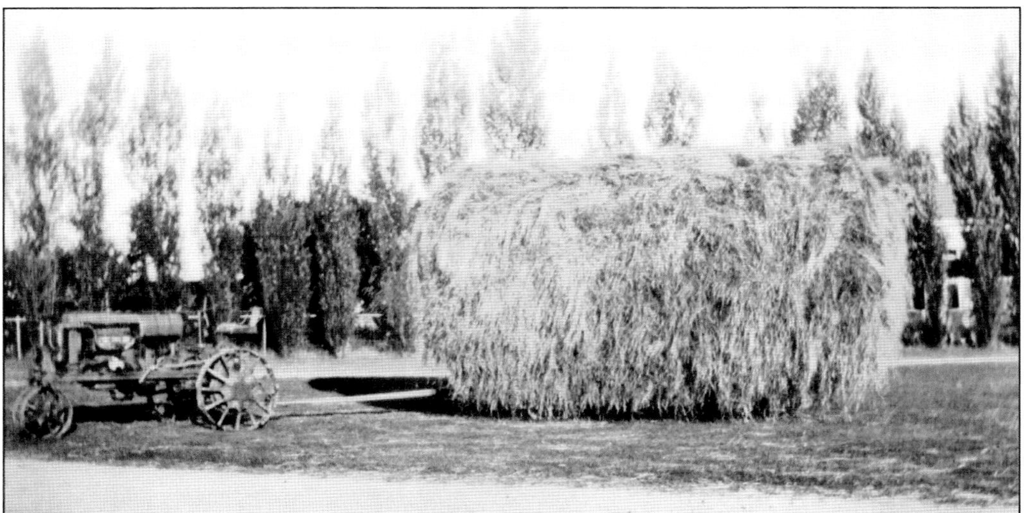

Farmers were proud of their accomplishments, and a record wagonload of hay deserved a photograph. The margin of this photograph, taken at the Stock Farm in the 1920s, notes that there are 4,850 pounds of hay on the wagon. (Courtesy of Nancy Elliott Rogers.)

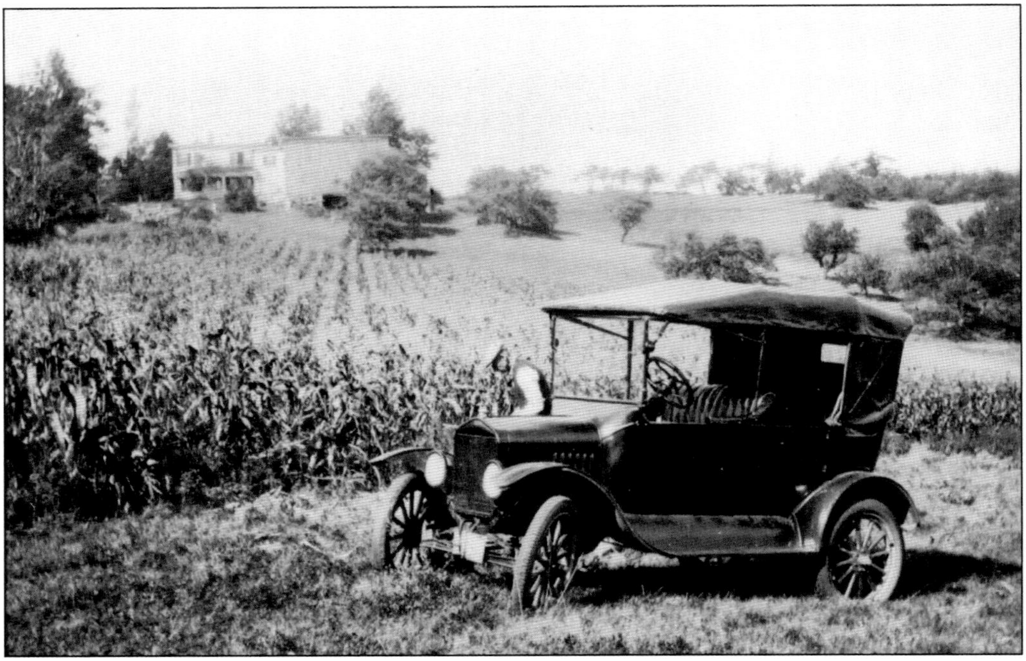

Ashby's economy in the 1920s was based on agriculture, wood mills, and tourism. Of the three, agriculture was the most important, and successful farmers had high status in the town. Many roads received their names from the family that owned the largest farm along the roadway. Here, John Elliott stands by his automobile on his farm about 1925. Elliott Road is behind the trees at the left of this photograph. (Courtesy of Nancy Elliott Rogers.)

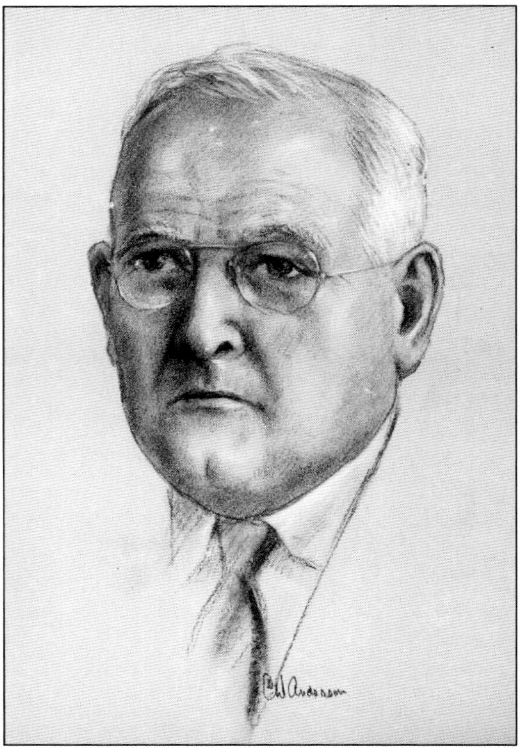

Frank Lyman was a successful businessman in the meatpacking and textile industries. He is shown here in a drawing by C.W. Anderson. Lyman lived at Brook Knoll along with his wife, Frieda, most of his adult life and was the last of the Lymans to occupy the house. (Courtesy of Warren Lyman.)

Florence Lyman was the daughter of Jesse and Mary Chapman Lyman. Born in 1888, she would marry Robert Wallace of Fitchburg. (Courtesy of Warren Lyman.)

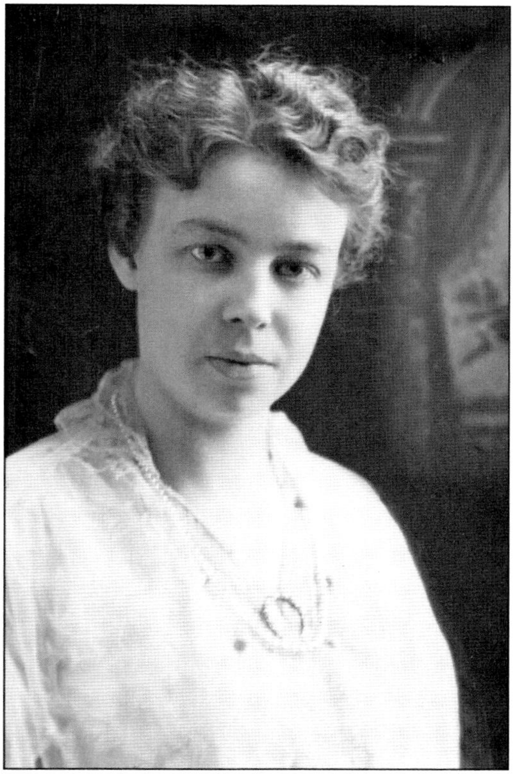

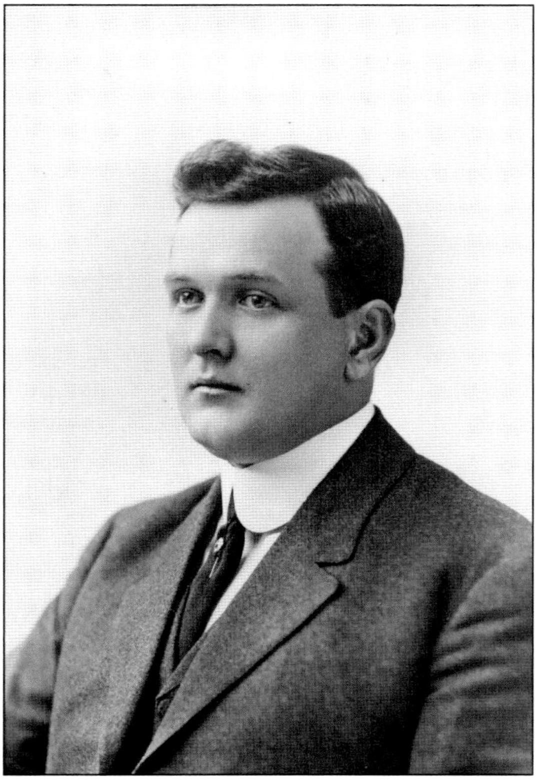

Jesse Lyman was a successful businessman who started his career in Chicago and moved to the Boston area. He lived at Brook Knoll on South Road from about 1906 to 1931 and owned the Ashby Stock Farm as well as the Blue Band Tea Room. He donated the land for the Lyman School. (Courtesy of Warren Lyman.)

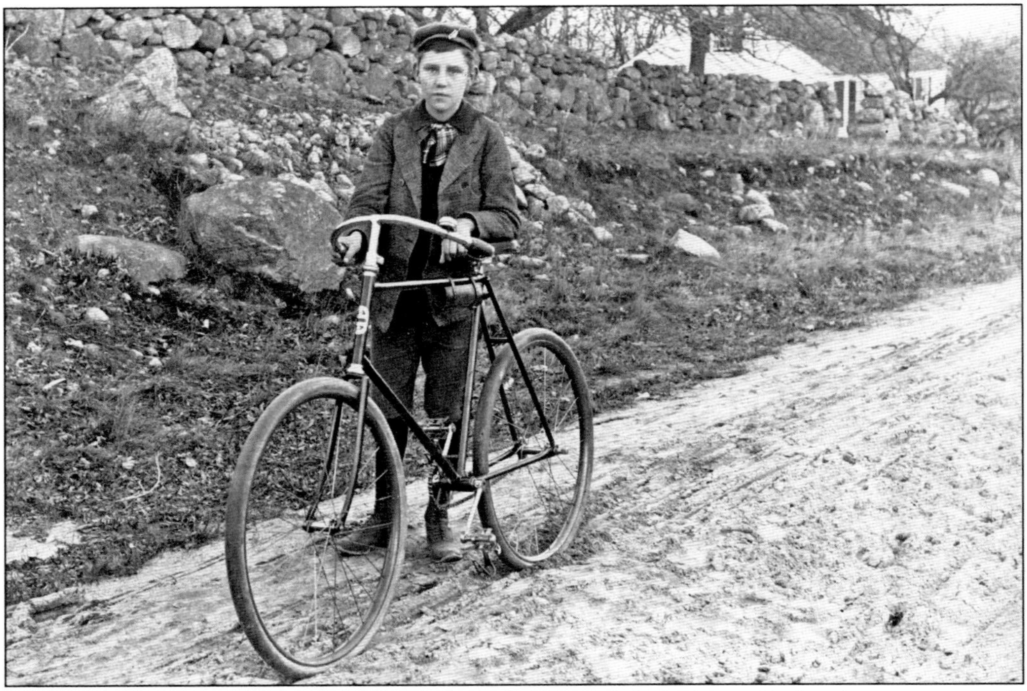

Carl Foster is pictured here traveling with his bicycle in 1898. Young Carl is fortunate enough to have the new "safety" bicycle with pneumatic tires. Despite the fact it had no brakes and the pedals were not freewheeling, it was safer than the high-wheeled ordinary bicycle of the day. Apparently, bicycling did Carl some good, for he lived to the age of 100.

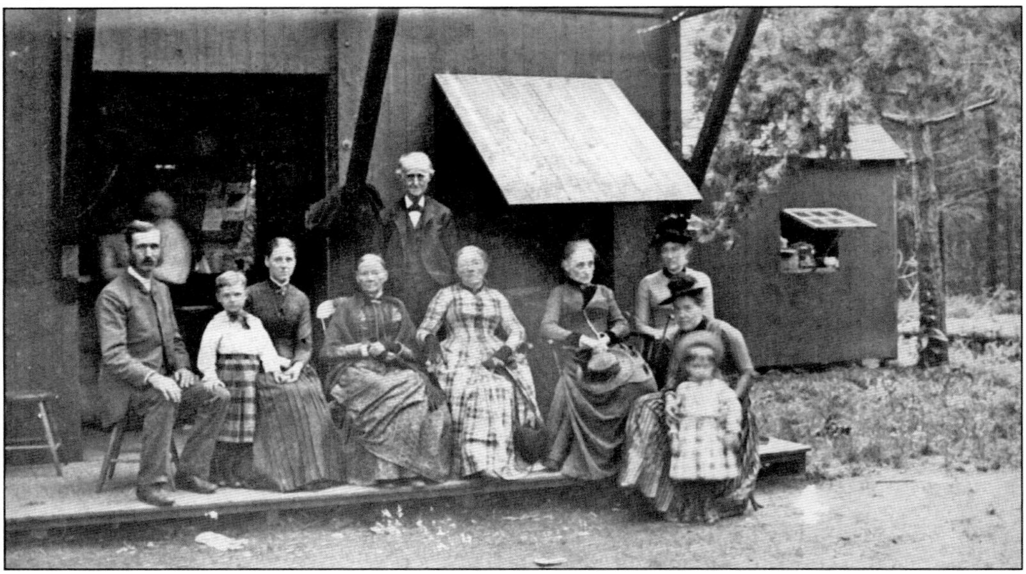

Rufus and Susan Wheeler operated a seasonal store at Damon Pond in the first years of the 20th century. The Willard Brook with its quick-moving waters and easy access by road attracted visitors in search of relaxation and cool, fresh air throughout the 19th and 20th centuries. Damon Pond, created by damming the brook, was a natural stop for swimming and picnicking. Ashby residents saw opportunity to make some extra money serving the travelers. (Courtesy of Carol Bennett Lielasus.)

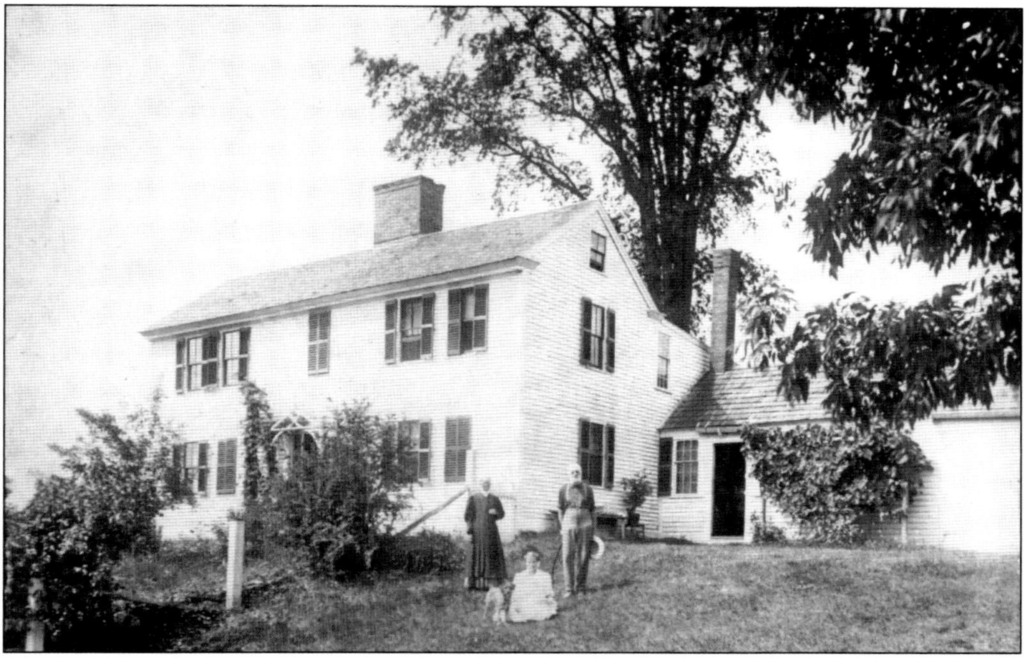

Francis and Mary Wheeler are pictured here with granddaughter Frances Louise Wheeler in front of their farmhouse on Wheeler Road in 1910. Francis was a veteran of the Civil War and served with the 53rd Massachusetts Volunteers. This farmhouse still stands on Wheeler Road. (Courtesy of Ken and Cathy Johnson.)

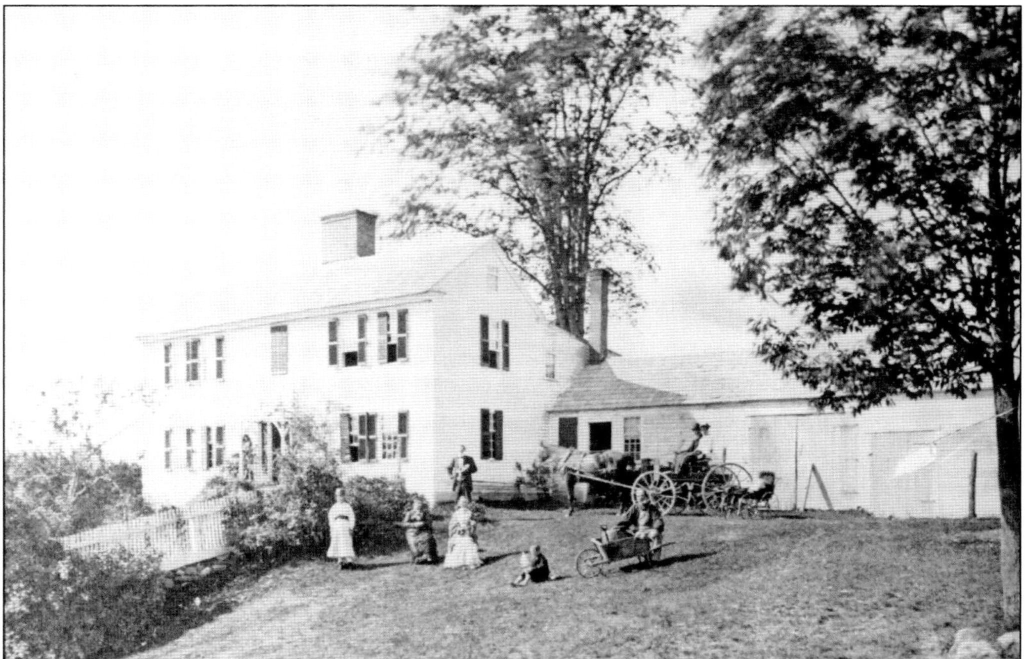

The family of Francis Wheeler is pictured here in front of their farmhouse in 1890. In 1775, this structure was the Samuel S. Stone Tavern, which served as a gathering spot for Ashby colonists chafing under rule from Britain. (Courtesy of Ken and Cathy Johnson.)

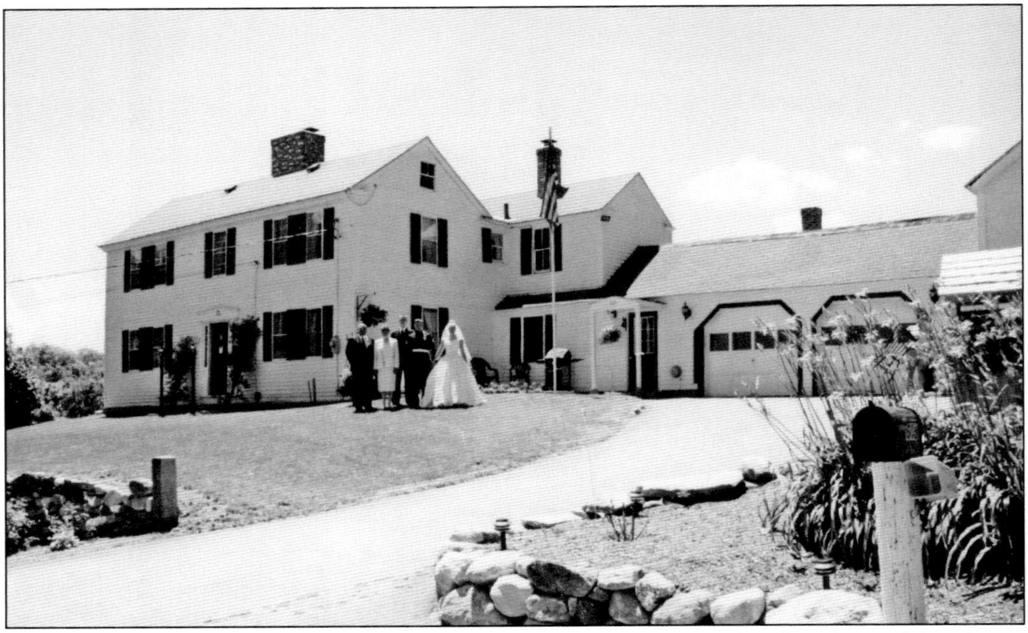

This is the only recent photograph in the book and shows the Johnson family in front of their home in 2001. It is the same building that had been the Samuel S. Stone Tavern in the 18th century and the Wheeler home in the 19th and 20th centuries. (Courtesy of Ken and Cathy Johnson.)

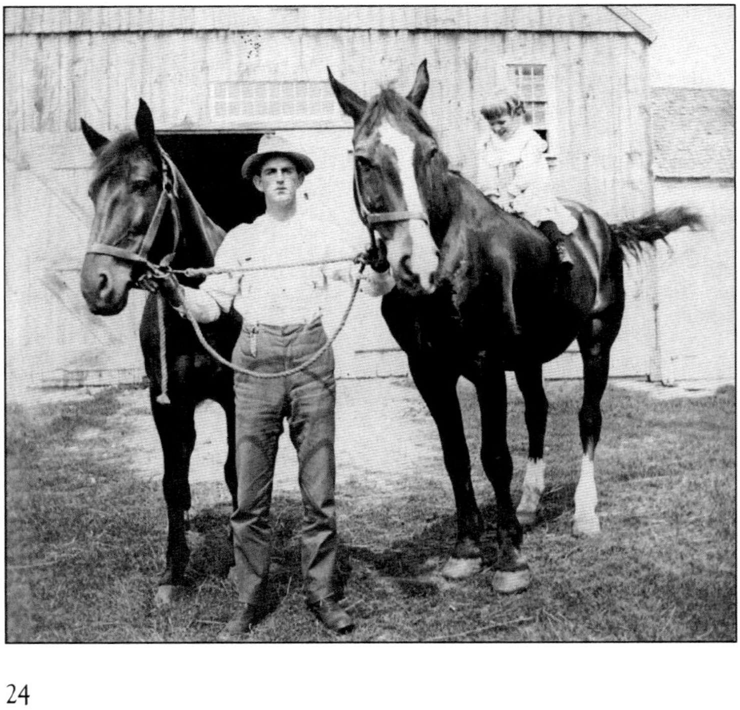

John Lawrence shows off two horses with a young girl, perhaps his daughter, straddling one about 1910. Part of growing up in Ashby was learning to ride a horse, as it was the primary means of transport. However, by the time this young girl grows up, the automobile will have replaced the horse on Ashby roads.

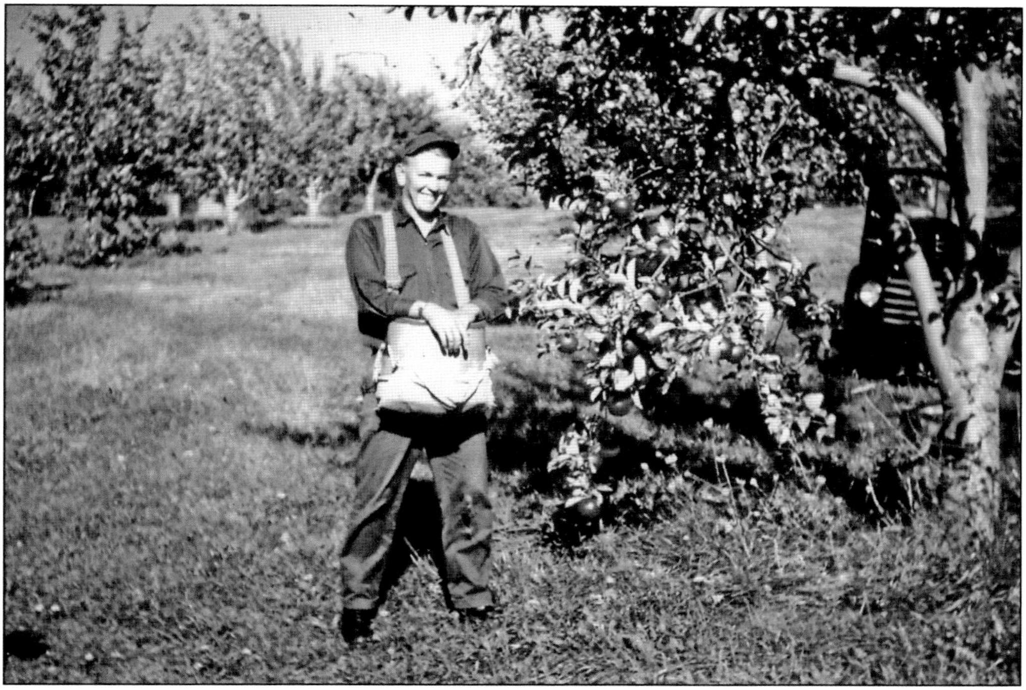

During the 20th century, several farms ran profitable apple orchards. Here, Richard Saari is picking apples at the Saari orchard in 1967. Farmers would need family members as well as hired pickers to get the apples in once they ripened. (Courtesy of George Saari.)

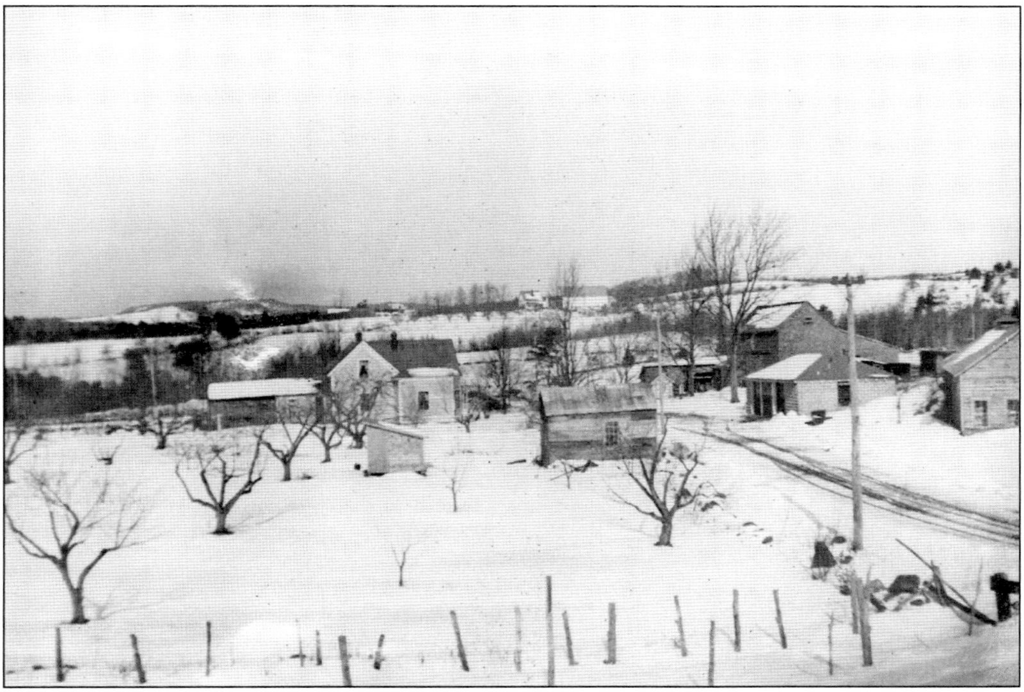

The Saari orchards, as seen in the 1930s, are located in the Foster Road and Greenville Road area. A variety of apples, including Macintosh, Cortland, and Delicious, were grown here throughout most of the 20th century. (Courtesy of George Saari.)

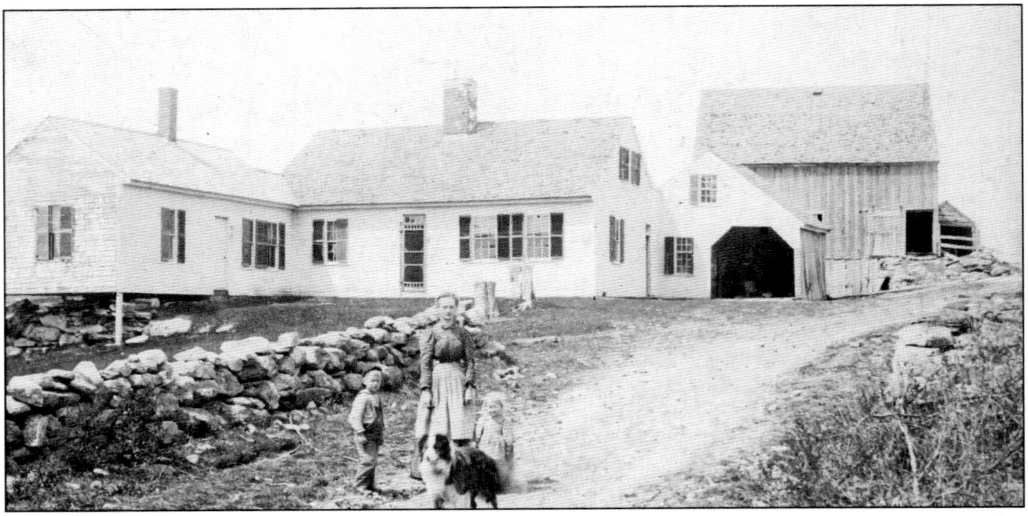

The Wellington home, on Ashby Rindge Road, has been in the family since 1759. Edith Fuller Wellington and her sons Charles and Harry are pictured here; in the photograph, Harry is wearing a dress. Boys often wore dresses until they reached the age of breeching, when they were allowed to wear pants or breeches. This custom facilitated potty-training in the days before the zipper.

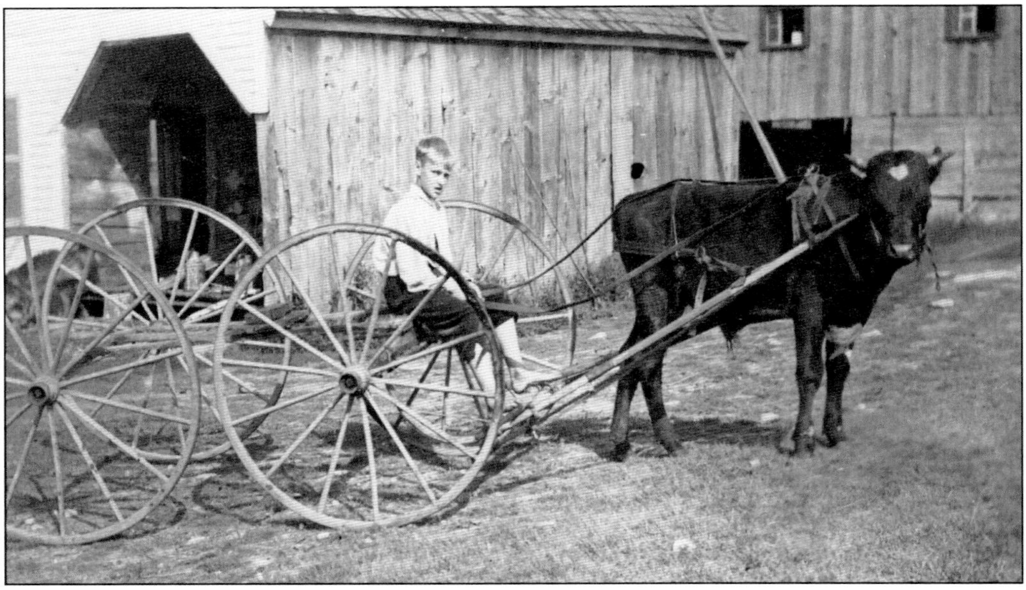

Charles Wellington is seen here working with a young steer pulling wagon gear about 1900. Farmers often bought just the wagon gear and outfitted it as needed. This gear could be outfitted as a buckboard, hay wagon, or farm wagon and might serve as any or all of them over the course of the year.

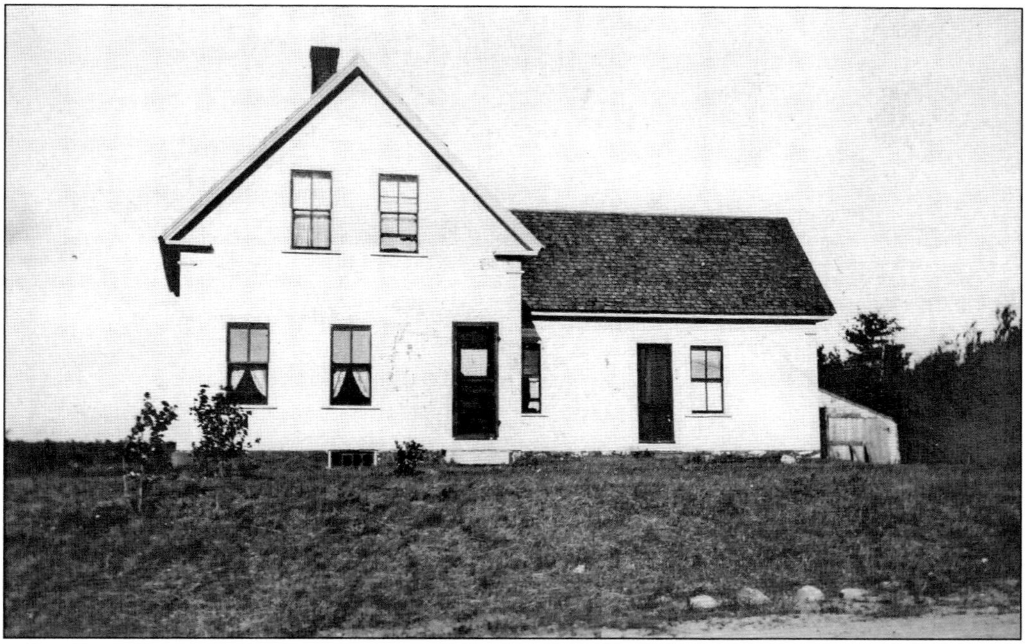

This is the house that Fred Stacy built for his family in 1900 on West Road. The house would serve as the family home until 1968. The family raised chickens and sheep and sold gasoline in addition to operating Stacy's sawmill. (Courtesy of the Stacy family.)

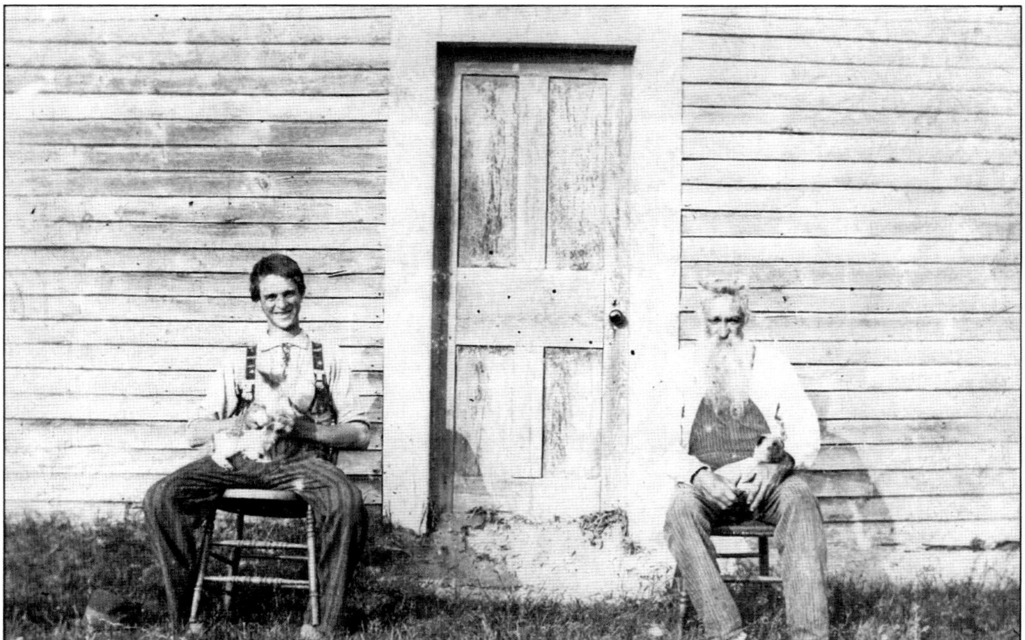

Fred Stacy (left) and Alvah A. Stacy are pictured here in 1894. The Stacy family owned a farm on the northern side of town, and young Fred would buy Holt's Mill in about seven years. (Courtesy of the Stacy family.)

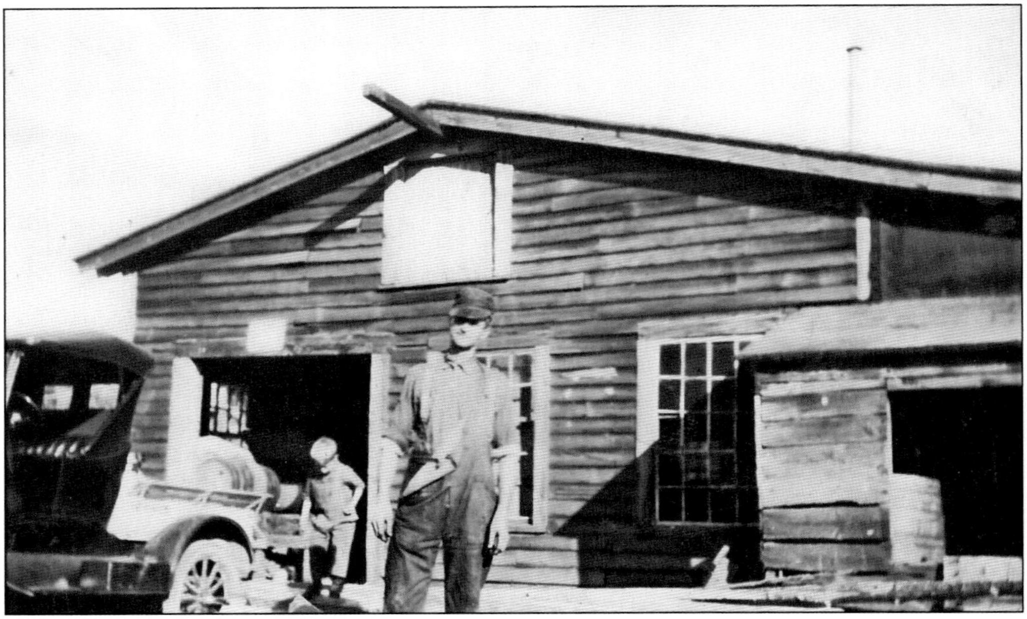

Fred Stacy stands here in front of his mill on West Road about 1922. Ashby's water-powered mills primarily processed the abundant timber of the town. Stacy's mill sawed lumber and made shingles. (Courtesy of the Stacy family.)

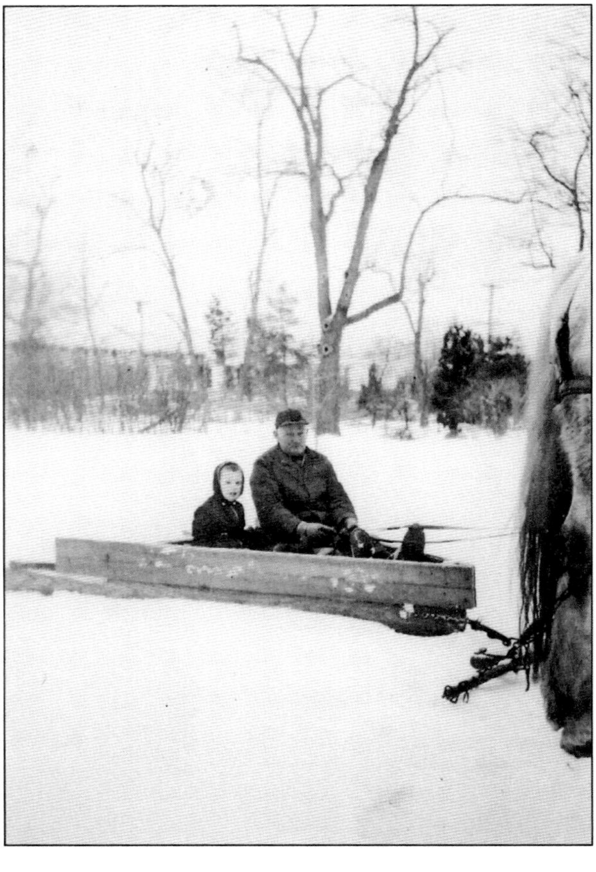

This horse-drawn snowplow was used to keep the roads passable during the winter. The plow would push away the loose snow and pack the remainder underneath it to provide a firm surface for sleighs and carriages. The driver was exposed to the weather, so plowing did not begin until the storm had ended. (Courtesy of the Stacy family.)

Two

BUSINESS

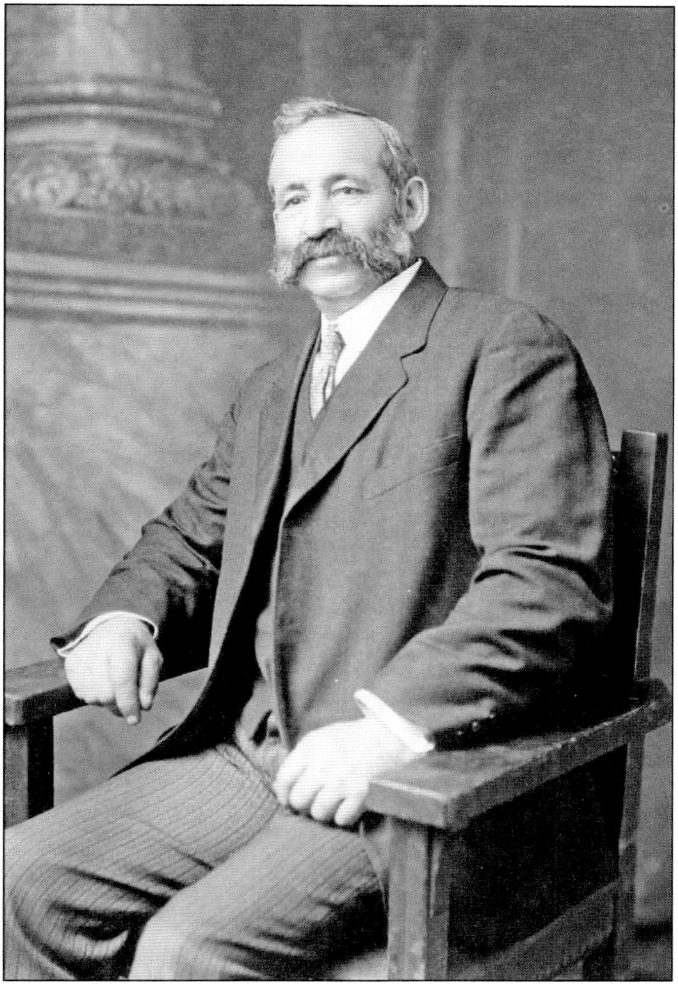

David Damon ran a successful construction company in the late 19th and early 20th centuries. He built the Ashby Library and the Lyman School in addition to working on the state highway.

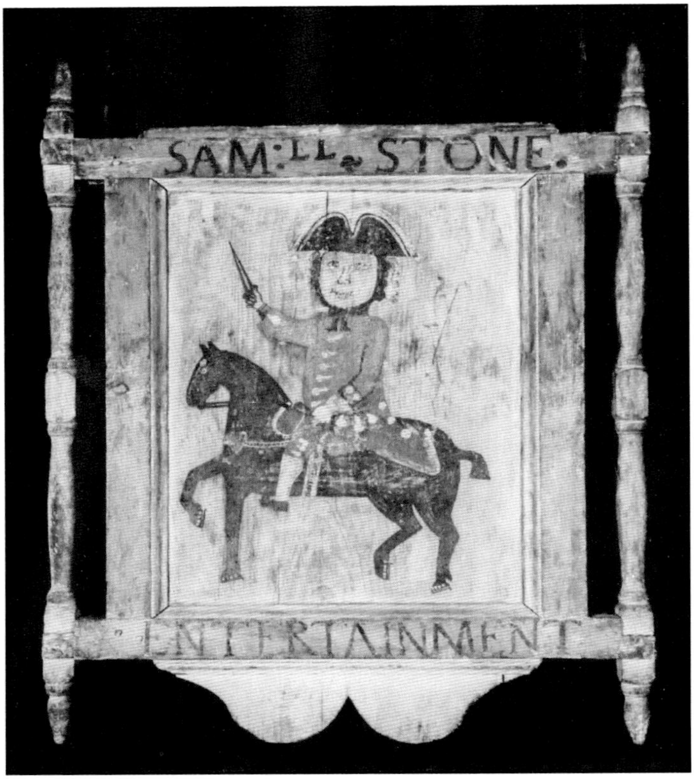

This pre–Revolutionary War sign advertises the Samuel S. Stone Tavern located on Wheeler Road near the Townsend line. The soldier is depicted in a red British officer's uniform, although Stone's tavern would become one of many gathering places for the rebellion against Britain.

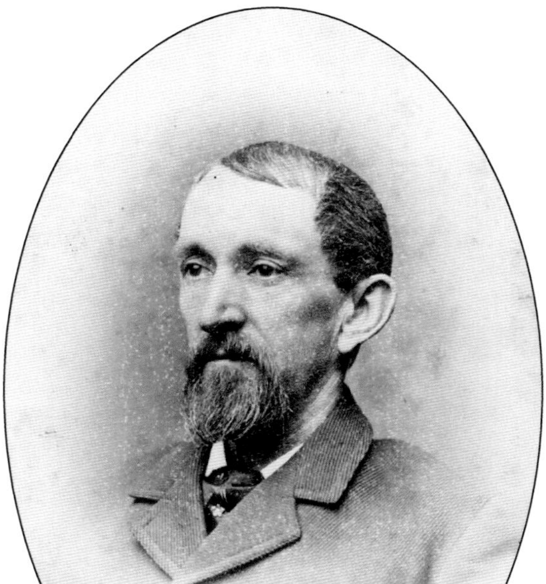

Charles O. Green was the proprietor of the store at the center of Ashby from 1865 until the 1890s. During research for this book, a handwritten note was found on the back of a register slip with the following: "Harry Bingham worked for C. O. Green. Harry was also close to C. O.'s daughter. One day C. O. told Harry to go home, get on his Sunday clothes and be back by 8:00. There is going to be a wedding tonight." (Courtesy of Ashby Free Public Library.)

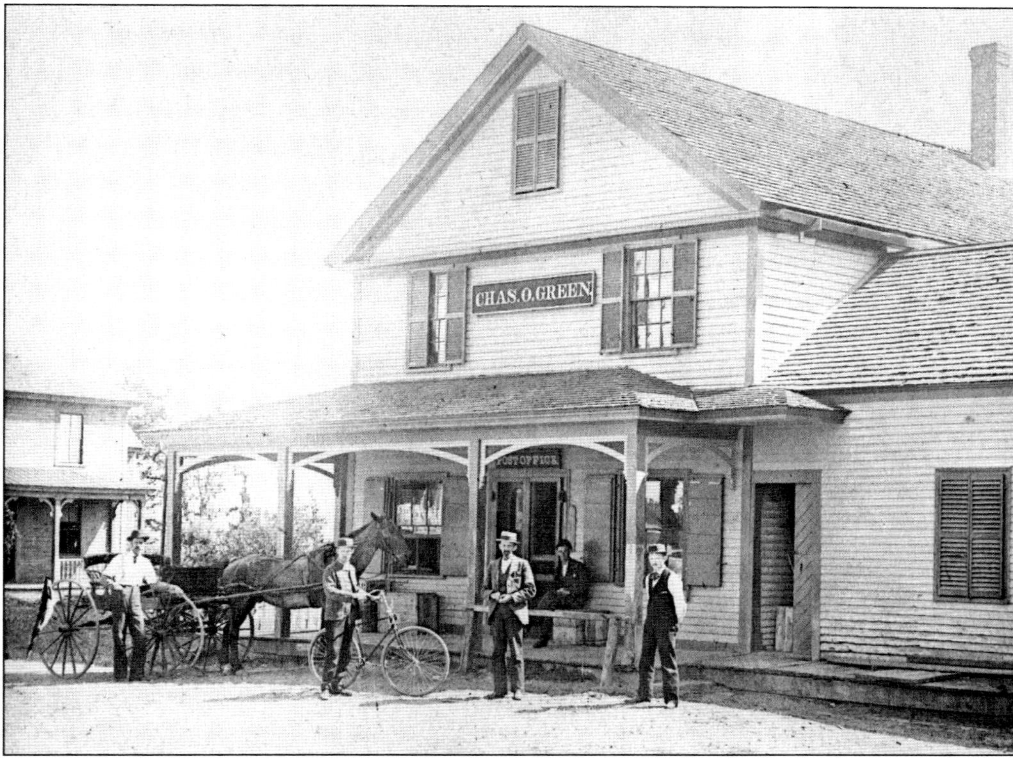

The earliest known photograph of the store in the center of Ashby was taken about 1890. The person at the center of the photograph is most likely Charles O. Green. The store also served as the post office. (Courtesy of Bill Arnold.)

CHAS. O. GREEN,

DEALER IN

GROCERIES, FLOUR AND GRAIN,

PRODUCE AND FARMING TOOLS,

WOOD ✢ AND ✢ LUMBER

AGENT FOR A. A. CARR'S WOODEN WARE.

ASHBY, MASS.

This leaflet from Charles O. Green's store shows the type of goods the store carried in the second half of the 19th century. It was customary at the time for local farmers to barter their produce and lumber for goods they needed from the store. Green was also the agent for woodenware produced at Carr's Mill, indicating he was selling these articles to merchants in nearby towns.

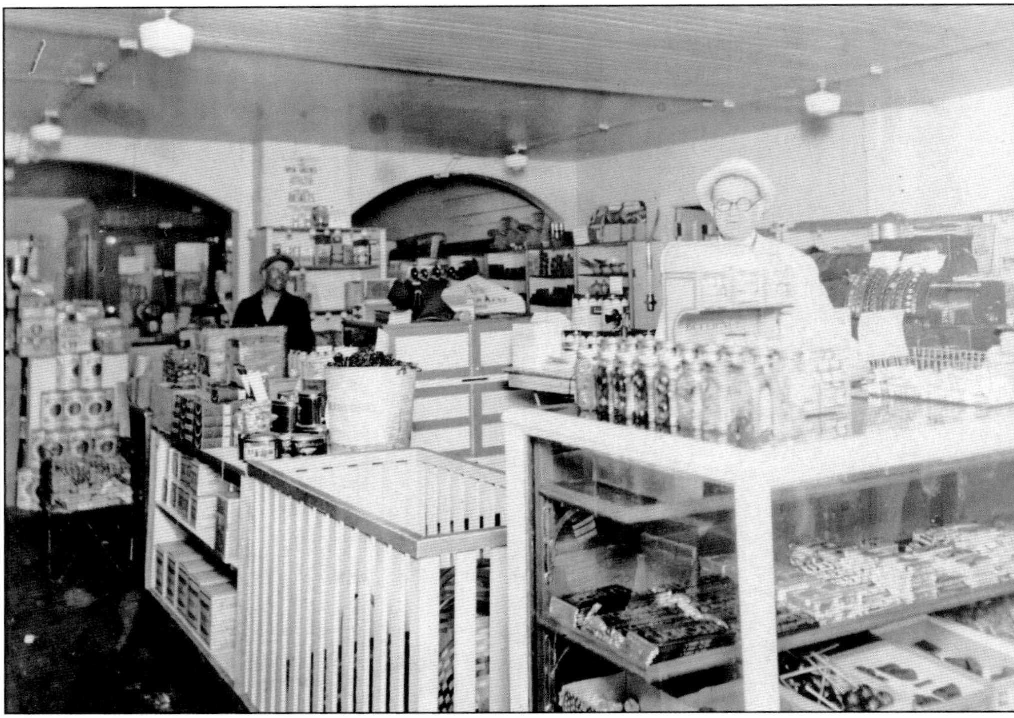

This is a photograph of the interior of the Ashby General Store in the 1930s. The large bin near the center of the photograph holds baskets so that patrons can select their own goods. Prior to this time, patrons would bring a list to the proprietor, who would get the products. (Courtesy of Bill Arnold.)

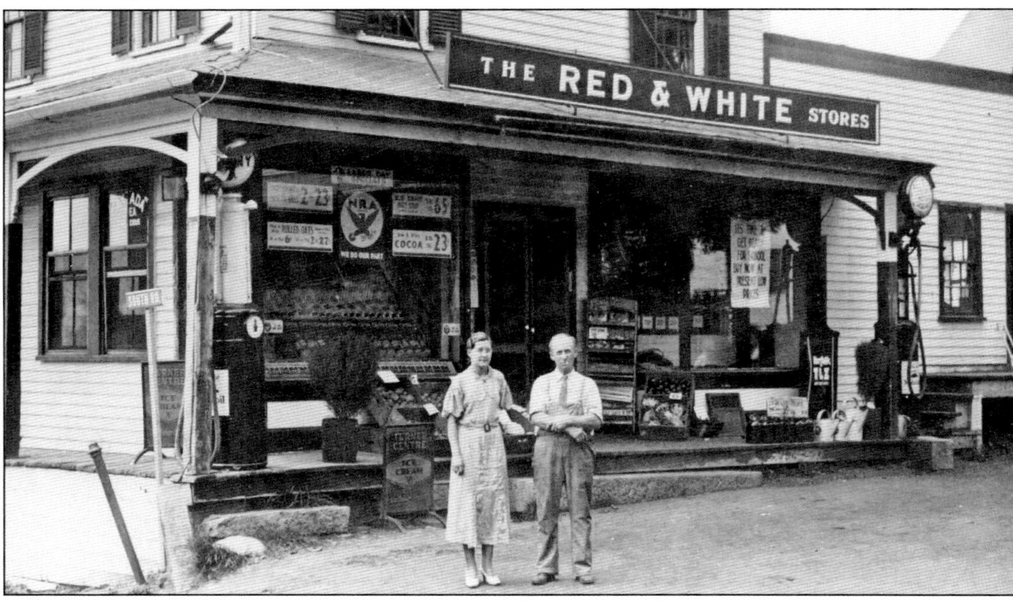

Lydia Bernhardt and John Leach pose in front of the Red & White Store in 1934. Gasoline pumps are on each end of the porch. The sign in the window to the left of the doorway with an eagle and the letters NRA stands for the National Recovery Act, a New Deal piece of legislation that was later struck down by the Supreme Court. (Courtesy of Bill Arnold.)

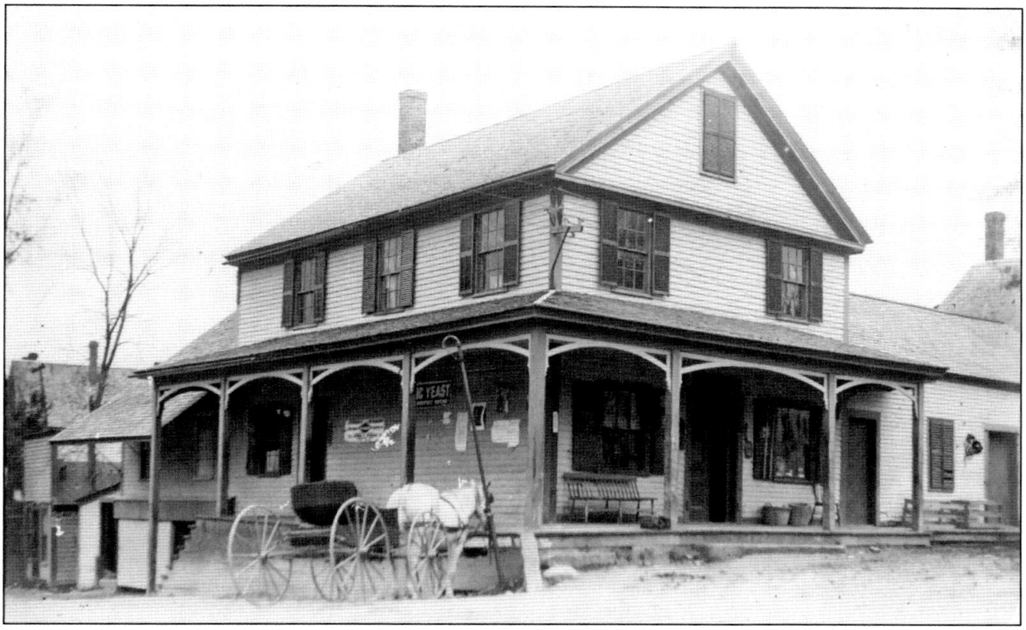

Pictured here is the Ashby village store in the first years of the 20th century. Local stores were the primary source of goods from outside the community. Transportation was slow, and shopping in the city would be a rare treat, so local merchants supplied most of the town's needs for goods. Located on Main Street opposite the town common, this was Ashby's largest and longest-surviving store. (Courtesy of William and Katherine Stanwood.)

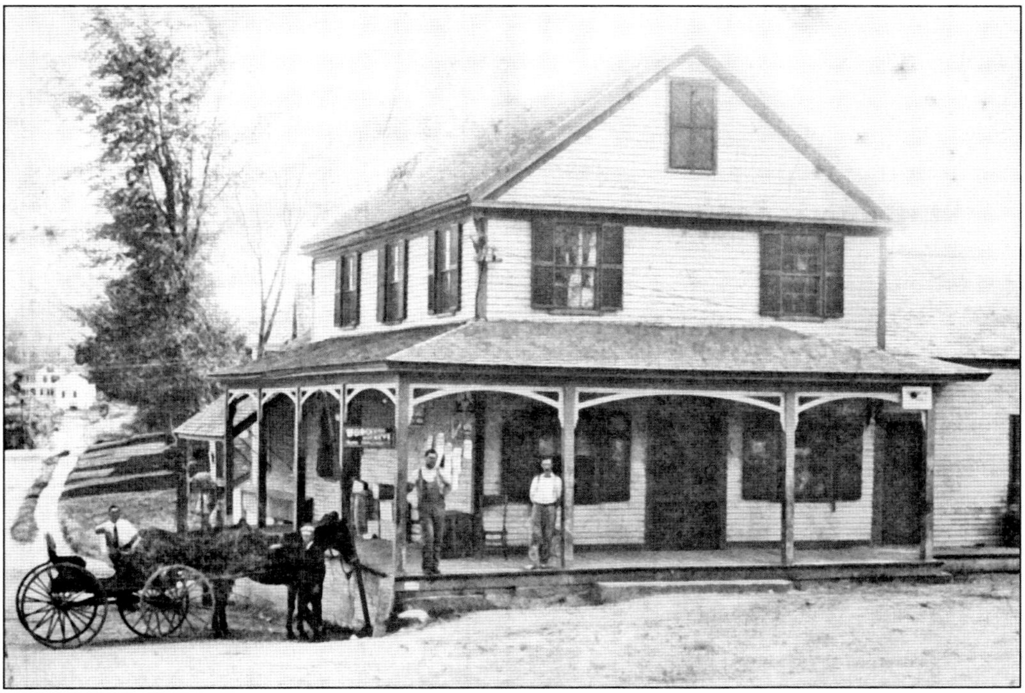

The store at the corner of Main Street and South Road is pictured here as it appeared around 1910. The owners apparently did not feel they needed a sign to identify themselves. The two signs on the outside of the building advertise Worcester Buckeye Farm Implements and ice cream.

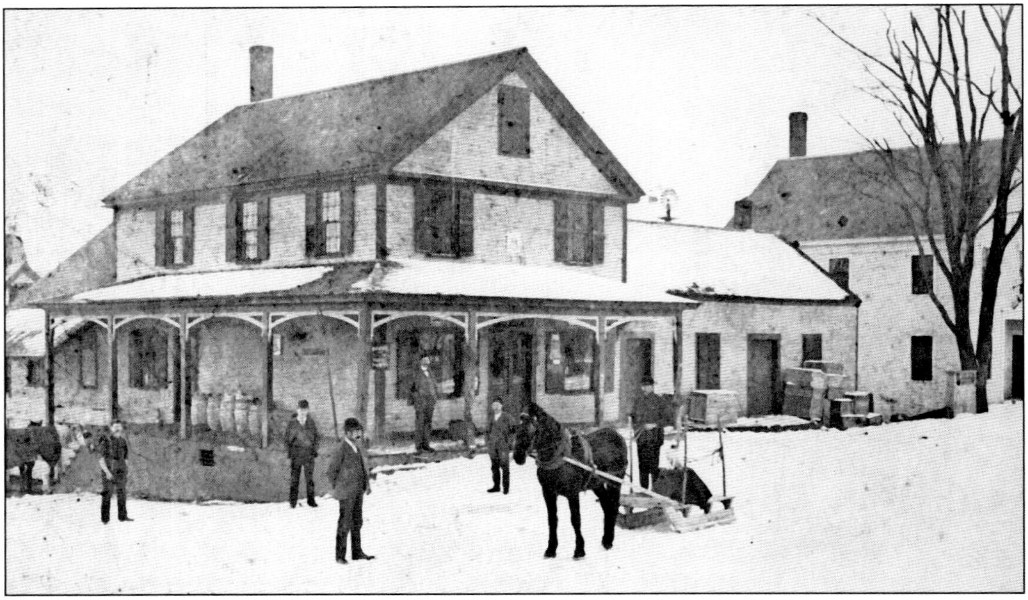

This is the Ashby Market as it looked in winter under the ownership of Goodnow, Derby & Hayes around 1910. The roads were not plowed then, and sleds were often used for transporting goods in winter.

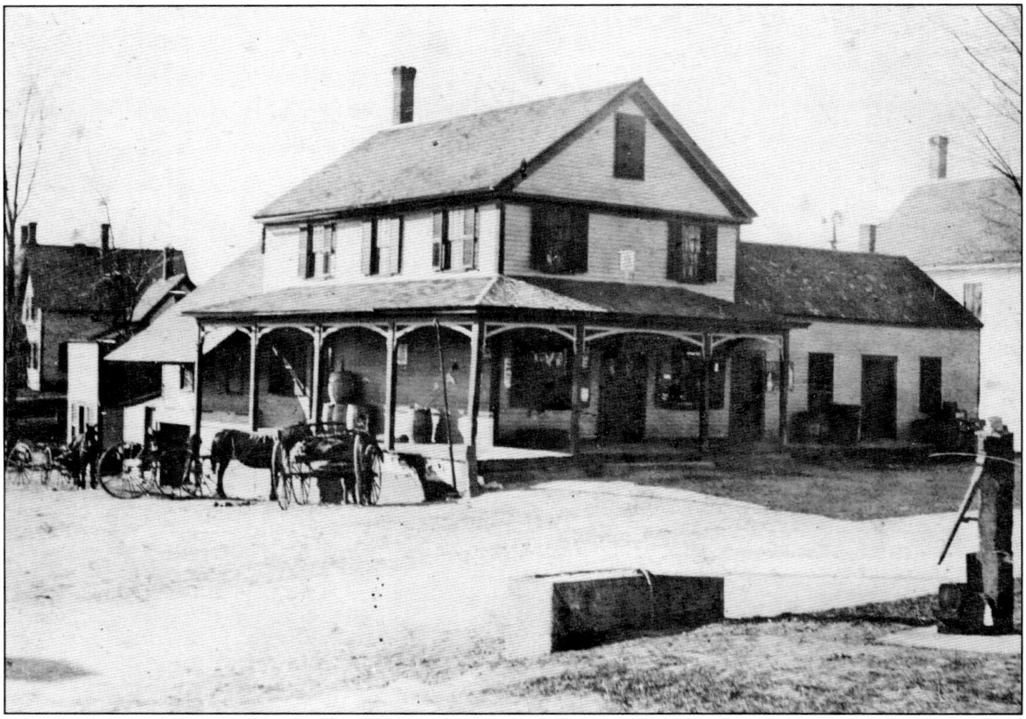

Pictured here around 1900, the general store in Ashby center has several buggies tied up by it. In the foreground are a pump and granite watering trough for the horses coming into town. These watering troughs were common along the roads, but few remain today. This trough remains in the same location but is now planted with flowers by Ashby Historical Society members. (Courtesy of Bill Arnold.)

ROGERS Silverware FREE to Customers

GOODNOW, DERBY & HAYES

"The Ashby Store"

DRY GOODS - GROCERIES - MEATS - SHOES
RUBBERS - MEN'S FURNISHINGS
HARDWARE - TINWARE - PAINTS - OILS
HAY - FLOUR - FEED
LIME AND CEMENT

Phone No. 24-2 **Ashby, Mass.**

This early 20th-century business card from the store now known as the Ashby Market shows goods being offered at the time. Goodnow, Derby & Hayes expanded the store to carry a wider range of goods than previous owners had provided. Investing in the latest technology required a caller to ask the operator to call "two-four-ring two."

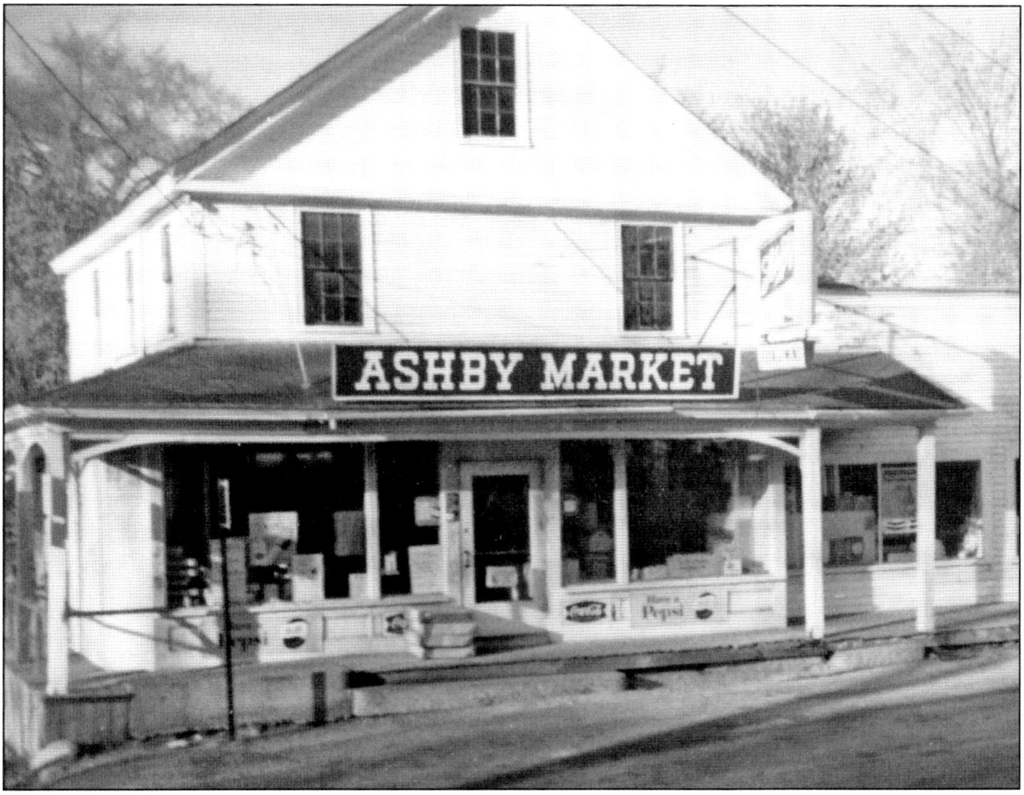

In the 1950s, the general store was owned by Wilfred J. Bedard and often staffed by his mother. Grandma Bedard would ring up purchases where she could watch the children come in to select their candy and then be off to school or a ball game. (Courtesy of Bill Arnold.)

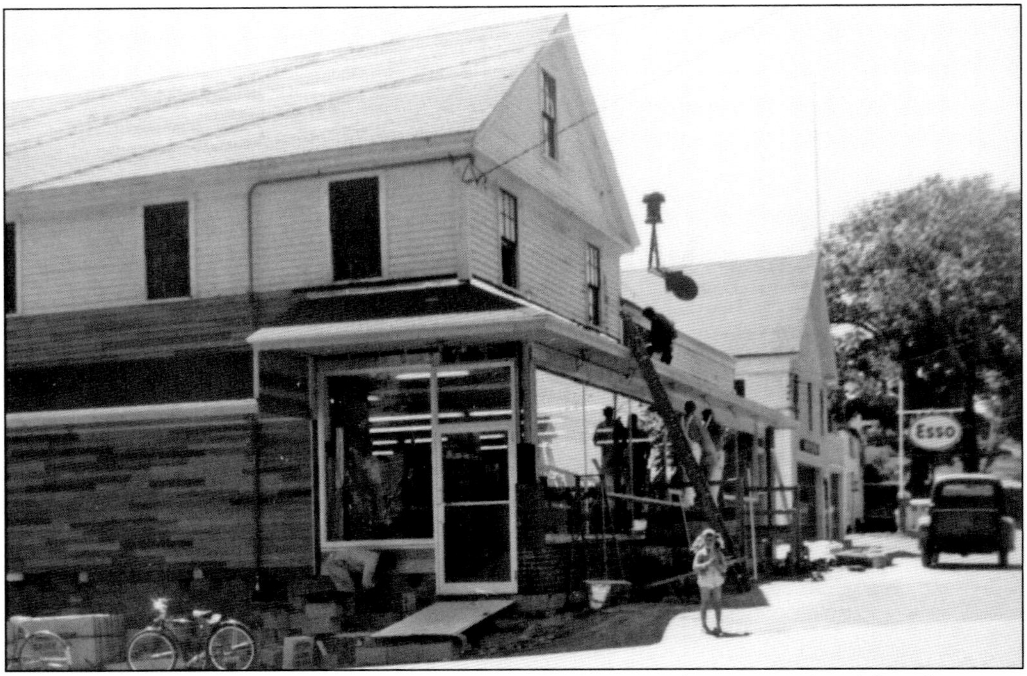

In the early 1960s, with Bernard Lizotte as the owner, the general store got a face-lift with a major reconstruction of the front of the first floor. The siren on the fire station next door was used to alert the volunteers to a fire and was blown daily at 6:00 p.m. Farther up the street, one can see the Esso sign at the Walnut Garage. (Courtesy of Bill Arnold.)

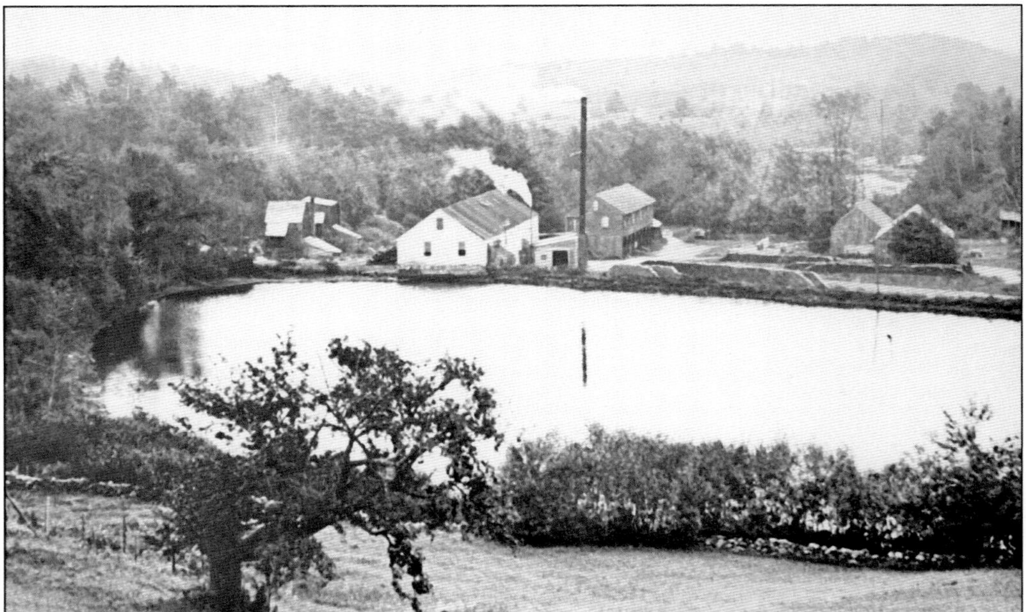

Carr's Tub Mill was one of the largest mills in Ashby. It was located on Valley Road and produced wooden tubs and other wooden products. At the height of its prosperity, it employed 30 people. In the late 1930s, it burned to the ground and was never rebuilt. (Courtesy of William and Katherine Stanwood.)

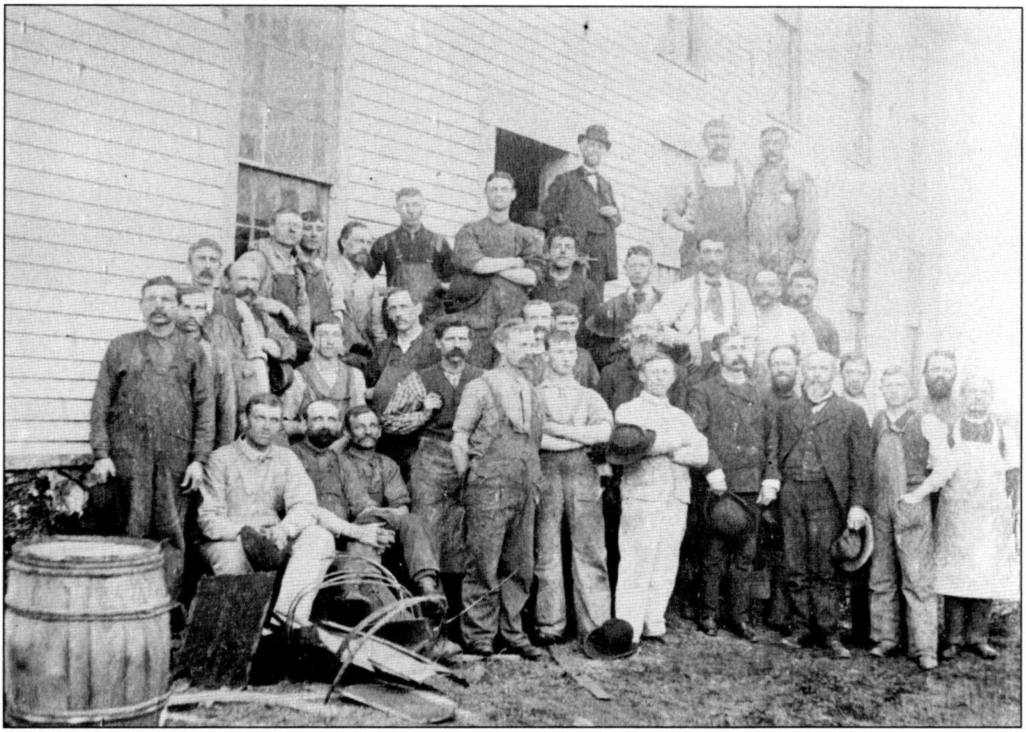

The workers at Carr's Tub Mill are shown in this photograph from the early 20th century. The factory employed from 10 to 30 workers depending on the business climate and the amount of water available to power the mill. (Courtesy of Carol Bennett Lielasus.)

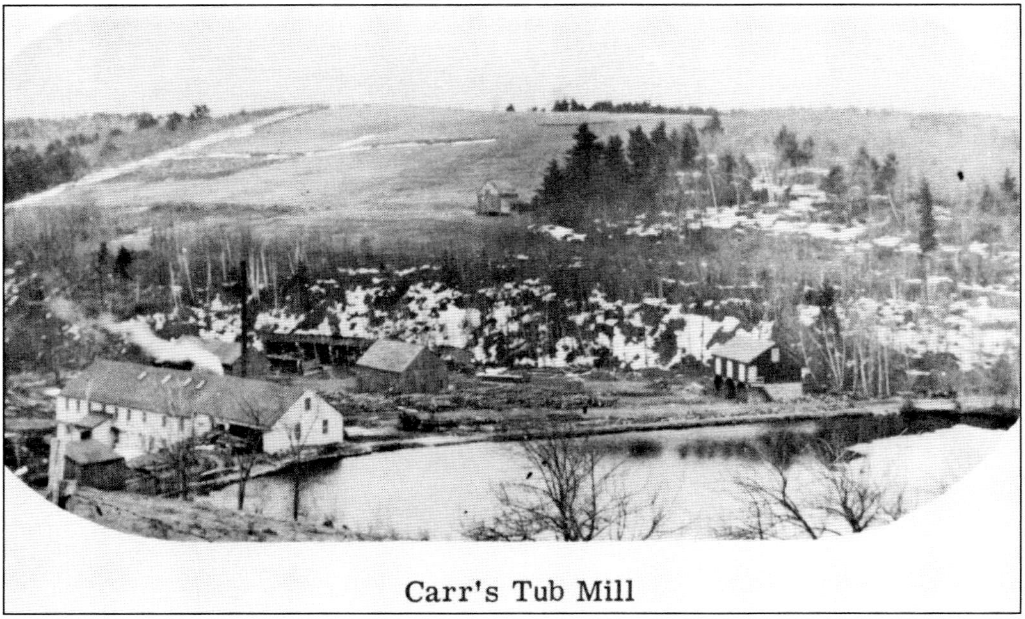

In 1930, the tub and pail factory of Alonzo Carr was a major employer in Ashby. It was started as a sawmill, but in 1853 began the manufacture of wooden tubs, which would continue until it burned down in the late 1930s. (Courtesy of Carol Bennett Lielasus)

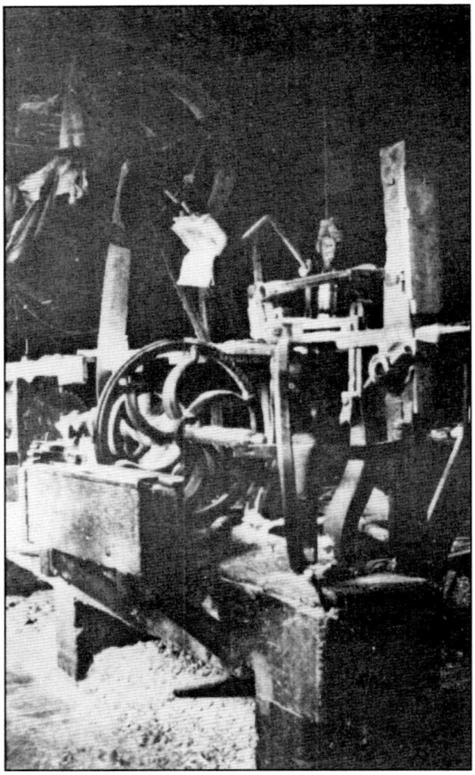

The outside tub lathe was one of the machines used to form the tubs at Carr's Tub Mill. The factory was powered by water and later steam. The power was transmitted by shafts, pulleys, and belts to the machines. This photograph is from 1914.

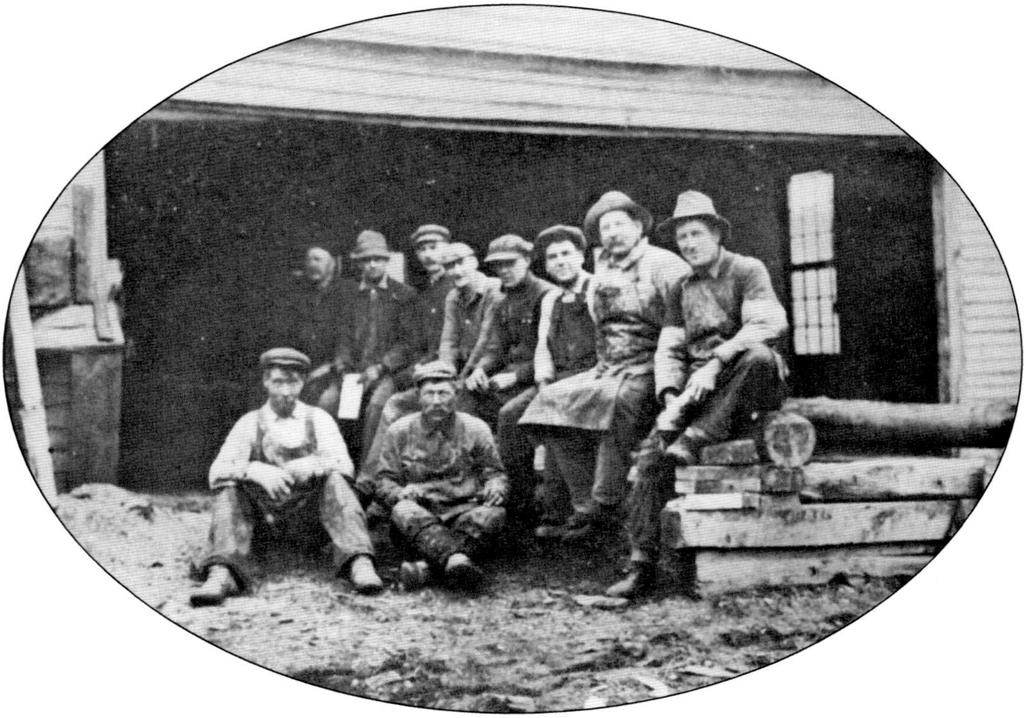

Workers are pictured here sitting on the ways at Carr's Tub Mill in 1914. The ways are the wooden structure used to bring logs into the mill. The logs were then sawn into staves for the tubs.

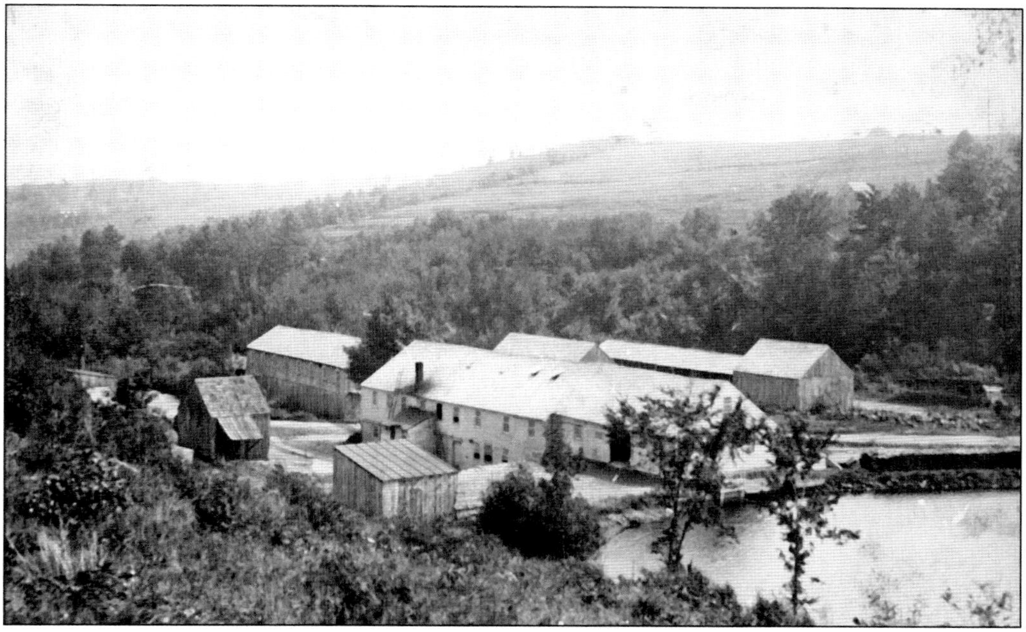

This is a view of Carr's Pail and Tub Mill from about 1880. Between the two trees near the center is the sluice gate to allow water into the turbine that powered the mill. The buildings around the main building were used to store lumber and bend the wood prior to making the staves. Later photographs show a tall chimney next to the building that may have housed a steam engine, a more reliable source of power.

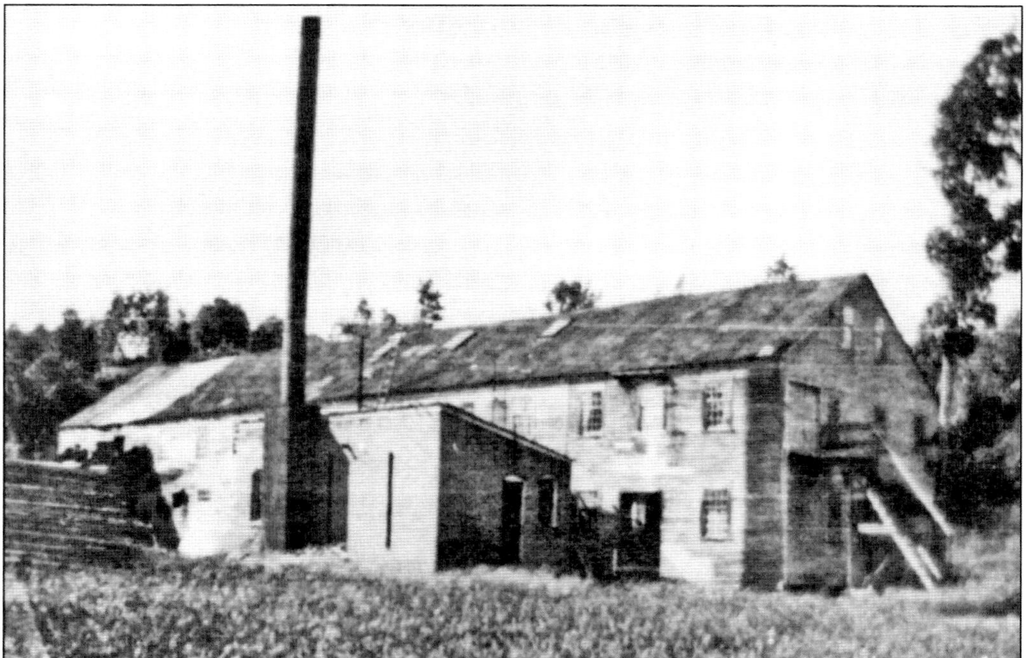

Carr's Tub Mill on Valley Road produced wooden tubs. Originally, the mill was powered by water, but the building in the foreground suggests that by the time this photograph was taken it was using steam power.

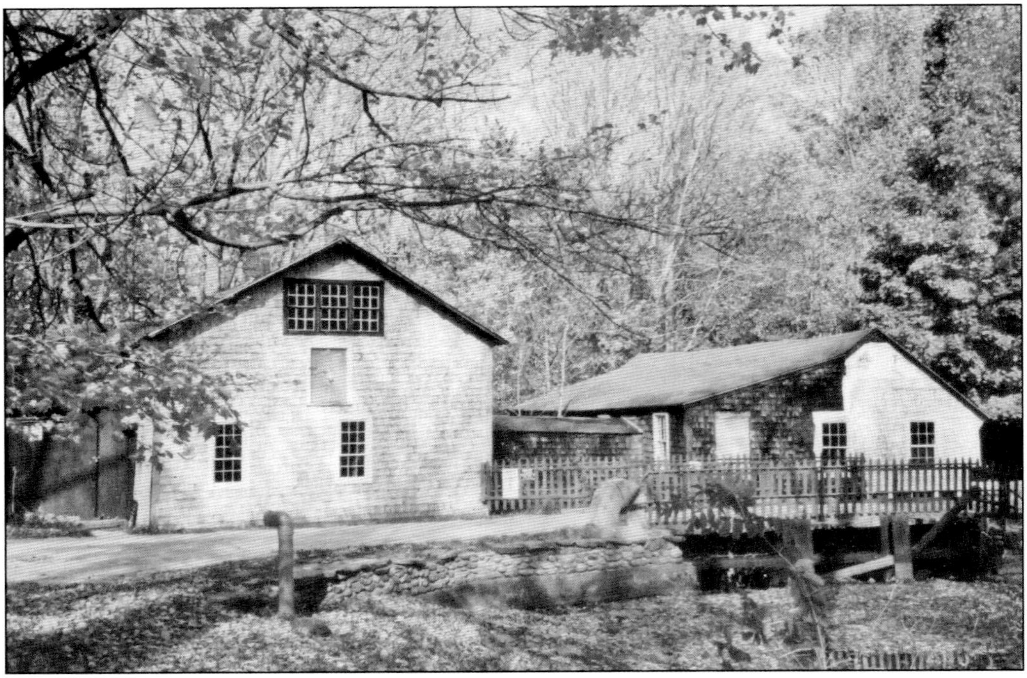

The former Loveland Saw and Gristmill is pictured here in the mid-1970s, by which time it had become a 4-H summer camp. Although the mill buildings no longer serve their original purpose, they continue to be used and maintained by the camp.

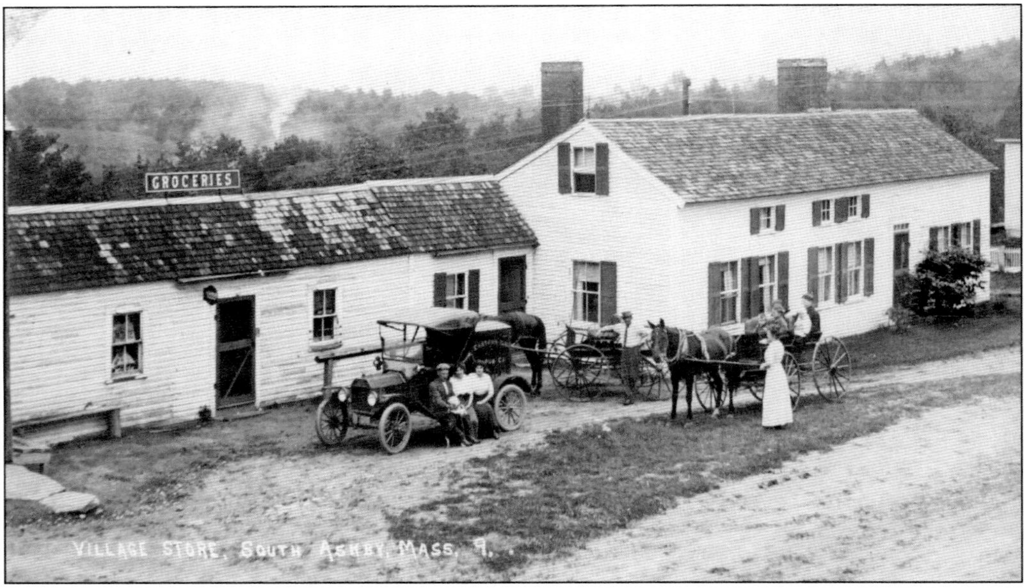

This store operated until the early 1960s. Located on the corner of Erickson and South Roads, it served the South Village area. The house still stands, but the grocery section is gone. The automobile in the photograph is from about 1918 and is lettered on the side "Eastern Ill. Pub. Co." There are two carriages—one driven by a single man and the other with a family with children seated on it. This nicely illustrates the change from horse-drawn to motorized vehicles, a change that would have a major impact on the way people worked and lived in Ashby. (Courtesy of William and Katherine Stanwood.)

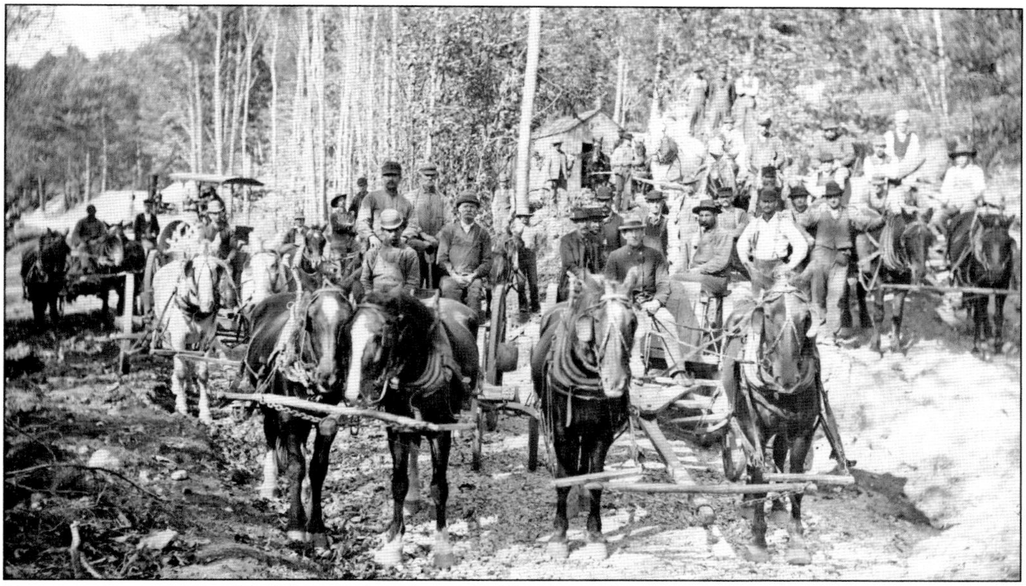

Here, a crew is assembled for roadwork, probably along the Willard Brook State Forest section of Ashby Road (Route 119). This photograph was probably taken during the 1894 highway improvement. Toward the left, behind the horses, a steamroller can be seen. It appears to be the only mechanized piece of equipment on the job.

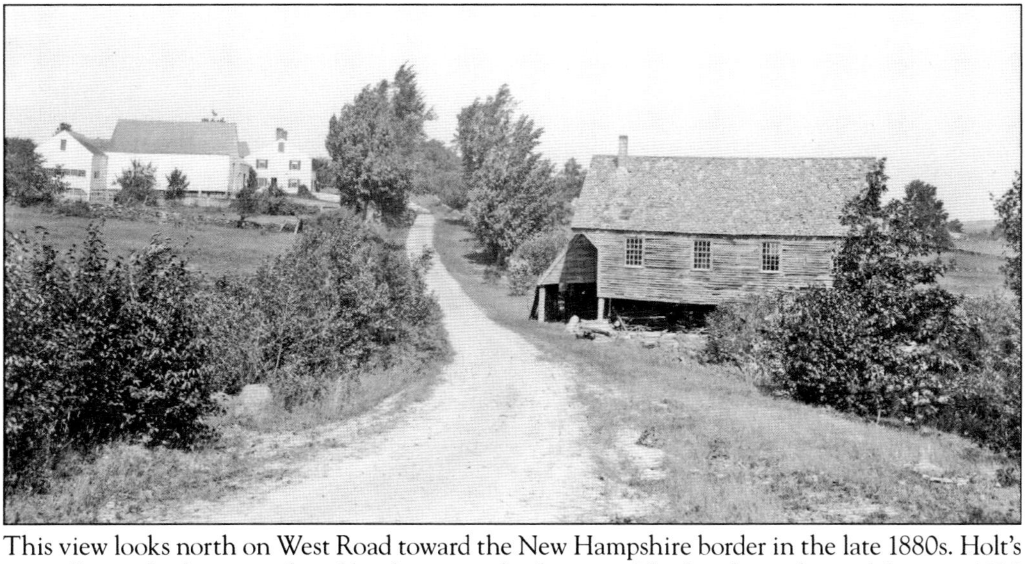

This view looks north on West Road toward the New Hampshire border in the late 1880s. Holt's sawmill is in the foreground, and his farm is in the distance. The farmhouse burned down in 1890 and was replaced with a smaller family home, which is now a part of an alpaca farm. The mill building seen here burned in 1895. The mill site was then purchased by Fred Stacy, who rebuilt the mill to make wood shingles.

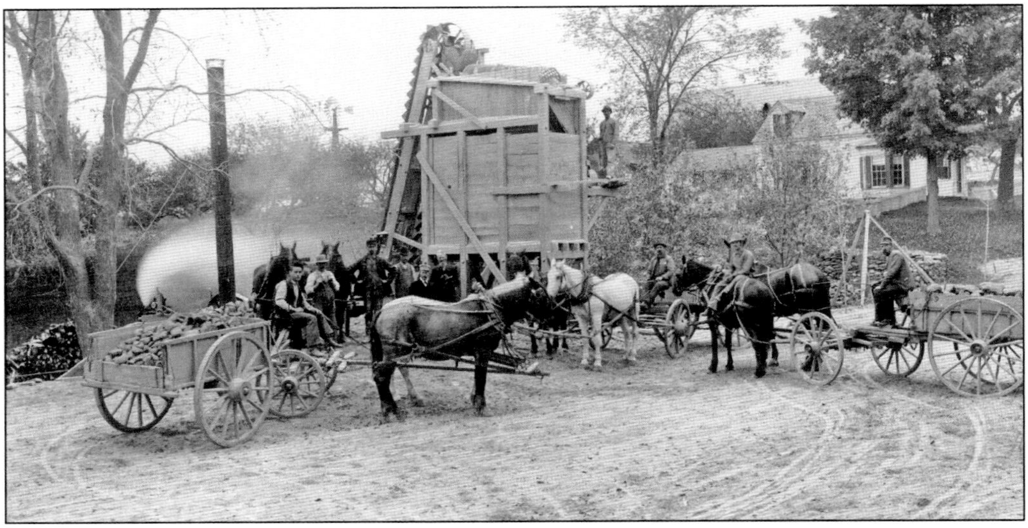

David Damon's steam-powered rock crusher is seen here about 1890. The jaw-type crusher is located near the top of the wooden structure, which is the hopper. The articulating wagons, specially made to handle heavy loads, pull up by the bucket conveyor to unload. As the rocks are crushed, they are directed by a slide into a wagon on the far side of the machine.

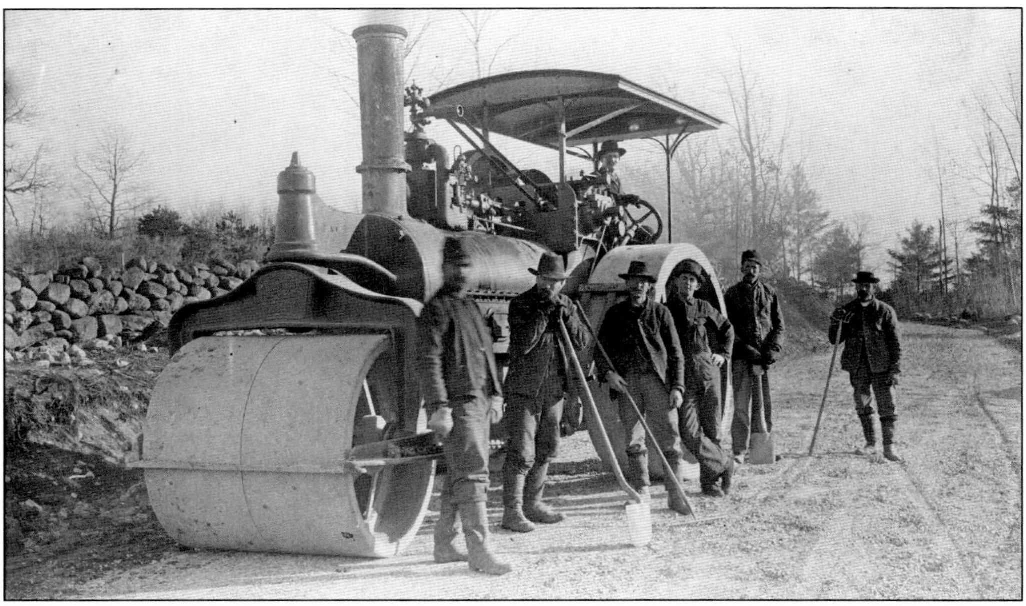

Although one mile of state highway had been paved in 1894, much of the highway system was still gravel. Part of maintaining the state highways was compacting the gravel to prevent ruts from developing. A six-man crew is working with a steam-powered roller in Ashby around 1905.

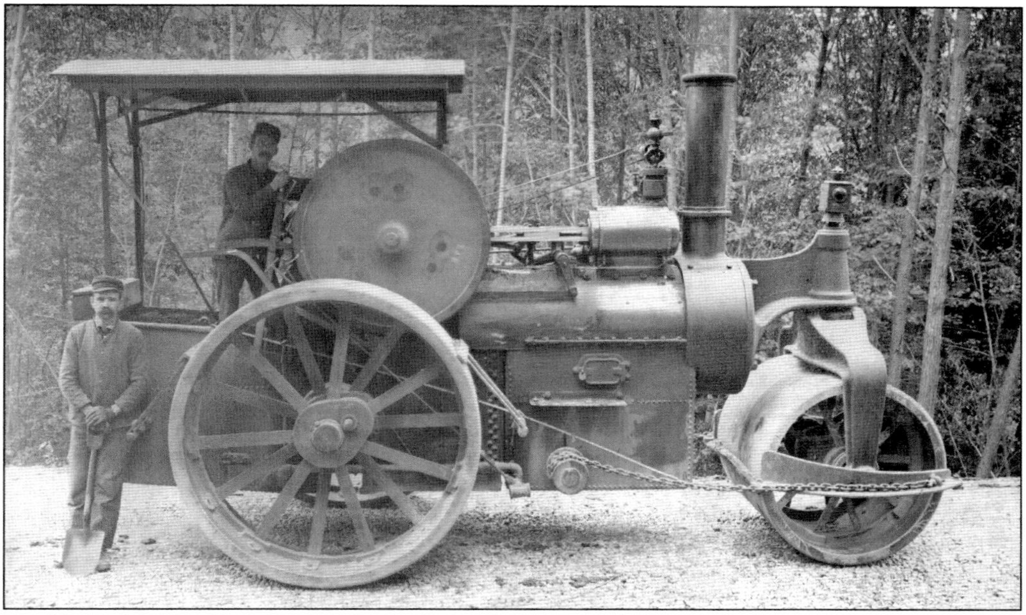

It is likely that the first motorized vehicle Ashby saw was the steamroller sent out to smooth and compact Main Street prior to paving in 1894. The machine was operated by a driver and a fireman. Steamrollers like this weighed 15 to 20 tons and could move along at a brisk walking pace.

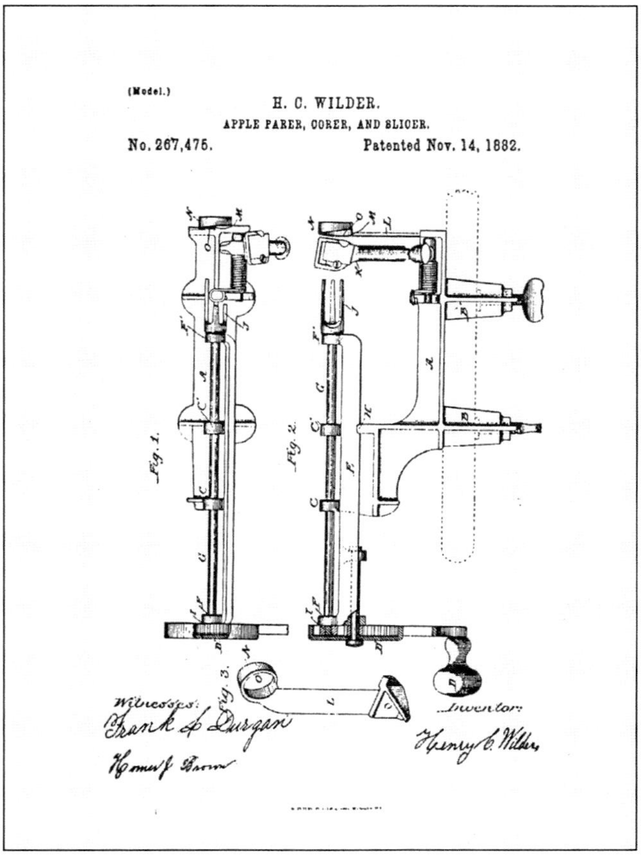

In 1881, Henry C. Wilder of Ashby patented an apple parer, corer, and slicer. Wilder notes that his invention is particularly useful for creating even slices in preparation for "evaporating," or drying, the apples. Many home apple peelers sold today are based on this design. (Courtesy of Ashby Free Public Library.)

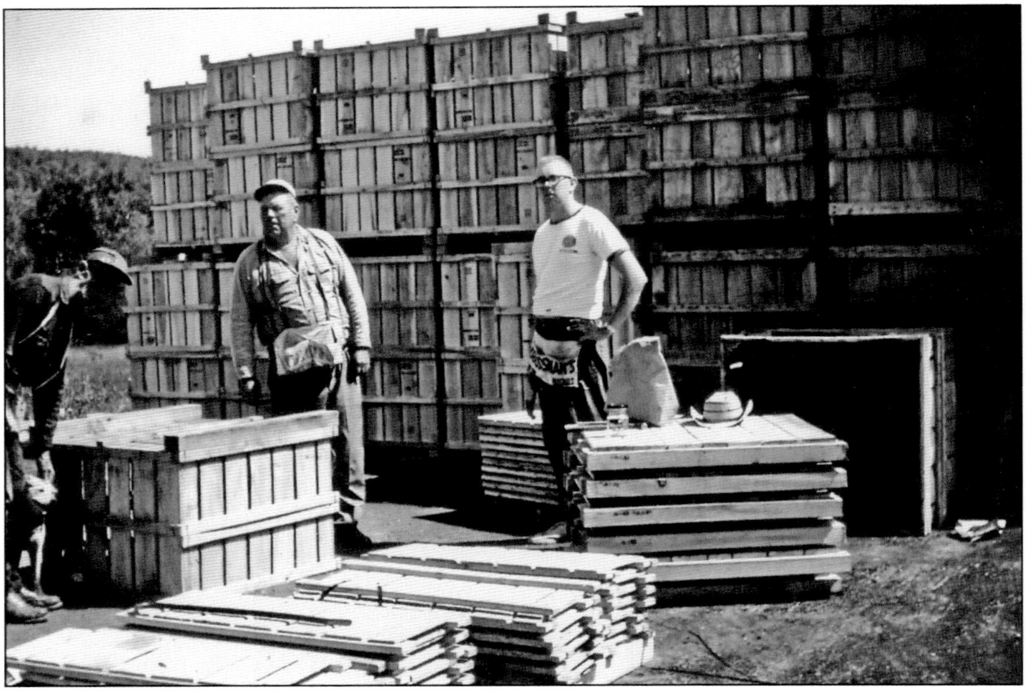

Making the bulk bins to ship the apples was one of the chores on the apple farm. In 1965, Tip Tyler (left), Richard Saari (center), and George Saari are seen assembling the bins in preparation for the harvest. Over 1,000 bins would be needed to store and ship the apples. (Courtesy of George Saari.)

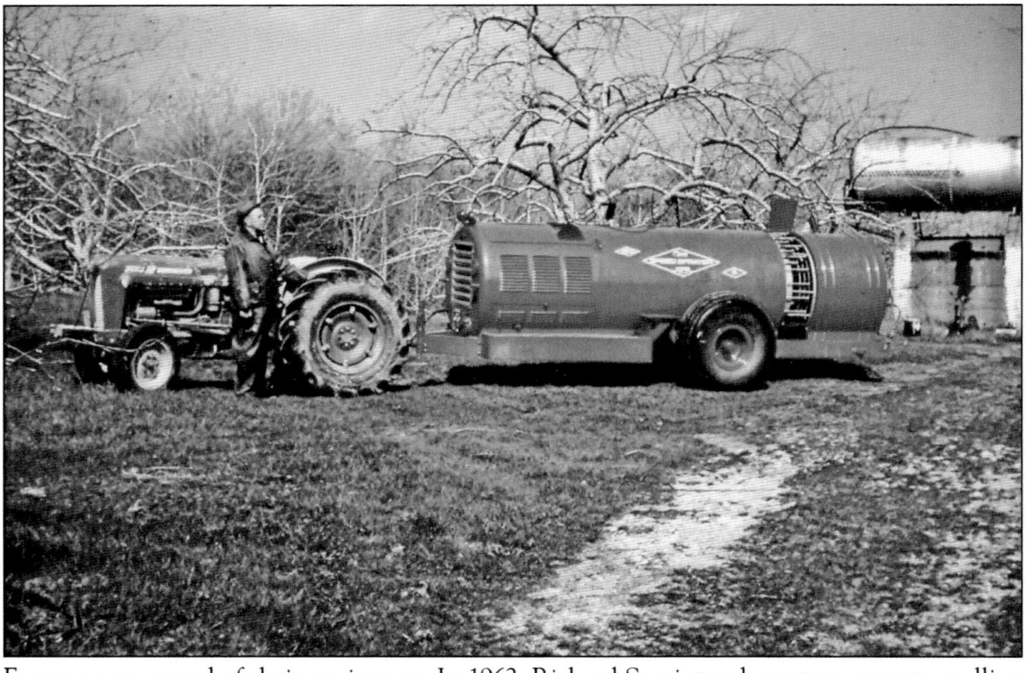

Farmers were proud of their equipment. In 1962, Richard Saari stands next to a tractor pulling his new air-blast sprayer. This sprayer allowed faster and more effective spraying of the orchard than the high-pressure spray guns it replaced. (Courtesy of George Saari.)

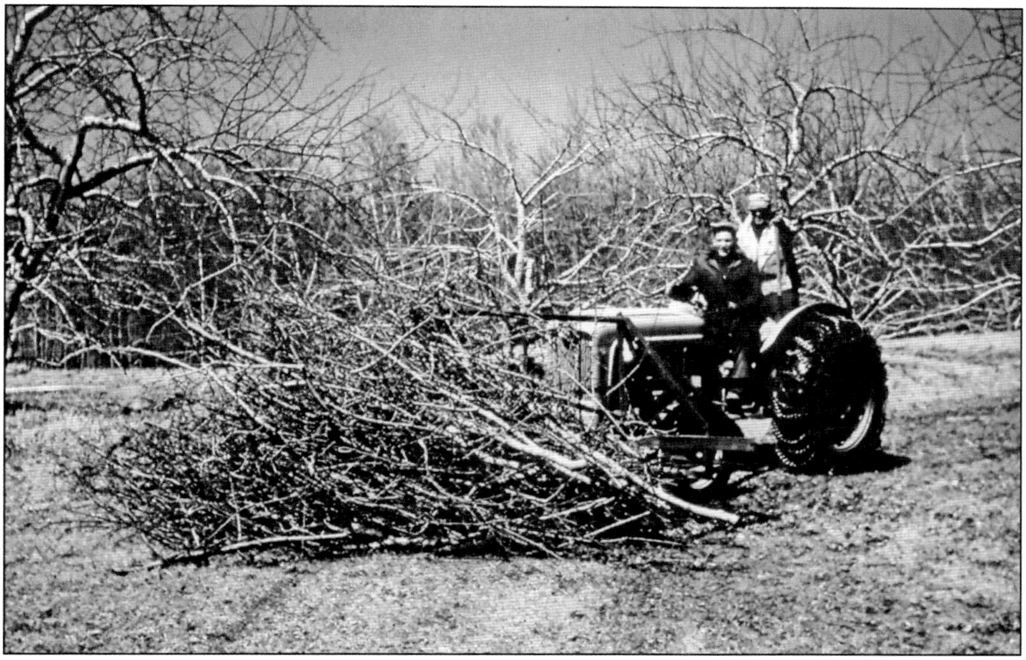

Here, Richard Saari Jr. (left) and George Wisti pick up brush in the spring of 1965. Each winter, the trees were pruned, and the pruned branches were thrown aside. In the spring, the tractor was outfitted with a brush fork, and the branches were collected and pushed out of the orchard. (Courtesy of George Saari.)

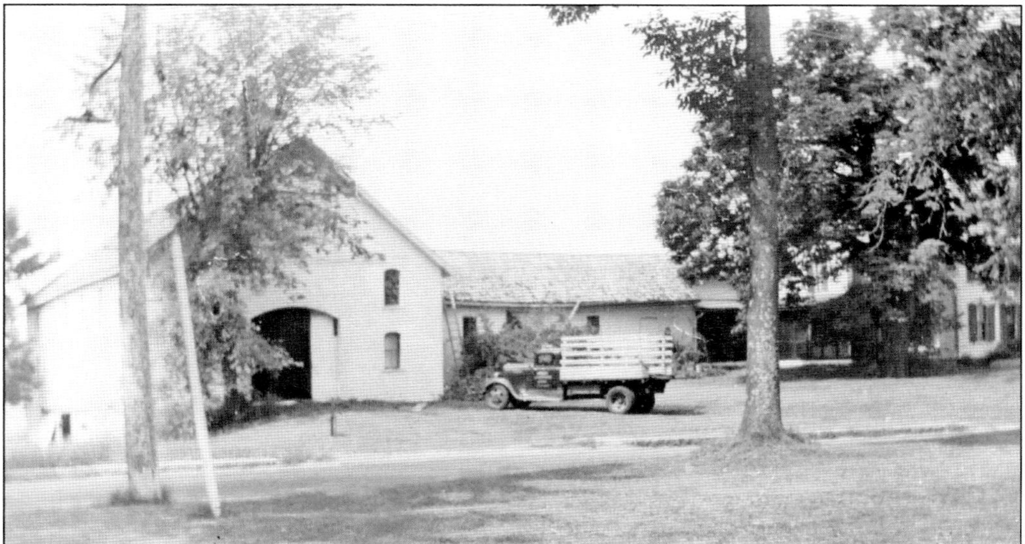

This photograph from 1942 shows the massive 38-by-77-foot barn at the corner of Main Street and Allen Road owned by Jim and Carrie Allen at the time. The middle portion of the ell between the house and barn housed the A. & C. Edwards clock shop between 1793 and 1820. The barn and a portion of the ell were torn down around 1950. This photograph was sent to Ray Wilkinson, who was serving in the Pacific during World War II, by his mother. This message was inscribed on the back: "A glimpse of old Main St. I know you wish you could see it yourself and believe we wish you could too. Maybe it won't be too long." (Courtesy of Tom Dorward.)

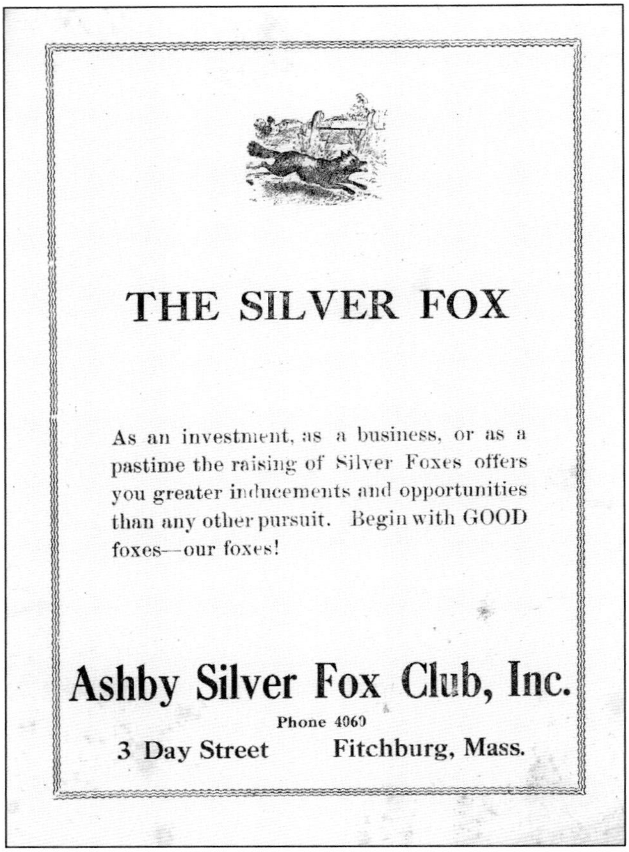

In the 1920s and 1930s, fox fur was in great demand, and the silver fox was the most desirable, commanding hundreds of dollars per pelt. Even more money could be made selling the live foxes to others who wanted to get in on the action and start their own farms. This advertisement offers foxes through the Ashby Silver Fox Club. (Courtesy of Carol Bennett Lielasus.)

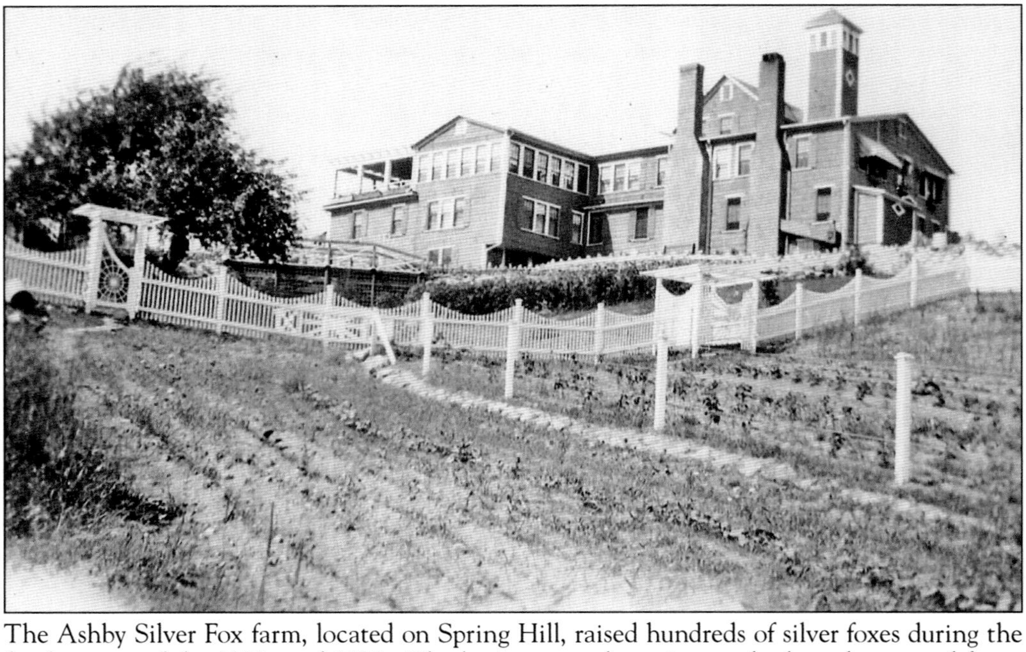

The Ashby Silver Fox farm, located on Spring Hill, raised hundreds of silver foxes during the fox-fur craze of the 1920s and 1930s. The business was lucrative, as the large house and fancy fencing around the garden attest. (Courtesy of Carol Bennett Lielasus.)

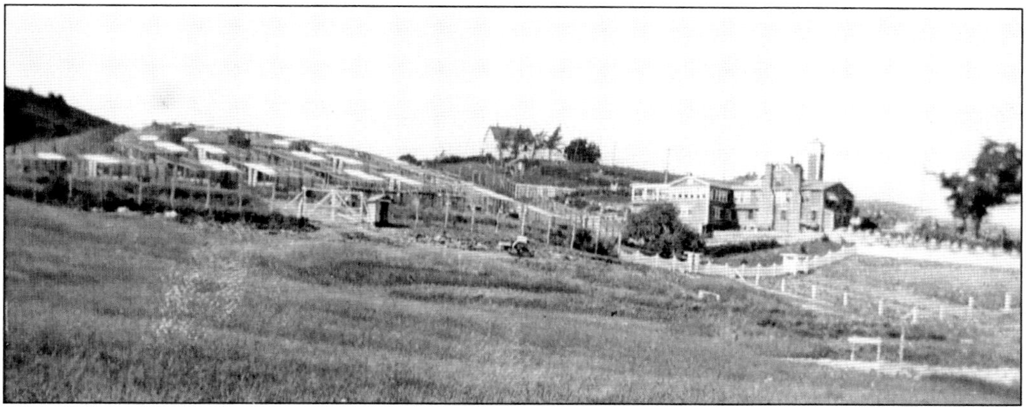

The Ashby Silver Fox Farm was a profitable venture in the mid-1930s. The pelts and breeding stock of the silver fox were in great demand and commanded high prices. The silver fox is a natural variation of the red fox, the only difference being the fur color is silver to black. The fox pens are seen on the hill on the left.

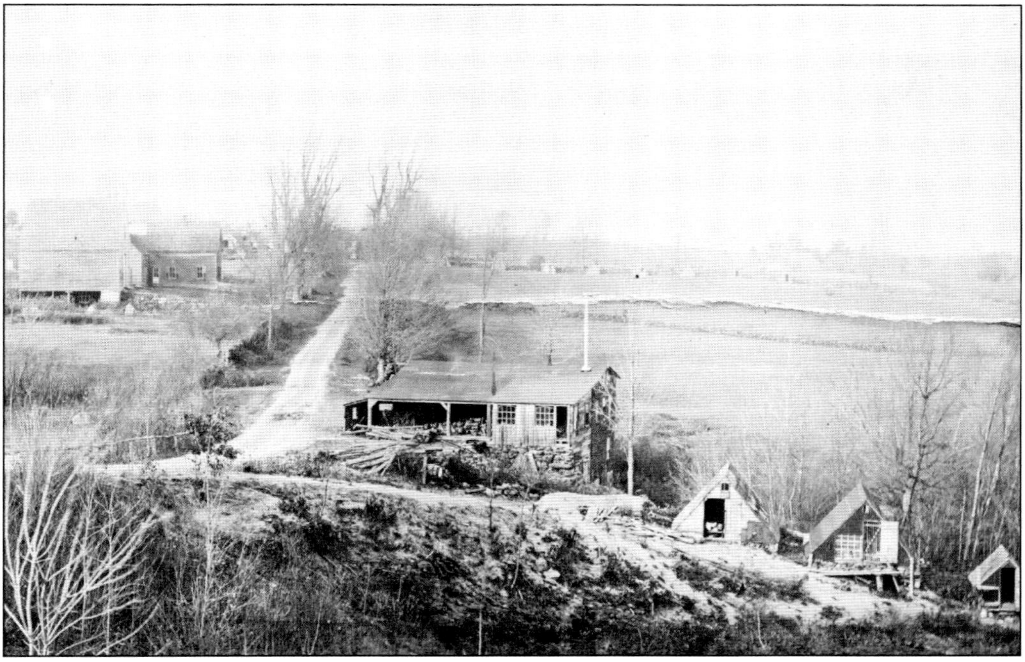

This photograph is of Stacy's Mill on West Road. Fred Stacy purchased the mill from Asa Holt in 1896. The original Holt mill building was moved to another location, and Stacy built a smaller mill building for the sawmill. It was here that he ran a lumber and shingle mill until 1942. (Courtesy of the Stacy family.)

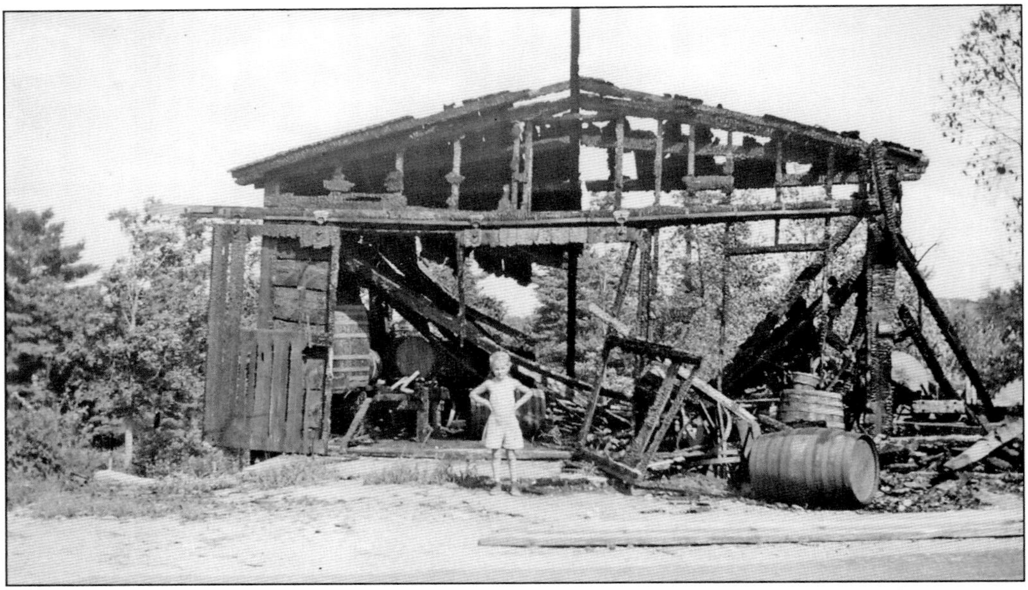

Fred Stacy operated the mill he bought from Asa Holt in 1896 until 1941, when the structure was burned down along with several other buildings by an arsonist. The mill had sawn lumber and shingles and pressed cider. It was the last mill to operate on waterpower in Ashby. (Courtesy of the Stacy family.)

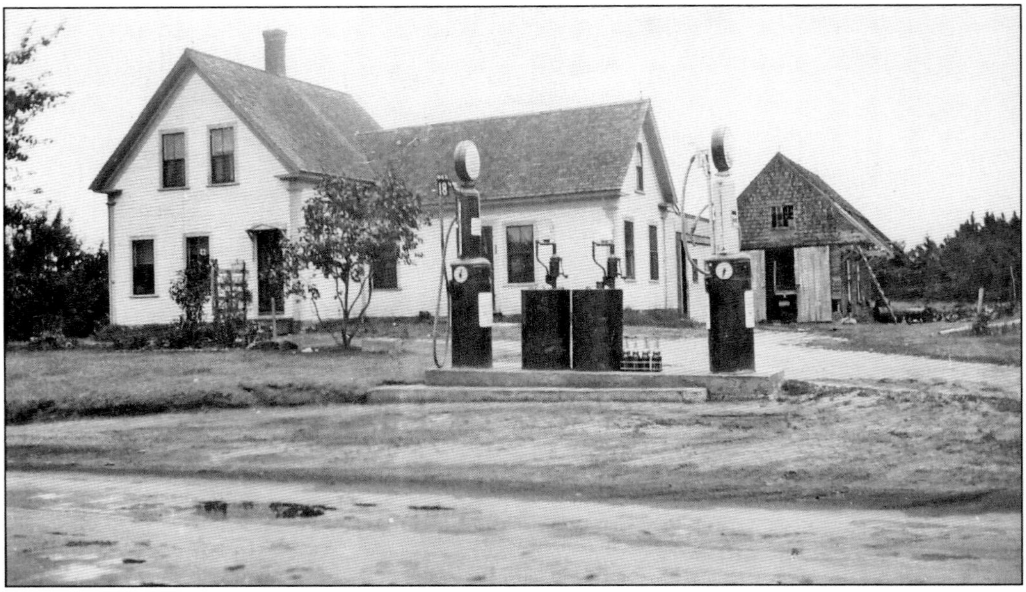

The Stacy house on West Road was built by Fred Stacy in 1900. The gasoline station, which operated in the 1920s, provided a place to fuel up on the way to New Hampshire. These pumps were hand-cranked, with a dial to indicate the quantity of gasoline. (Courtesy of the Stacy family.)

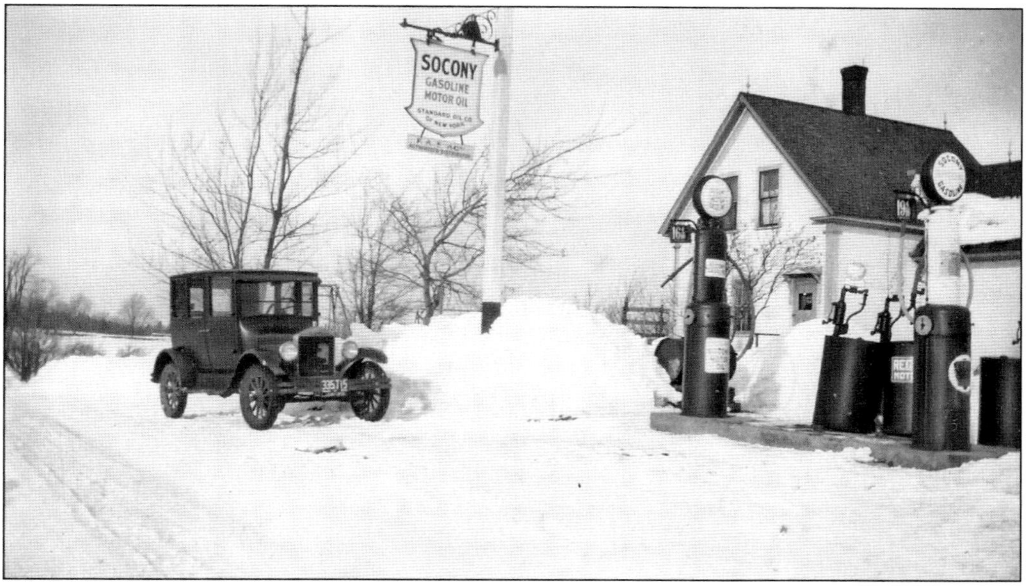

Stacy's Filling Station on West Road sold Socony gasoline, kerosene, and motor oil in the 1920s and 1930s to motorists in West Ashby. Socony would go on to become Mobil Oil Corporation. (Courtesy of the Stacy family.)

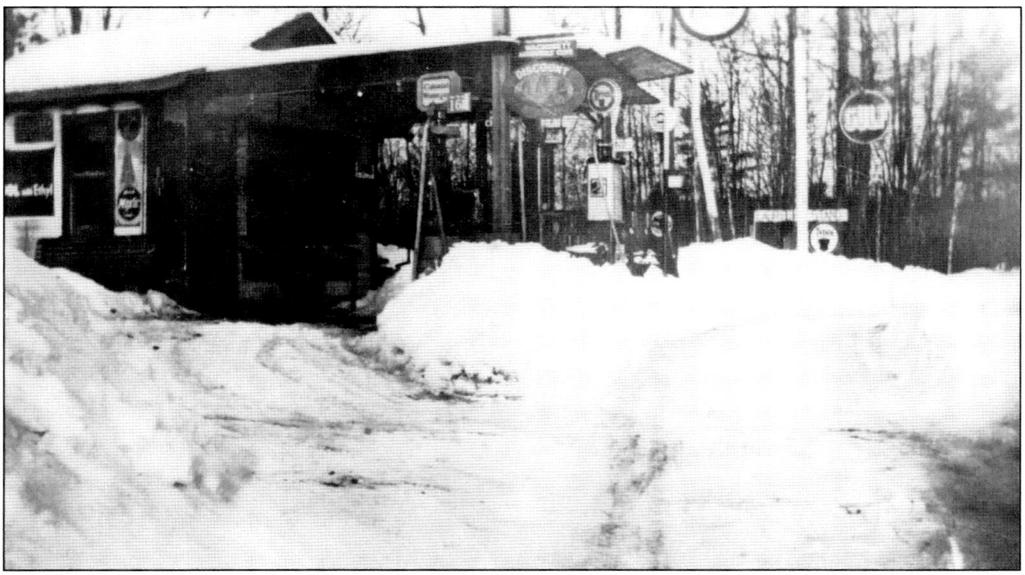

The Laurel Hill Stand and Duncklee Filling Station, located on Main Street on Sheldon Hill, is pictured here in 1931. The Duncklee Filling Station was one of several small filling stations located around town to serve the local needs. At this time, the price of gas is 16.4¢ per gallon. (Courtesy of Nancy Elliott Rogers.)

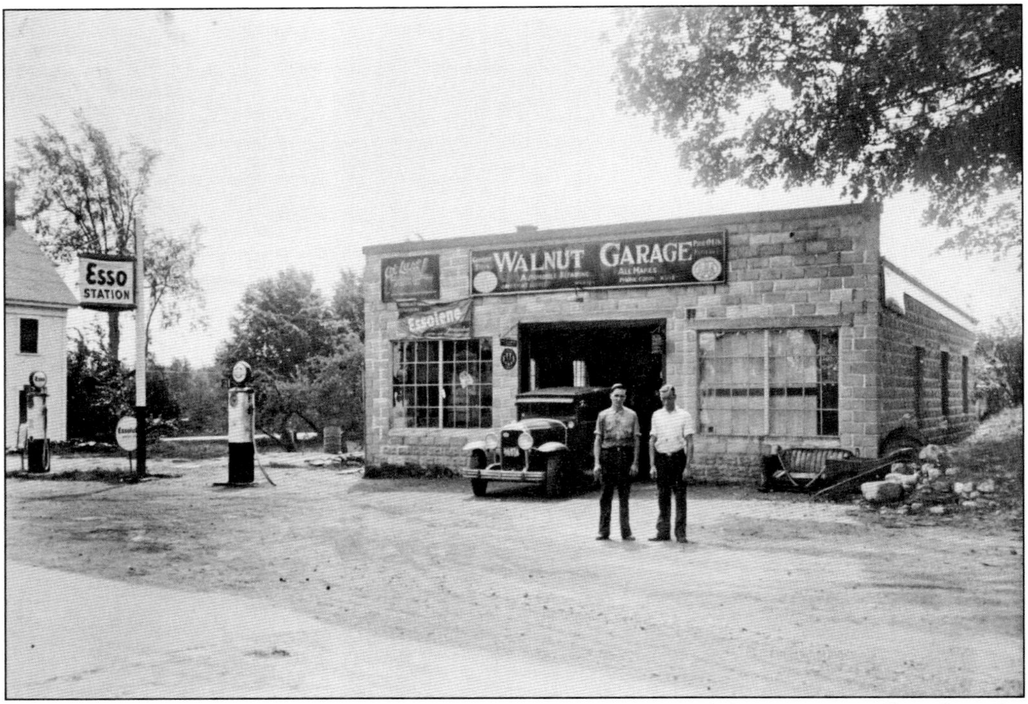

In 1931, the Walnut Garage sold gasoline and advertised automobile repairs on all makes. For many years, the garage was owned by Irving Miller.

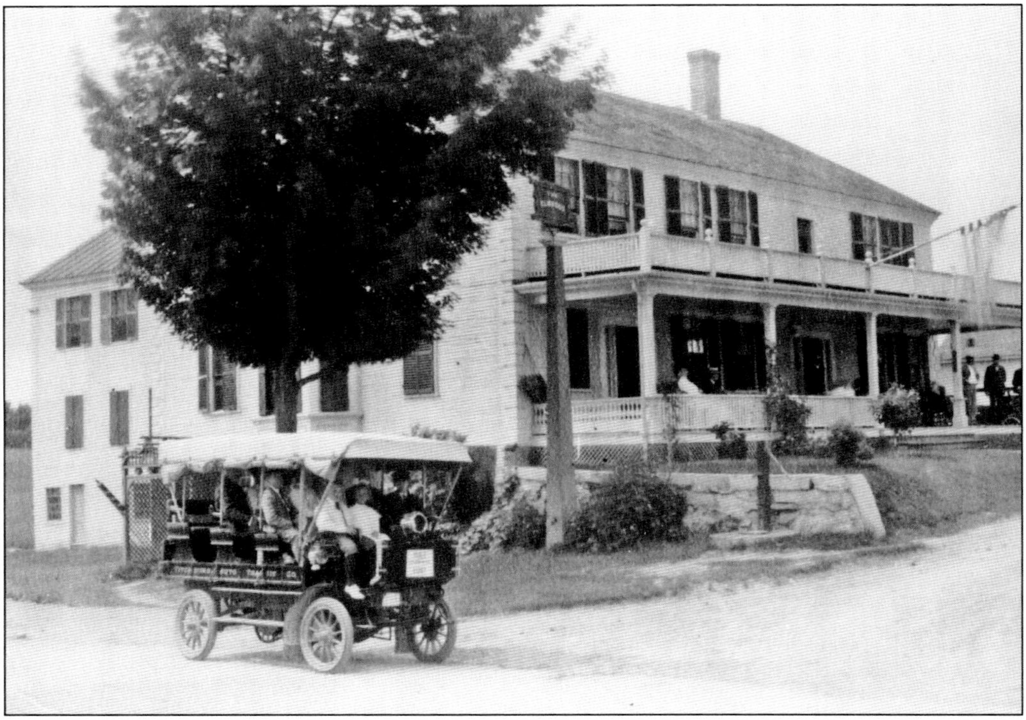

A Fitchburg Auto Transit jitney is carrying passengers from the Elmwood Inn to Fitchburg in 1907. Jitneys were the forerunners of the ubiquitous city bus of today.

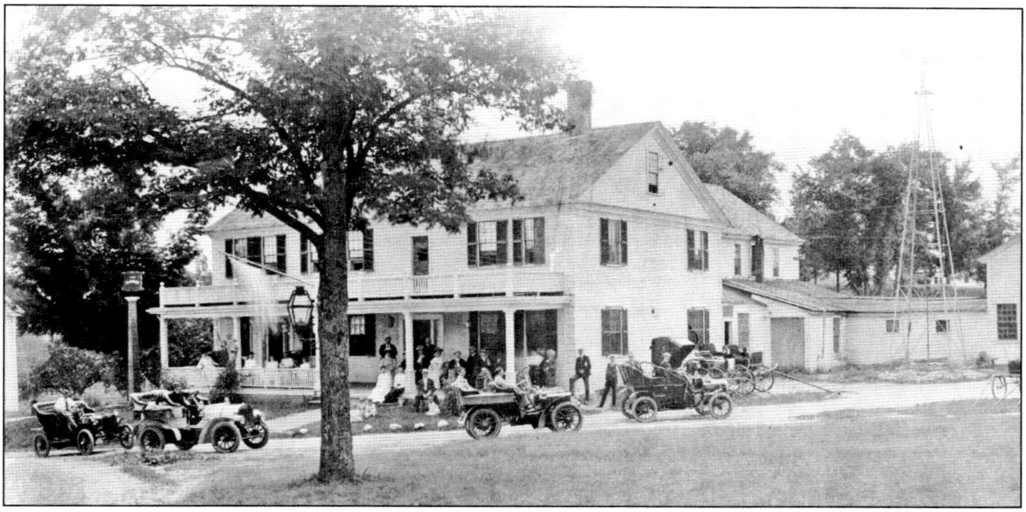

The Elmwood Inn attracted many visitors with good food and entertainment in the evening. In this photograph taken about 1905, automobiles with their drivers are lined up to either drop off or pick up patrons.

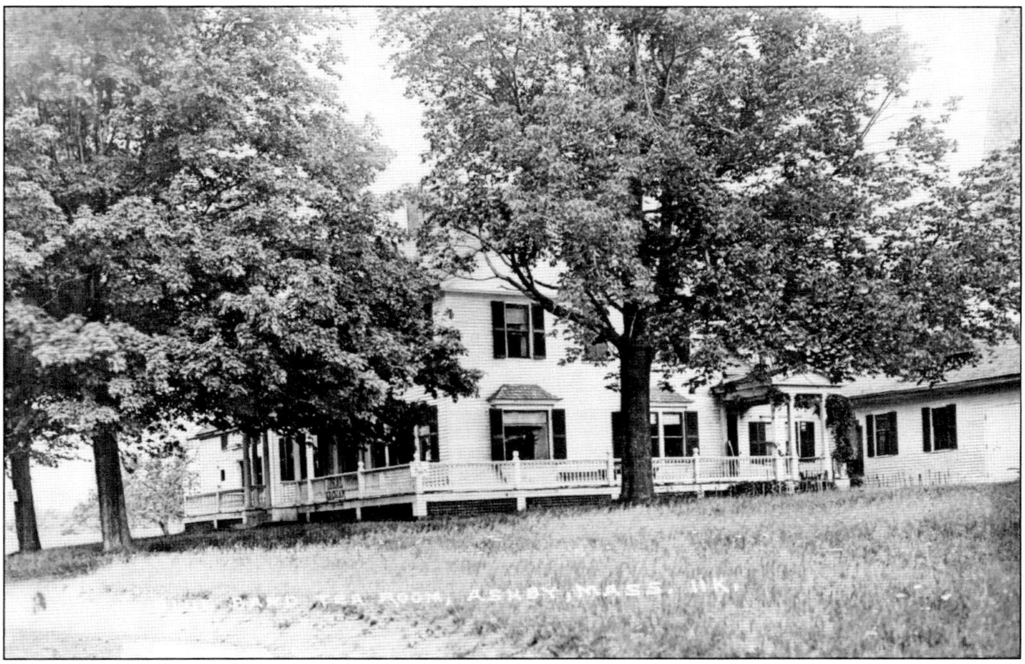

The Blue Band Tea Room was located about a half mile west of the town common, on Main Street. It was started by Jesse Lyman, a wealthy Boston industrialist who resided in Ashby. He had Arthur Wass operate the facility. With his Boston connections, Lyman was in a position to encourage acquaintances from the city to patronize his tearoom when they visited Ashby. Today, the structure is a private home and business. (Courtesy of William and Katherine Stanwood.)

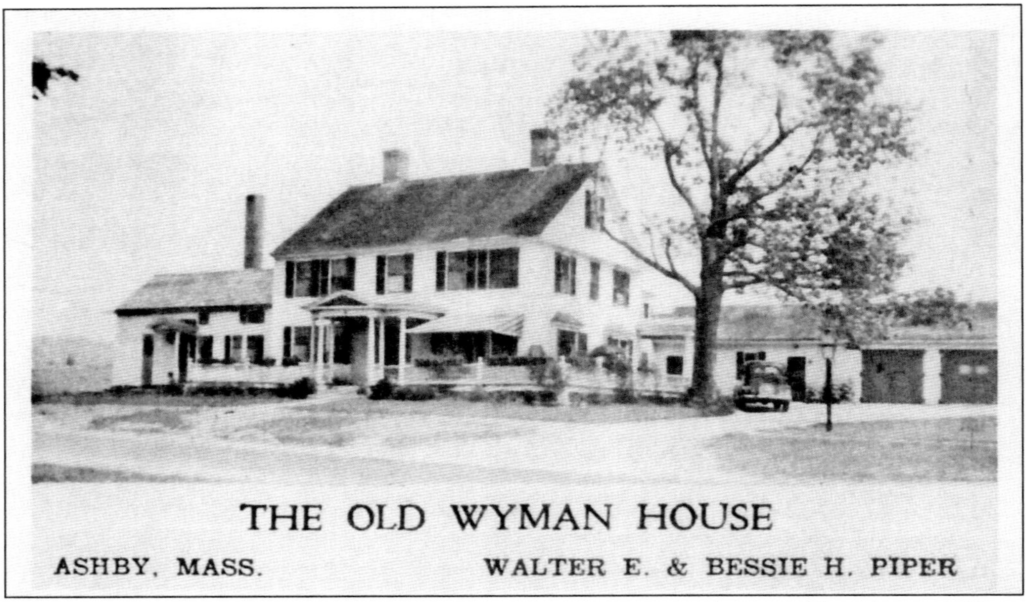

The Old Wyman House, located at 1031 Main Street and presently owned by John and Claire Lavin, was both a restaurant and boardinghouse. Many teachers in the Ashby schools boarded here, within easy walking distance of the Lyman School.

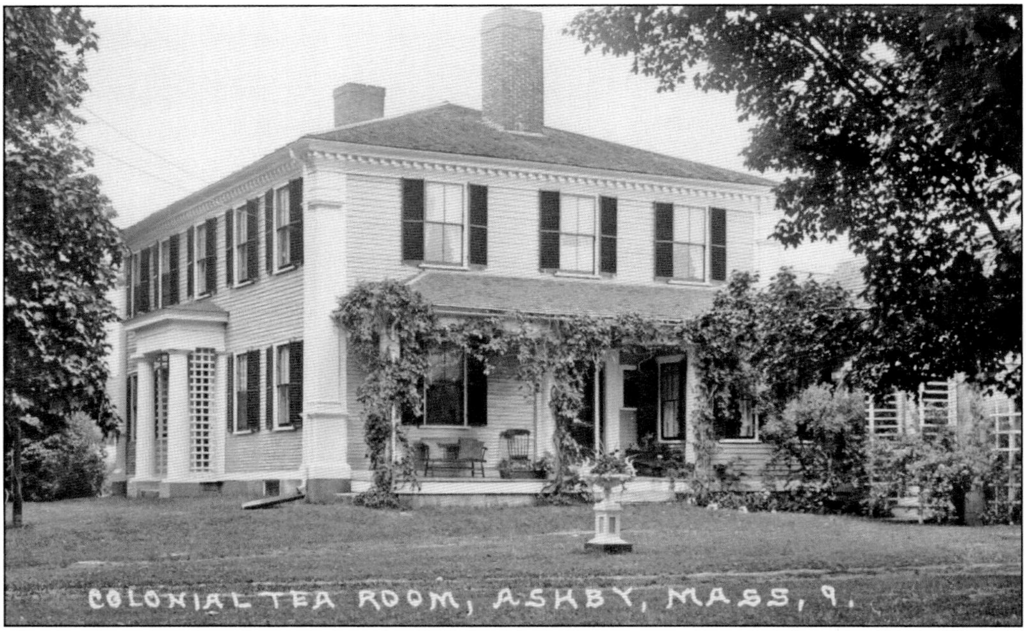

The Colonial Tea Room is pictured here in the late 1920s. The Colonial was the better known of two tearooms that served visitors and those residents who could afford to have tea and a bite to eat. Ashby was a favored stop for city residents able to escape the summer heat of the city. In the winter, the Colonial let out rooms to local teachers required to live in town. (Courtesy of William and Katherine Stanwood.)

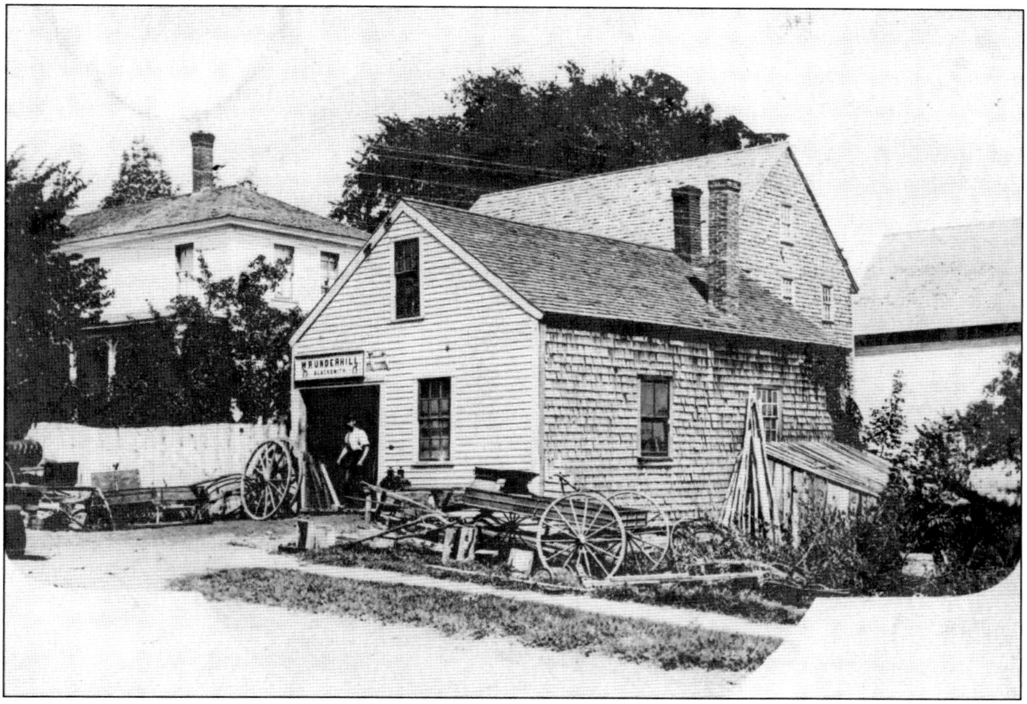

Blacksmithing was an important trade in a community where the horse and wagon was the primary mode of transportation. William R. Underhill specialized in repairing wagon wheels, although he did all types of blacksmith work. In this photograph, it can be seen that Underhill is keeping up with the times, as he has electric wires running to his shop. (Courtesy of William and Katherine Stanwood.)

When-
ever you are
in need of any General
Blacksmith or Wheelwright
Work of any description neatly
done at short notice and Rock
Bottom Prices, W. R. Under-
hill's shop is the place to go.
Central location. Tele-
phone connection.
Ashby.

This 1904 advertisement is for Underhill's blacksmith and wheelwright work. Underhill's shop was located behind the house on the corner of Main Street and South Road. The wheelwright's skill was always in demand, and Underhill kept Ashby's carriages and wagons rolling.

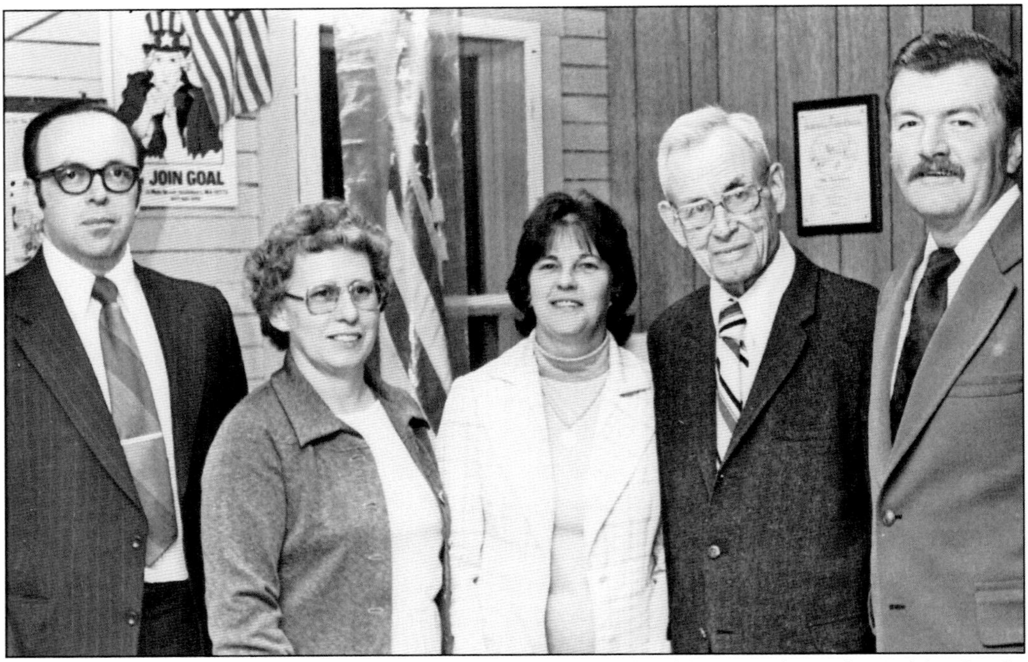

A small group of Ashby residents was organized by Alfred Tebbetts to form the Ashby Credit Union in 1969. Tebbetts had recently moved to Ashby and recognized the need for a banking facility. Shown here, the officers of the Ashby Credit Union are, from left to right, Richard P. Catalini, G. Lillian Whitney, Ann Seymour, Dr. Burnham S. Walker, and Elmer Fitzgerald. The credit union served the community for about 20 years before merging with the Lunenburg Credit Union and eventually becoming part of Worker's Credit Union. (Courtesy of Richard and Nancy Catalini.)

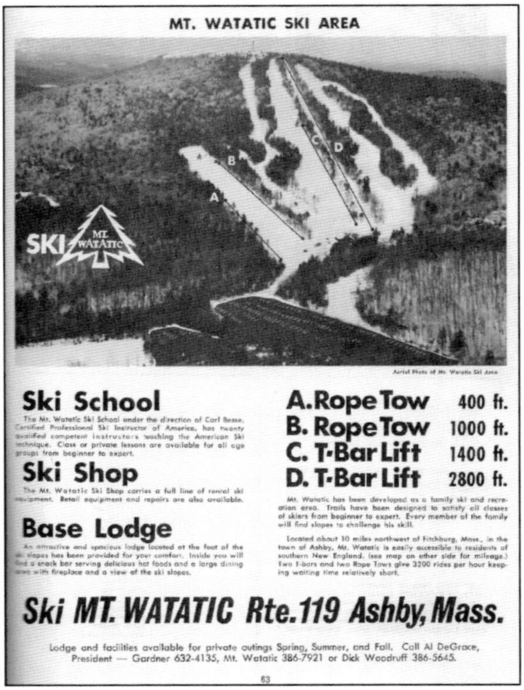

Mount Watatic Ski Area was operated as a successful ski business from 1962 until 1982. At its height in the early 1970s, the ski area had a lodge, ski shop, and ski school with as many as 20 instructors. (Courtesy of Carol Bennett Lielasus.)

Three

Around Town

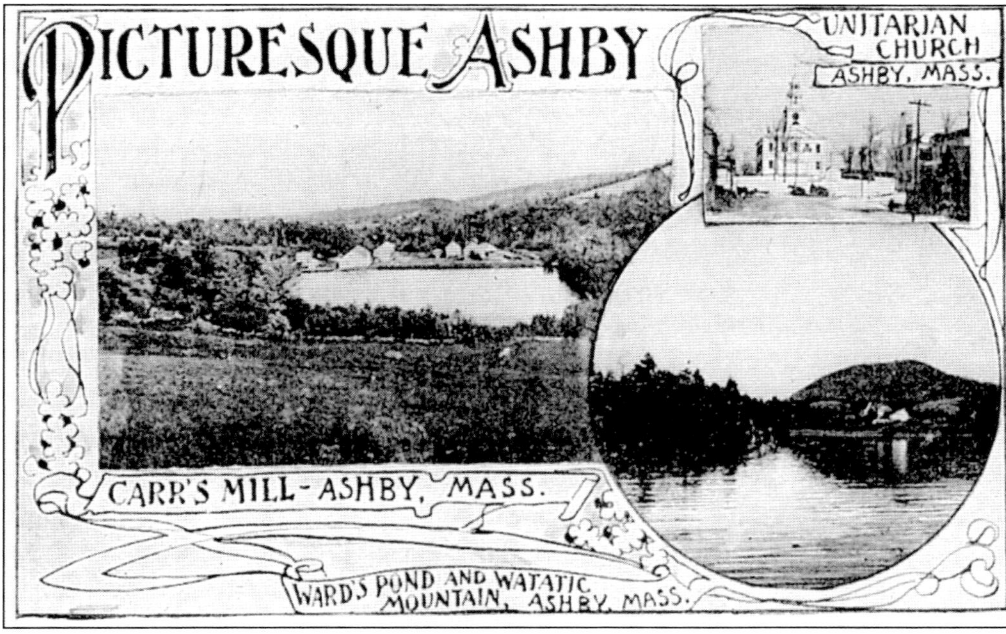

Postcards were a popular means to communicate with friends while traveling. This promotional postcard from the early 20th century lets the folks back home know what a quaint and attractive place the sender is visiting. The designer has even included Ward's Pond in neighboring Ashburnham as one of Ashby's attractions.

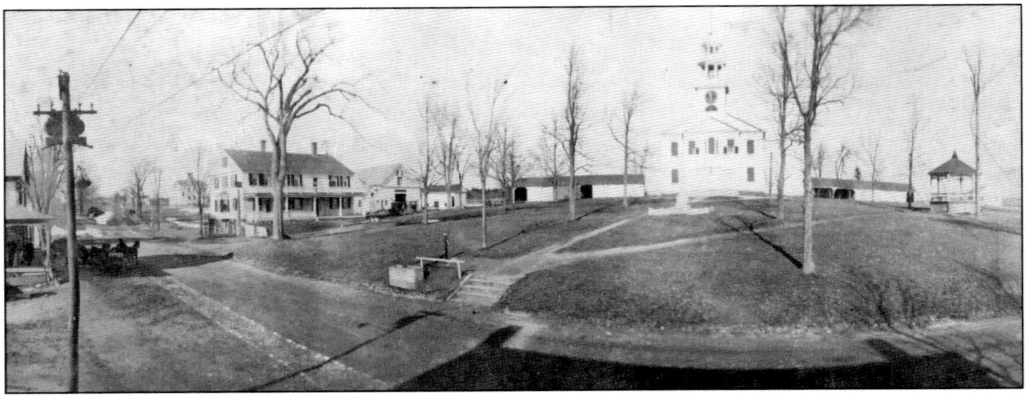

This is a panoramic view of the common taken about 1908. Electricity is being generated at Loveland's Saw and Gristmill, and wires have been strung to the south side of Main Street, but electricity has yet to reach the church, tavern, or school on the north side of the common. The watering trough just to the left of the steps was a common feature along roads in the early 1900s. Today, the trough and pump remain in their original location. The young trees seen in this image are now being replaced a century later as they succumb to age and disease.

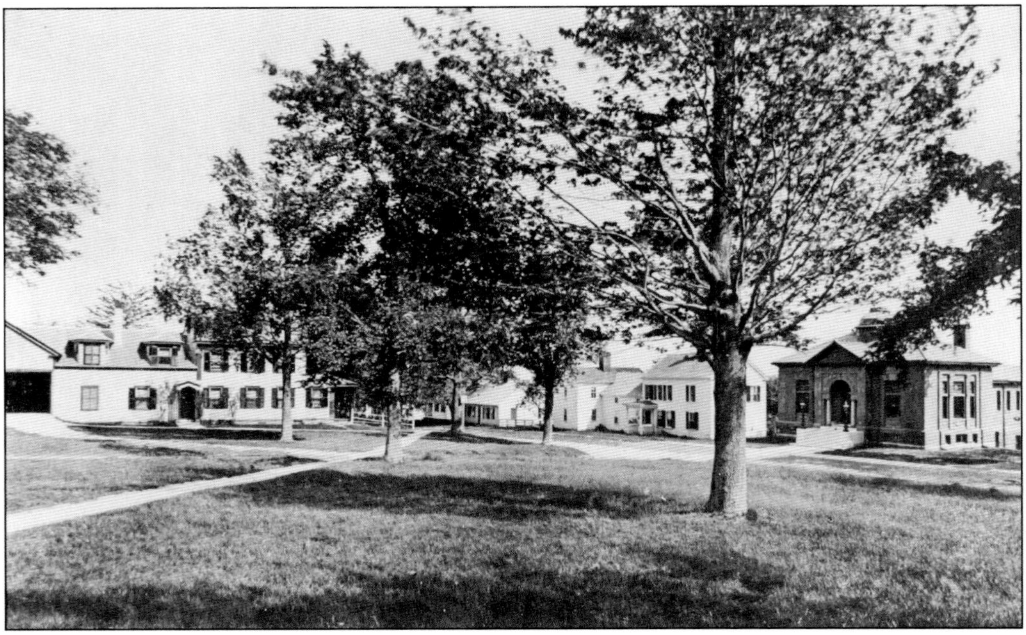

This view from the town common of the Ashby Free Public Library (right) and Edwin Chapman's home (left) was taken in 1903. Chapman funded the construction of the library, which served the town for over 100 years before it was expanded. (Courtesy of Ashby Free Public Library.)

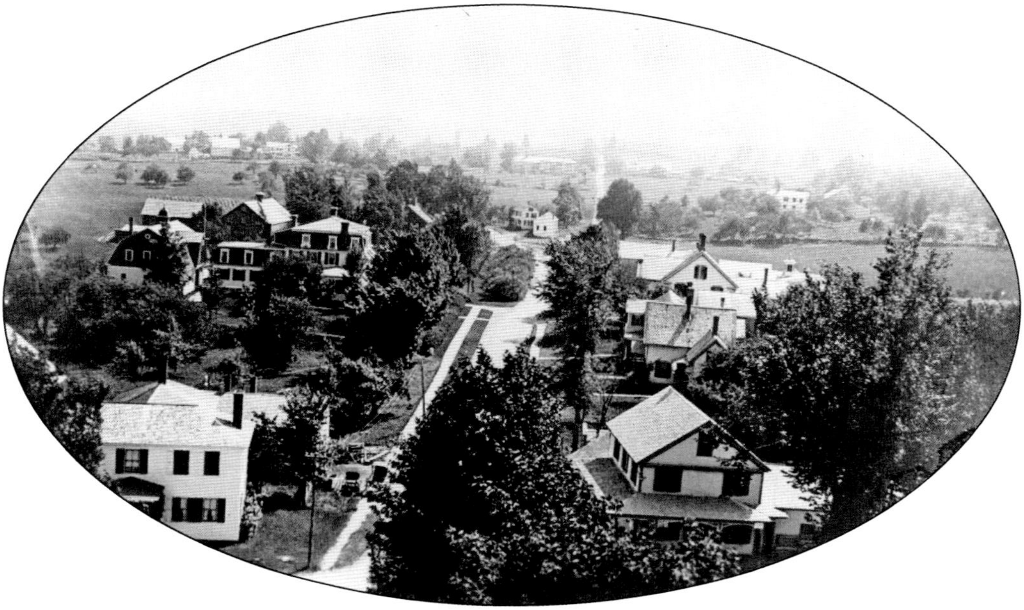

This view looking south from the belfry of the First Parish Church shows South Road in 1915. Although some of the barns are gone, all of the houses remain today much as they were back then. The newly installed electrical lines can be seen along South Road. The coming of electricity and the automobile had a major impact on the way of life in Ashby.

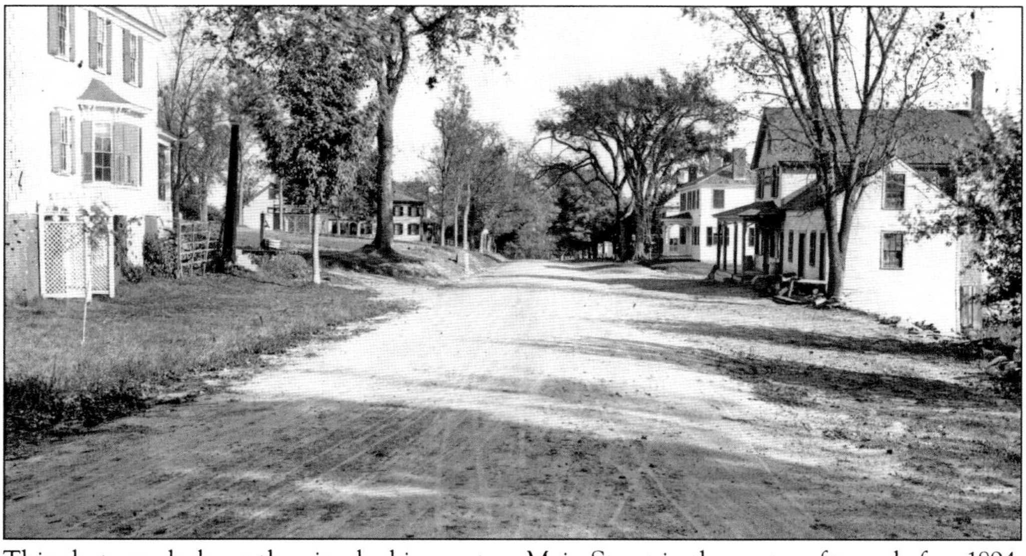

This photograph shows the view looking east on Main Street in the center of town before 1894. On the right is the store that is now the Ashby Market. On the left is the Elmwood Inn, now the post office. The fire station, now the historical society, has yet to be built on the right side of the street. The photograph clearly shows the elm trees that once lined Main Street.

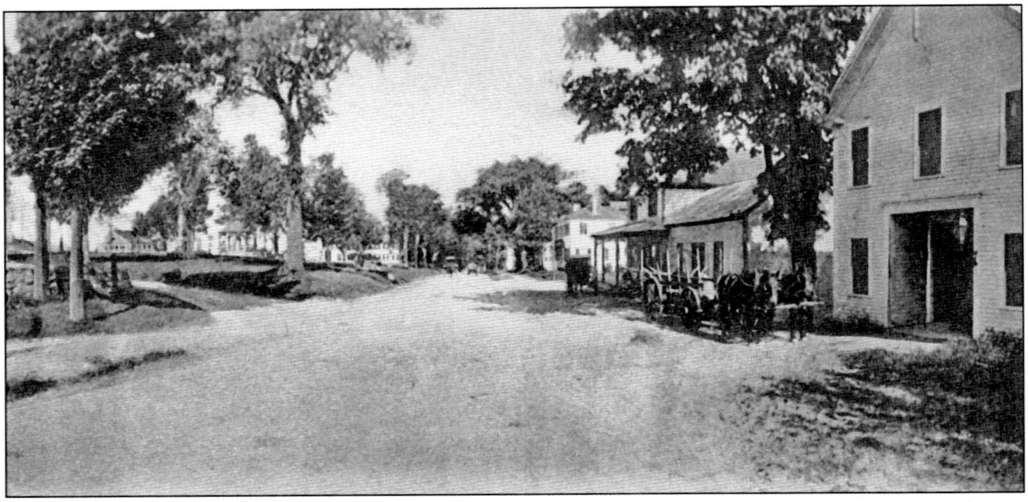

This is a photograph of Main Street about 1901. In this photograph, all the vehicles are horse-drawn and the new fire station on the right has been built. Two years earlier, the town had purchased a Watatic hand-pumped fire engine for $300. (Courtesy of William and Katherine Stanwood.)

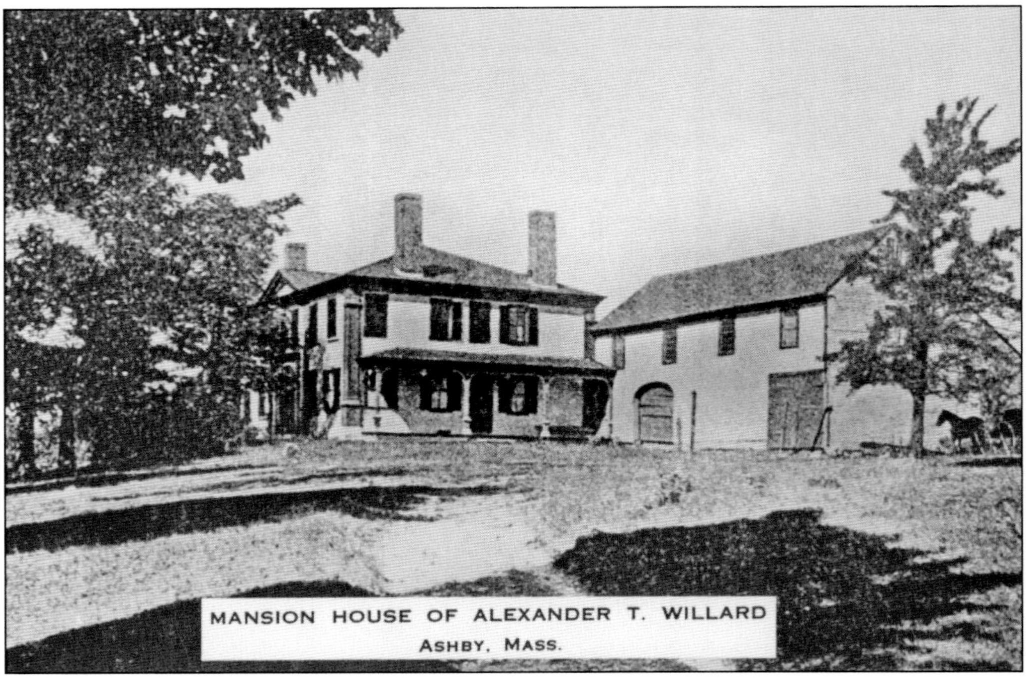

Built in the early 19th century, this elegant house belonged to Alexander T. Willard, one of Ashby's two clock-making families. The east and west ends of the house were brick and contained eight fireplaces. The clock shop was in a separate building just east of the house. The house was destroyed by fire in the early 1900s and replaced by a smaller home now on the Ashby Stock Farm. (Courtesy of Charles Parlee.)

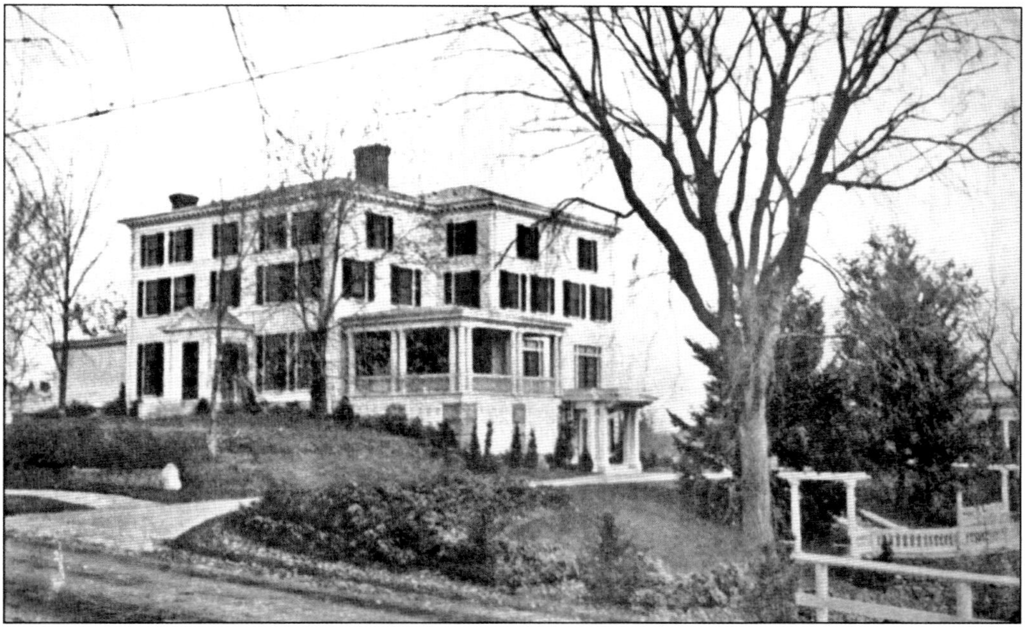

This is the Jesse P. Lyman estate, known as Brook Knoll, on South Road. The house served as a Lyman home for much of the 20th century.

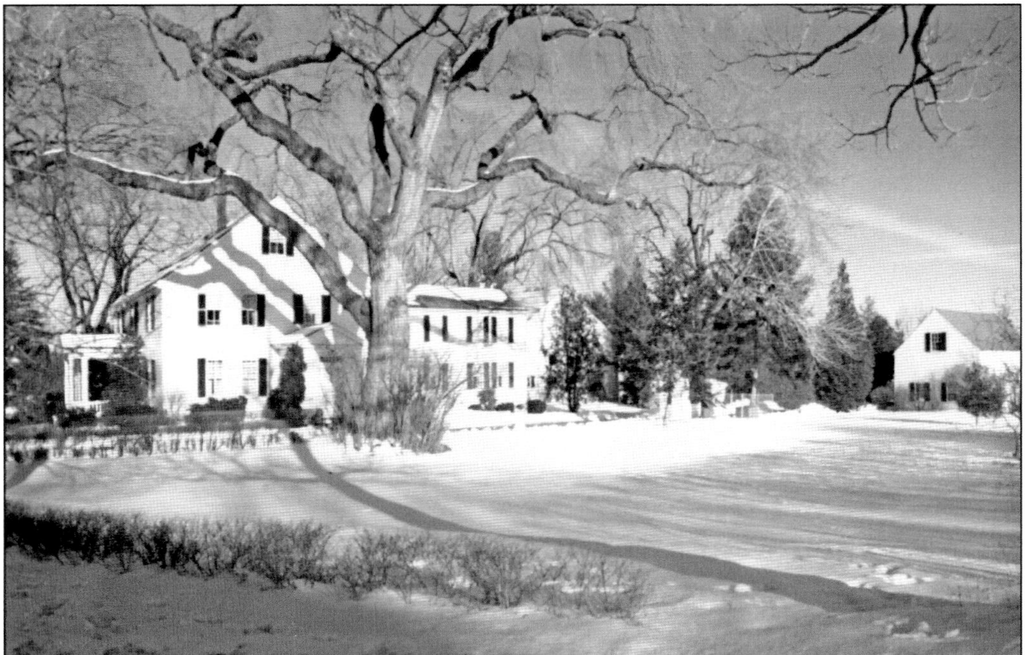

Elm Farm, on South Road, was the home of Edwin and Barbara Lyman for many years. (Courtesy of Warren Lyman.)

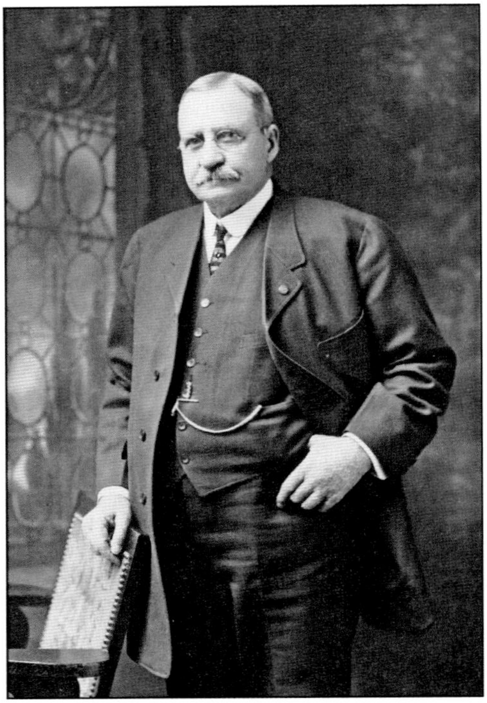

Edwin Chapman, who grew up in Ashby, moved to Boston and became a wealthy meat merchant. He maintained a home in Ashby as a summer residence. In 1901, Chapman became aware of the townspeople's concern for the safety and accessibility of the 3,000 or more books that constituted the town library, as they were moved from one private residence to another. He therefore purchased a piece of land directly across Main Street from his home and built "a nice building making it as near fire proof as possible and presented it to the town." It was dedicated in 1902.

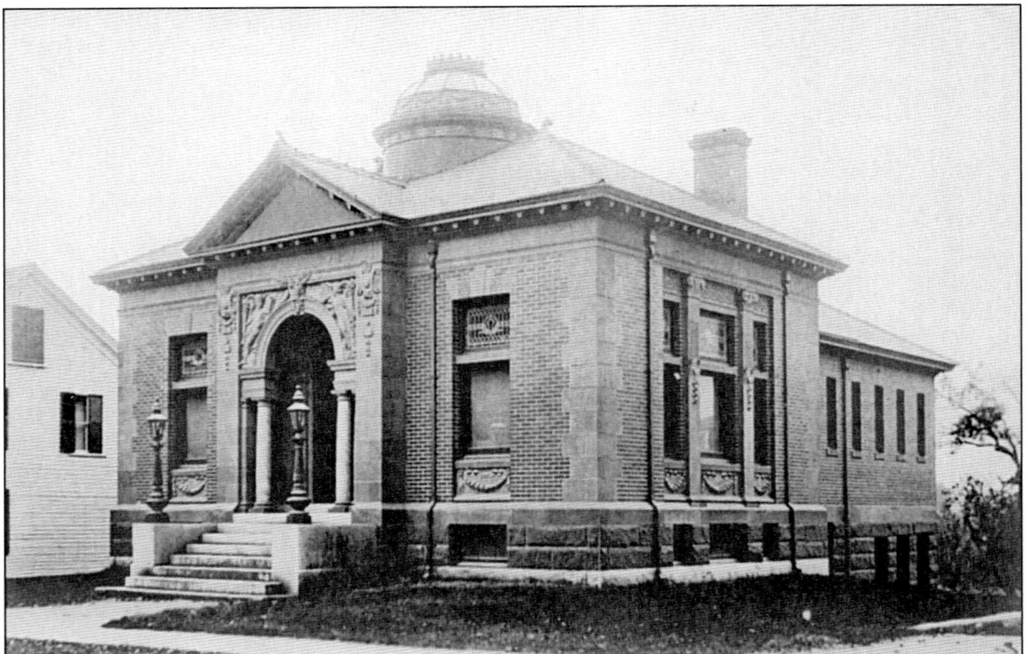

The Ashby Free Public Library was built in 1902 by Edwin Chapman, a wealthy meat and poultry merchant who divided his time between Ashby and Boston. Chapman, along with George Hammond of Ashburnham, pioneered the shipment of dressed beef in refrigerated railroad cars from Chicago to Boston. Prior to this, all beef was shipped live and slaughtered in the city. The building was constructed in the Beaux-Arts style by David Damon's construction company. (Courtesy of Nancy Elliott Rogers.)

This was the view as one entered the new Ashby Free Public Library in 1902. The entryway passed open rooms on both the right and left as patrons made their way to the librarian's desk, located between two massive columns of polished stone. The ornate lamp overhead provided light, and more came through the three south-facing windows behind the desk. (Courtesy of Ashby Free Public Library.)

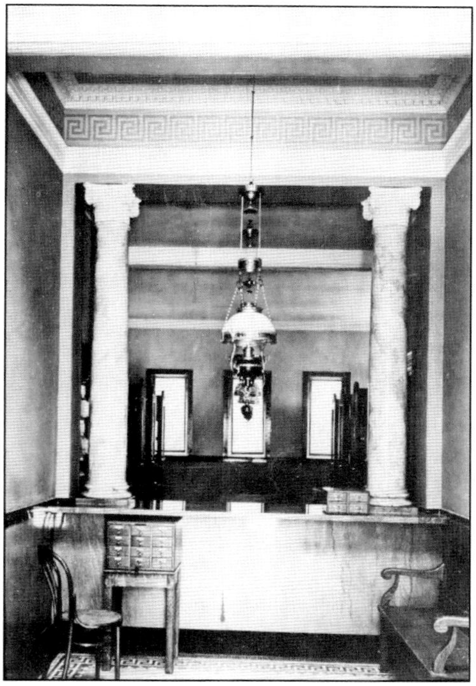

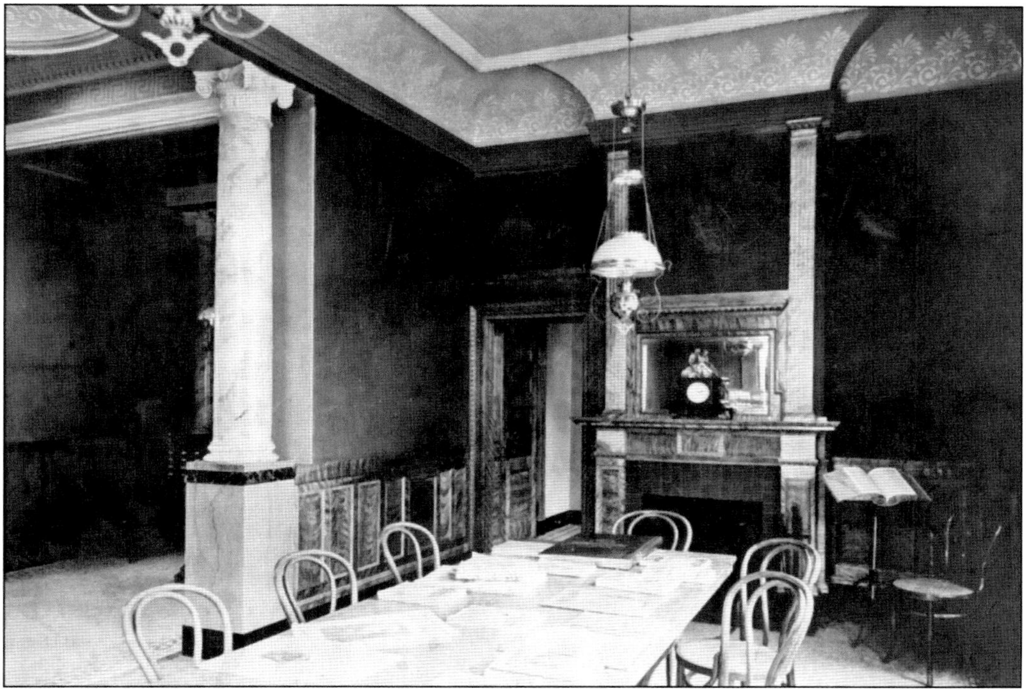

This view of one of the side rooms by the main hall shows the lengths Chapman went to in order to provide a first-class library. The architect, H.M. Francis, decorated the high wall and floor with classic designs that give it a feeling of elegance. Some minor changes were made during the first decade after the building was dedicated. A well was dug and water was furnished to the basement, the oil lamps were replaced with electric lighting, and the heating was changed from woodstoves to a coal furnace. (Courtesy of Ashby Free Public Library.)

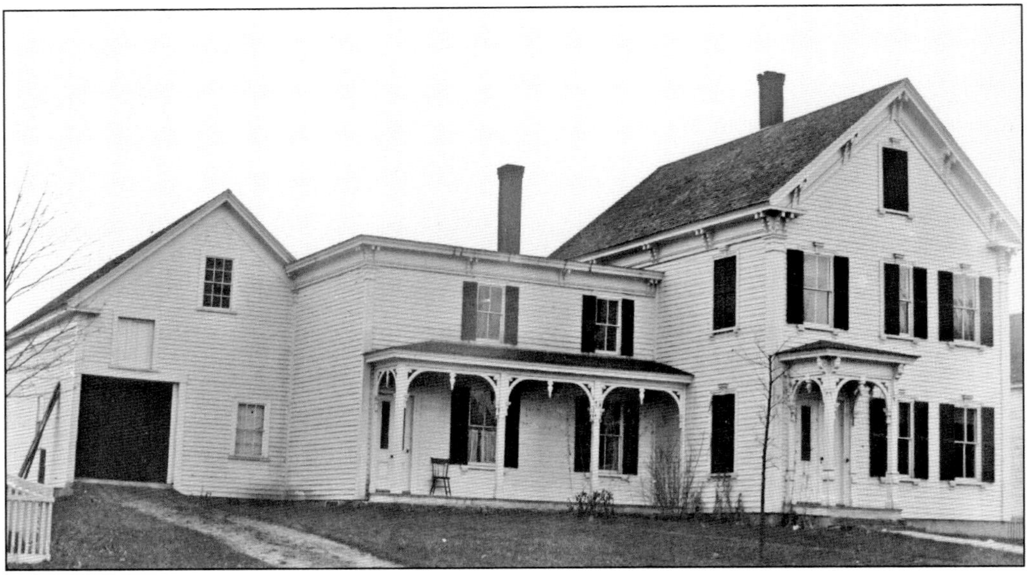

This home on Main Street demonstrates the creativity of local carpenters, who were not constrained by formal education in design. The house includes elements of Greek Revival and Carpenter Gothic styles combined to charming effect.

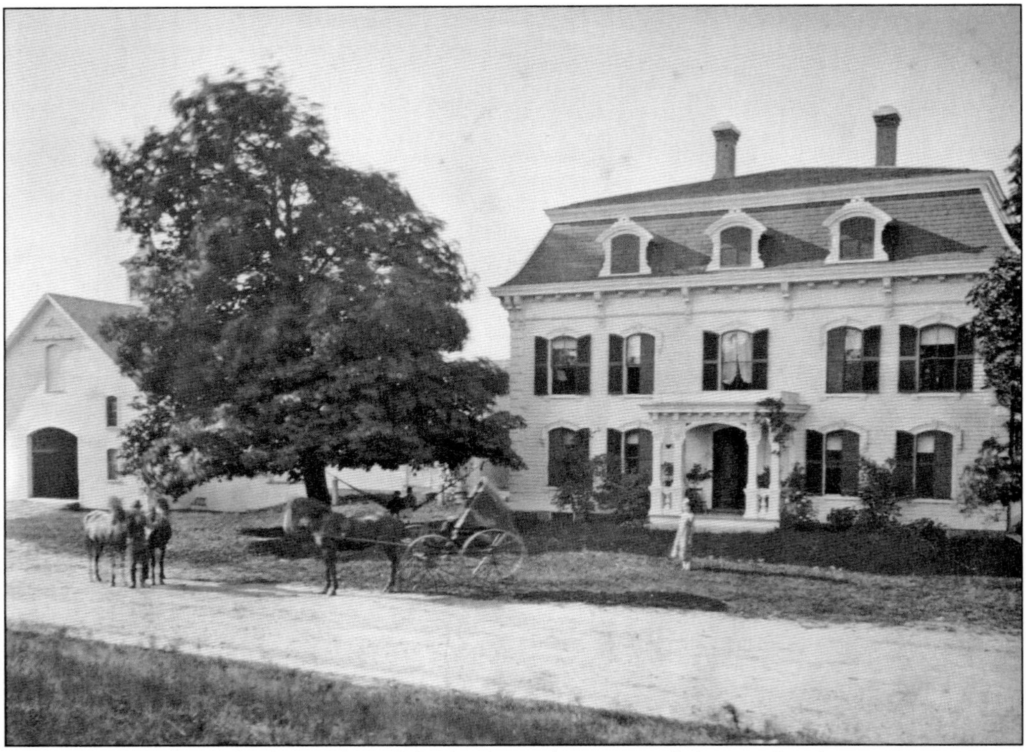

In 1793, Calvin and Abraham Edwards built a home large enough for two families on Main Street. They also built a clock shop in which they manufactured wooden-geared clockworks. In the 1860s, Francis W. Wright purchased the house and remodeled it in the then fashionable French Empire style. This photograph was taken about 1880, with F.W. Wright seated in the carriage behind his horse, Old Charlie, and Carrie Wright standing to the right. (Courtesy of Tom Dorward.)

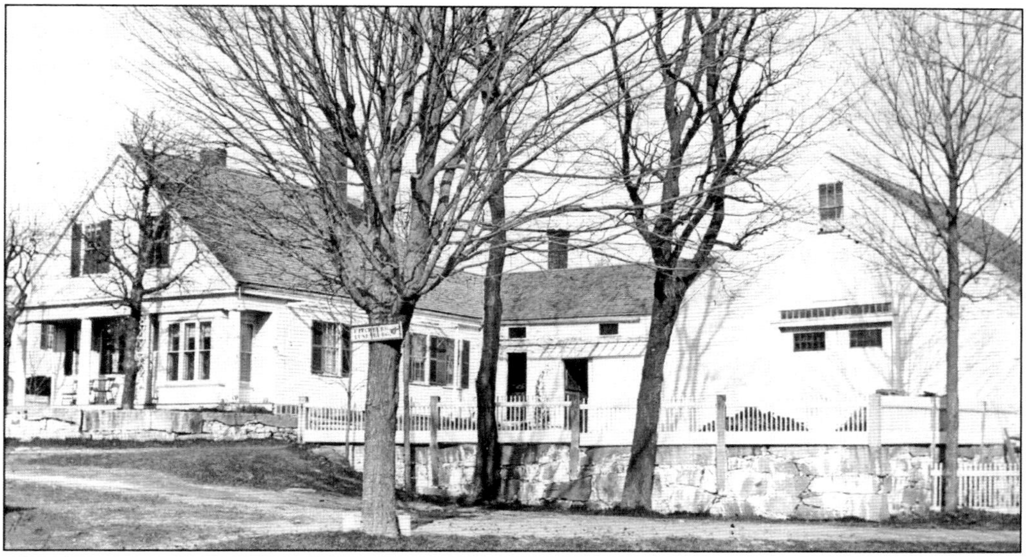

This house at the corner of Main Street and Turnpike Road is one of the few examples of Greek Revival architecture in town. The sign nailed to the tree points the way to Fitchburg and Lunenburg.

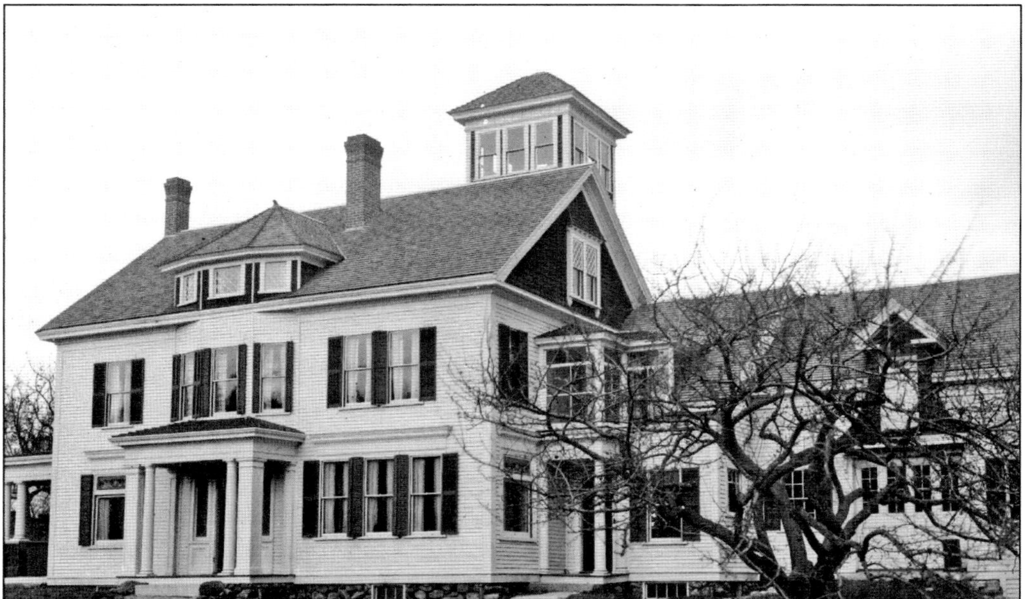

This house on Turnpike Road gained notoriety in the late 1950s when the owner applied for a building permit to construct a gas chamber to exterminate Jews. The permit was denied, despite the threat of a lawsuit.

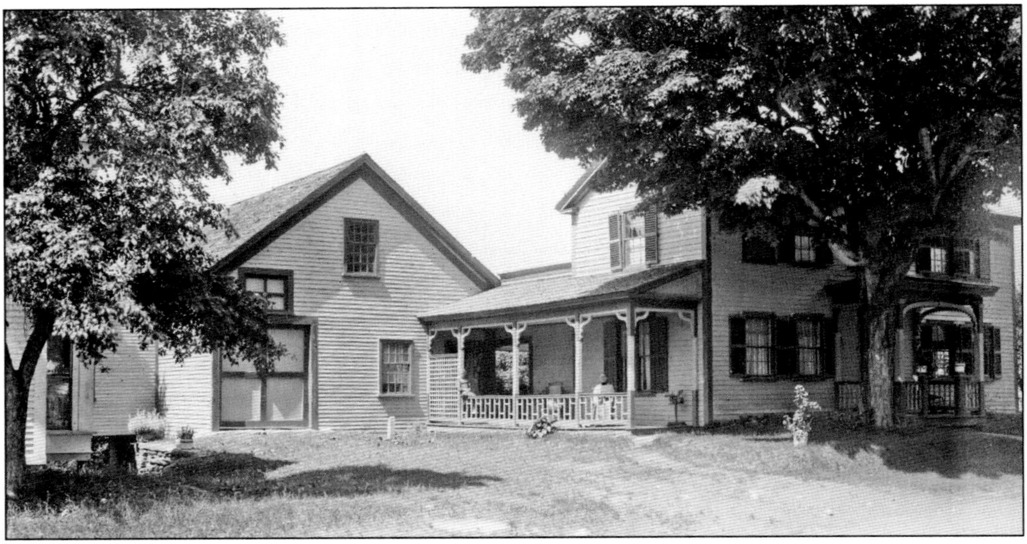

This is the home of George A. Hitchcock, who is noted for his diary of his time in the Civil War. The son of George L. Hitchcock and Eliza Sparhawk, he was born here in 1844. George L. was an abolitionist and a member of the Free Soil Party, espousing "free soil, free speech, free labor and free men."

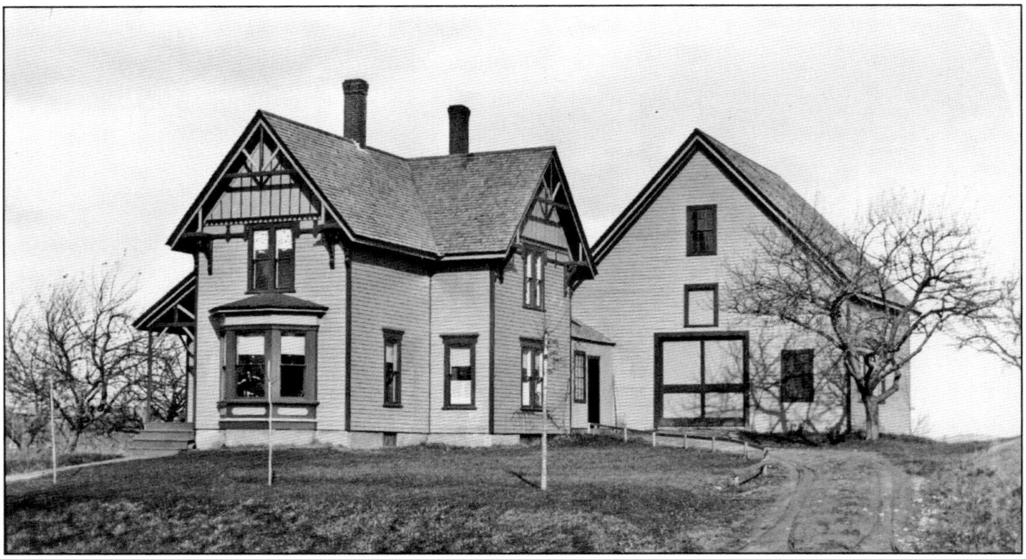

This house on Main Street is the only example in Ashby of Stick Style architecture, which was popular in the 1880s. At this time, Ashby's population had been in decline for 50 years, and few new houses were being built. Although the barn is gone, the house with its distinctive style still overlooks Main Street.

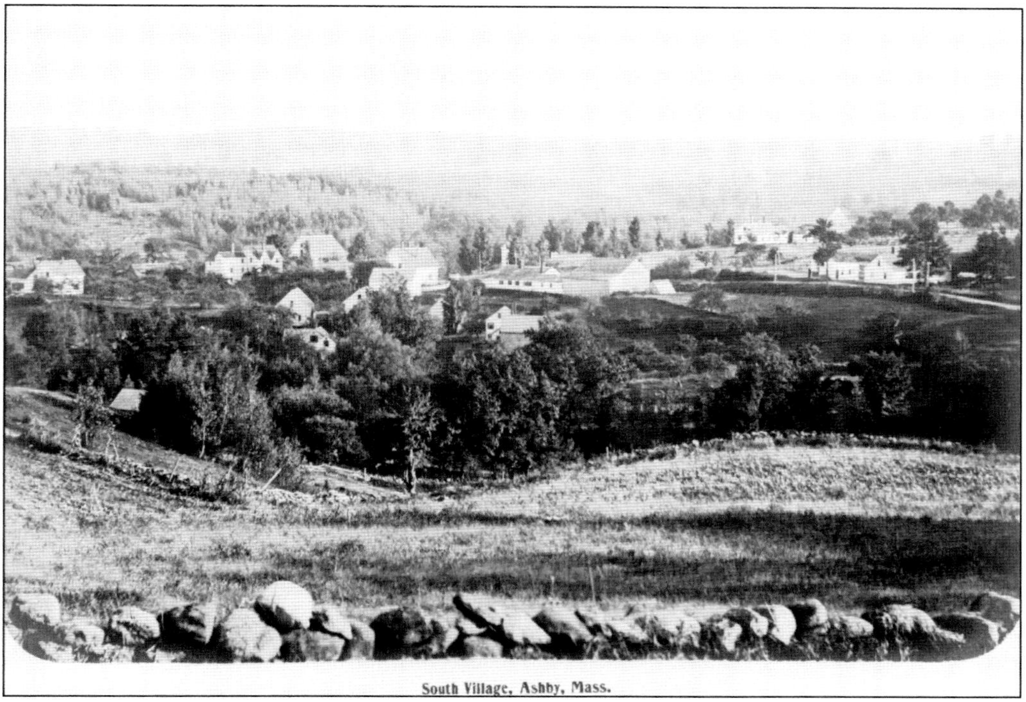

South Village, at the intersection of South and Erickson Roads, was a small village center close to the mills along Willard Brook. Many of the families living here either worked in or operated the water-powered mills nearby. (Courtesy of Richard and Nancy Catalini.)

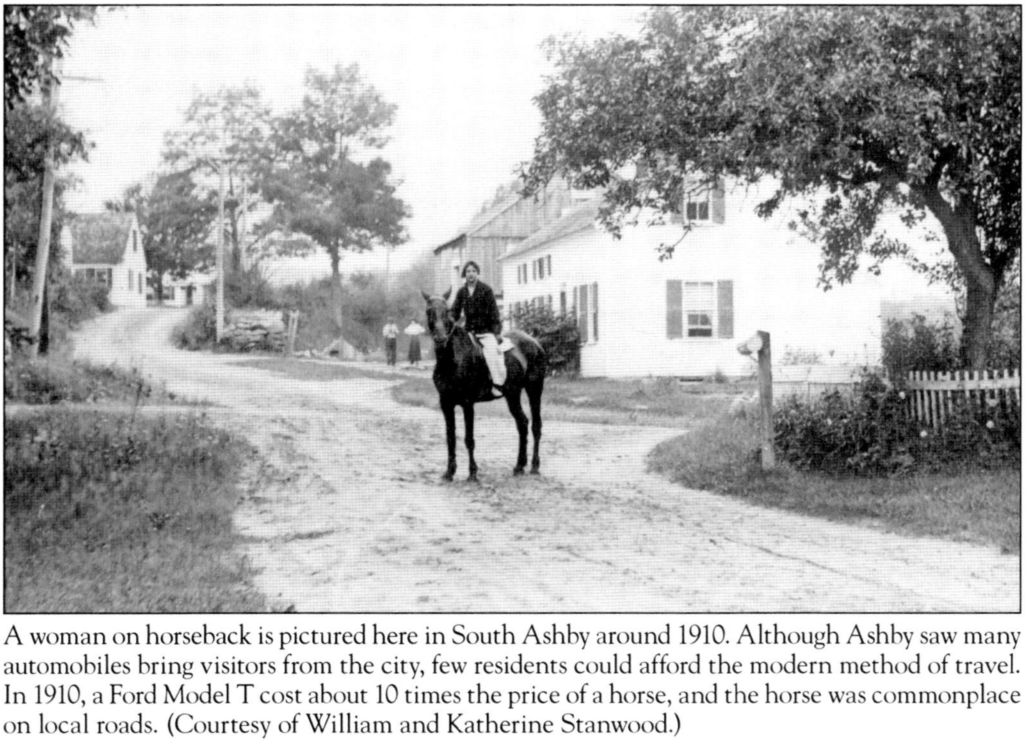

A woman on horseback is pictured here in South Ashby around 1910. Although Ashby saw many automobiles bring visitors from the city, few residents could afford the modern method of travel. In 1910, a Ford Model T cost about 10 times the price of a horse, and the horse was commonplace on local roads. (Courtesy of William and Katherine Stanwood.)

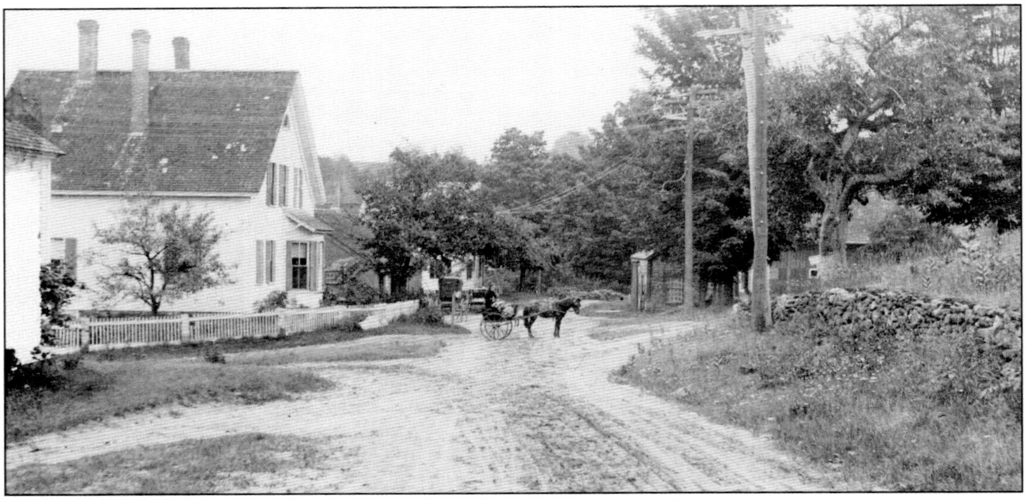

A woman in a cart drawn by a pony stops at the intersection of South and Erickson Roads. She is hauling a large sack placed on the floor of the cart at her feet. One can see utility poles along the street supplying electricity generated at Loveland's Mill, only a few hundred yards away, to local homes. Electricity was supplied intermittently, as the water flow from the millpond allowed. (Courtesy of William and Katherine Stanwood.)

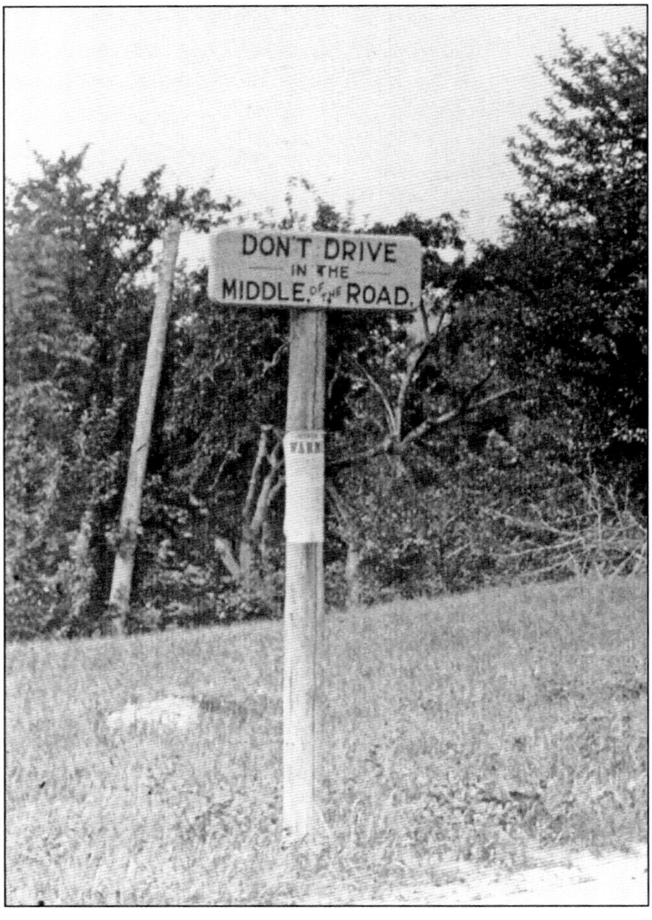

There were several signs along the state road like this indicating that driving in the middle of the road was a problem. At the time, Ashby had no police to enforce traffic laws. The arrival of the horseless carriage created new possibilities for collisions.

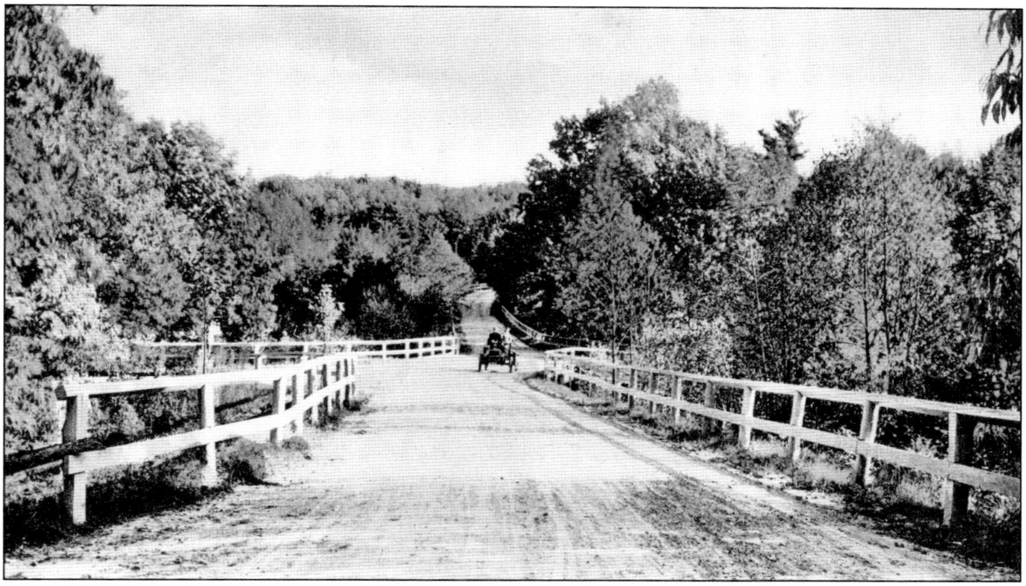

An early automobile is starting up the hill toward Ashby center on the "new" state road. The road, now Route 119, received a major upgrade in 1894. This was the beginning of improvements to state highways to accommodate the automobile. A better road allowed visitors from the Boston area to reach Ashby with relative ease. This encouraged the expansion and improvement of inns and teahouses to serve more guests. (Courtesy of William and Katherine Stanwood.)

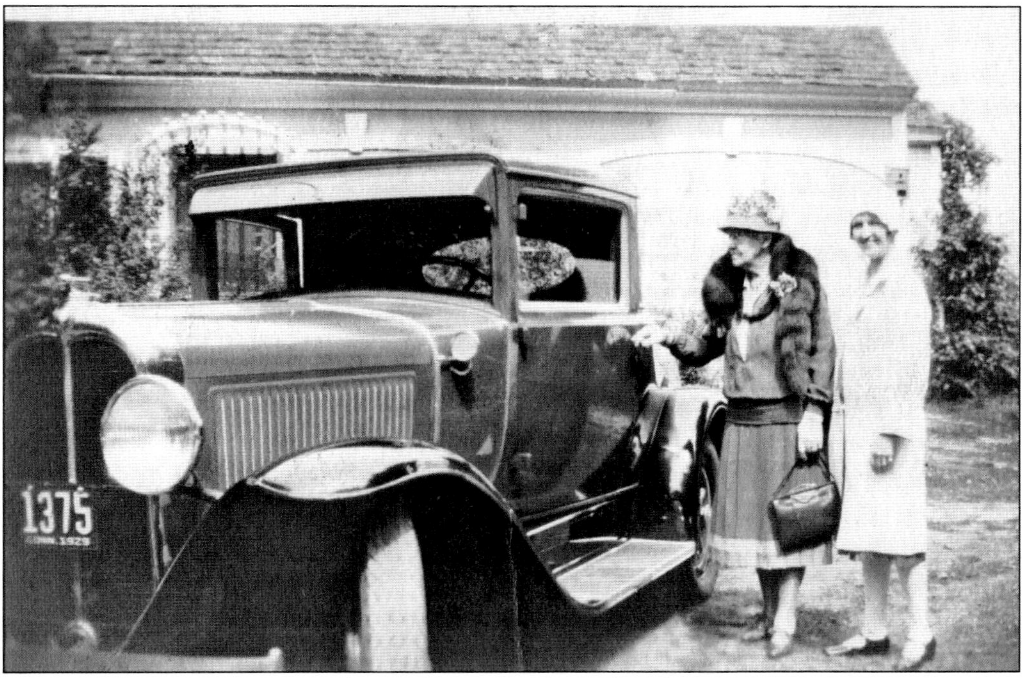

This photograph shows a Mrs. Olmstead, owner of the Colonial Tea Room on lower Main Street, and her daughter Grace Scoutin in 1929. The tearoom was one of several located in town during the 1910s and 1920s. A traveler could stop for the night or a bite to eat. Teachers, who were required to live in the town where they taught, could board there. Mrs. Olmstead was known for the elegant gardens around the house and her vegetarian fare.

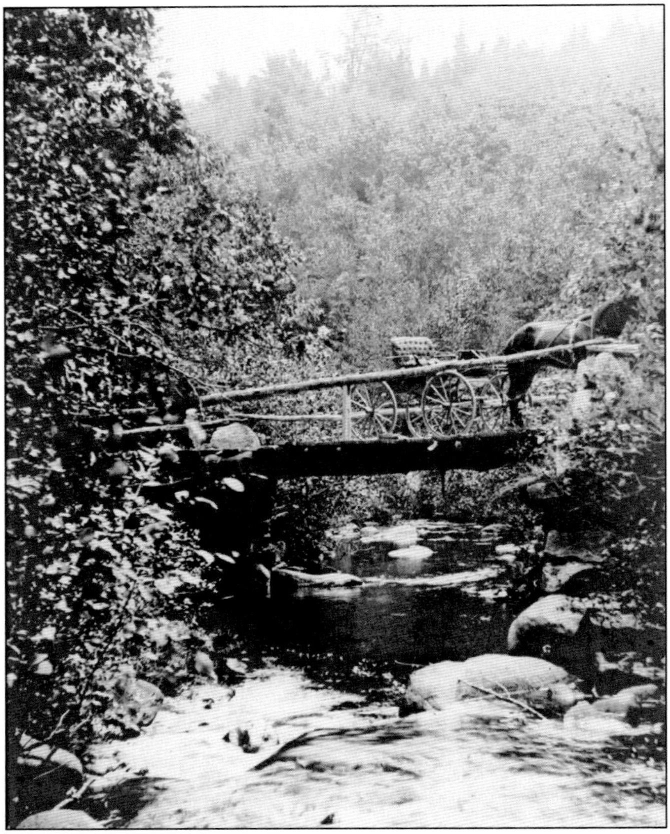

In the early 20th century, the Trap Falls Road Bridge was a wooden span between stone abutments. The bridge was later replaced with a steel bridge; it was removed, however, when rust weakened the steel, and it has not been replaced.

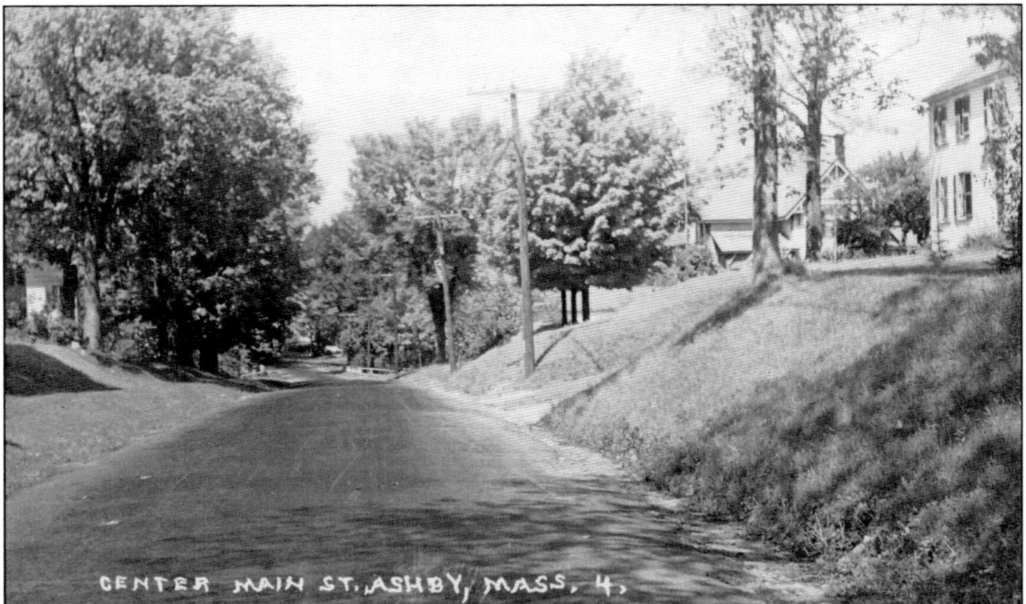

When the state paved the highway in 1894, substantial changes were made to the grade of the road to make it more level. When the houses along this section of road were built, their lawns were level with the road. The improvement left them standing well above the road.

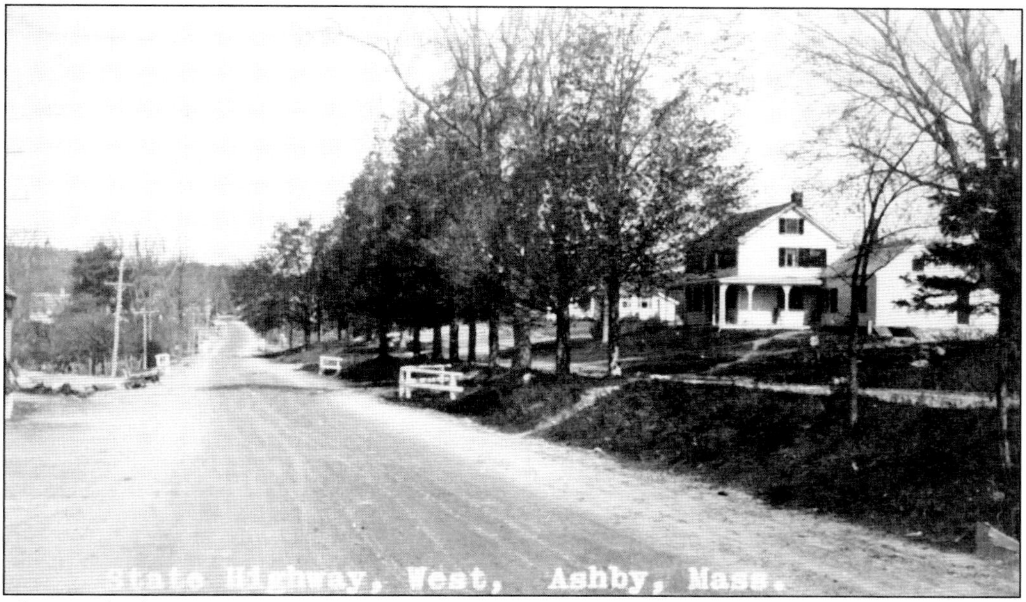

The state highway, now Route 119, was the main means of transportation to neighboring towns. In 1894, one mile of it in the center of Ashby became the first paved highway in the state. This was accompanied by needed improvements to the gravel portions of the road. This 1920s photograph captures a portion of the gravel highway. (Courtesy of William and Katherine Stanwood)

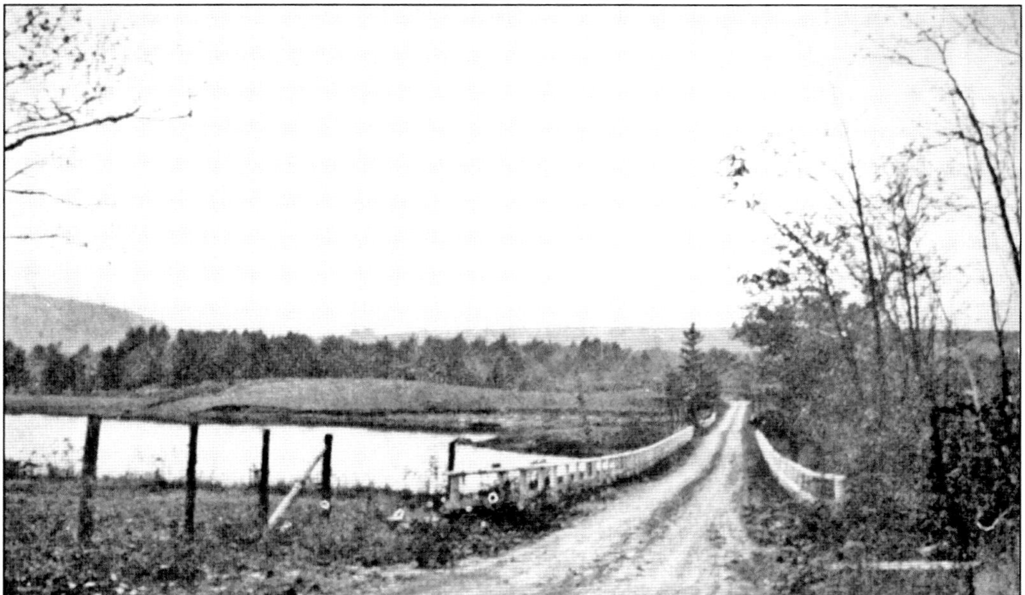

This view of Richardson Road shows the Ashby Reservoir, now the Fitchburg Reservoir, when it was operated by W. Loveland, A. Wilder, and A. Carr to supply water to their mills in South Village. In 1914, the City of Fitchburg would purchase the reservoir, raise the dam, and redirect the flow of water toward Fitchburg.

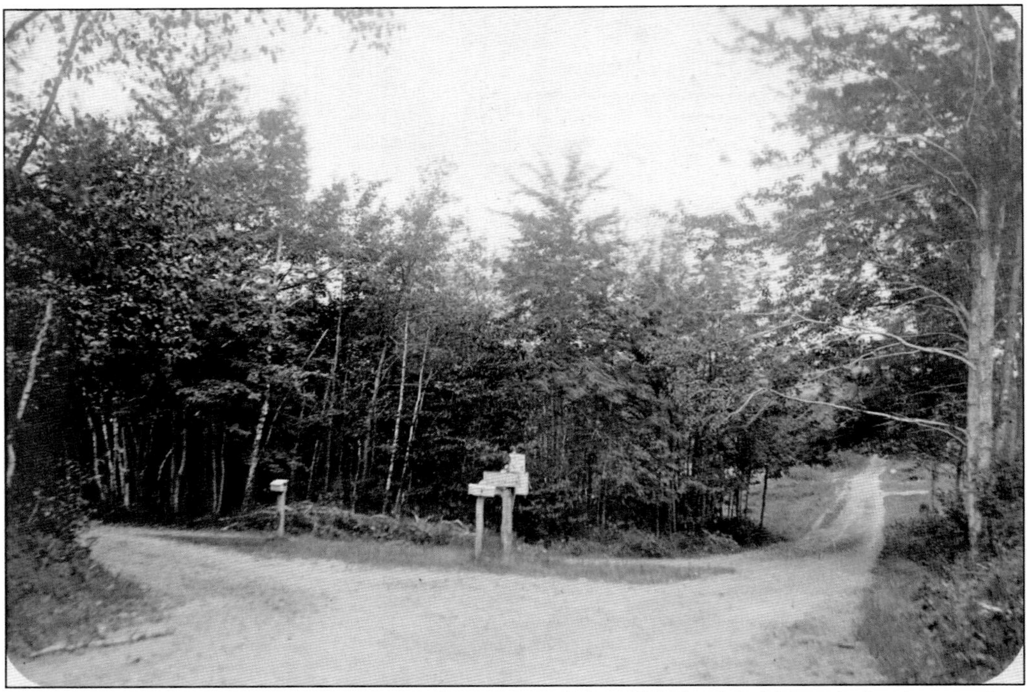

This intersection along the Rindge Road was part of the Old Northfield Road, the first road in what was to become Ashby. In the late 19th century, a railroad was planned for this area to serve Ashby. Financial backers could not be found for the project, and it was abandoned.

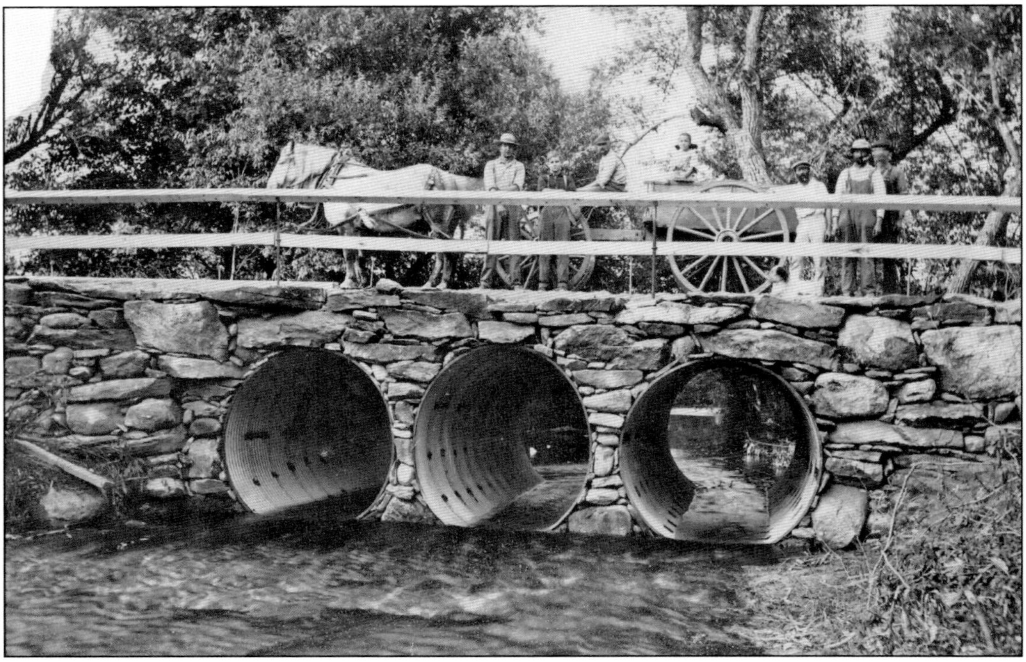

In 1894 through 1895, the state made major improvements to the Fitchburg Road, now Main Street, in Ashby. This photograph is of Sheldon Bridge in 1896. The use of steel culvert pipes channeling the stream were the newest drainage technology. The wagon on the bridge, used for hauling sand, gravel, and stone, appears to be giving a young girl a lift.

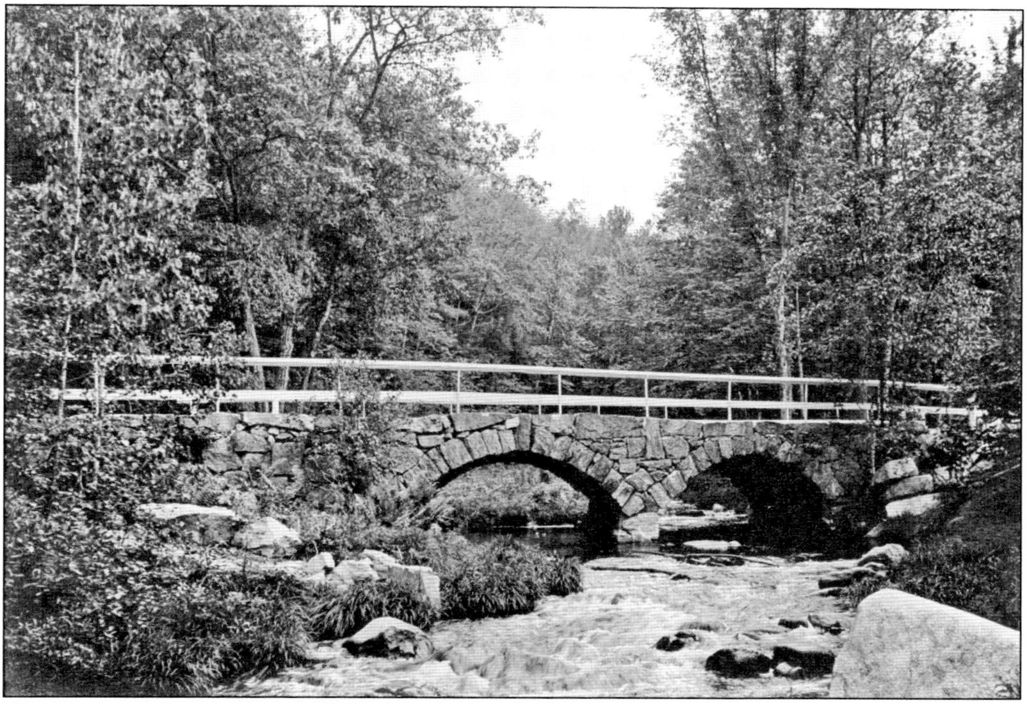

This is one of the drystone-arch bridges over Willard Brook on the Ashby Road, now Route 119. Built about 1850 with considerable skill and effort, this bridge saw service into the 20th century. The last drystone-arch bridge in use in Ashby was replaced in the 1970s.

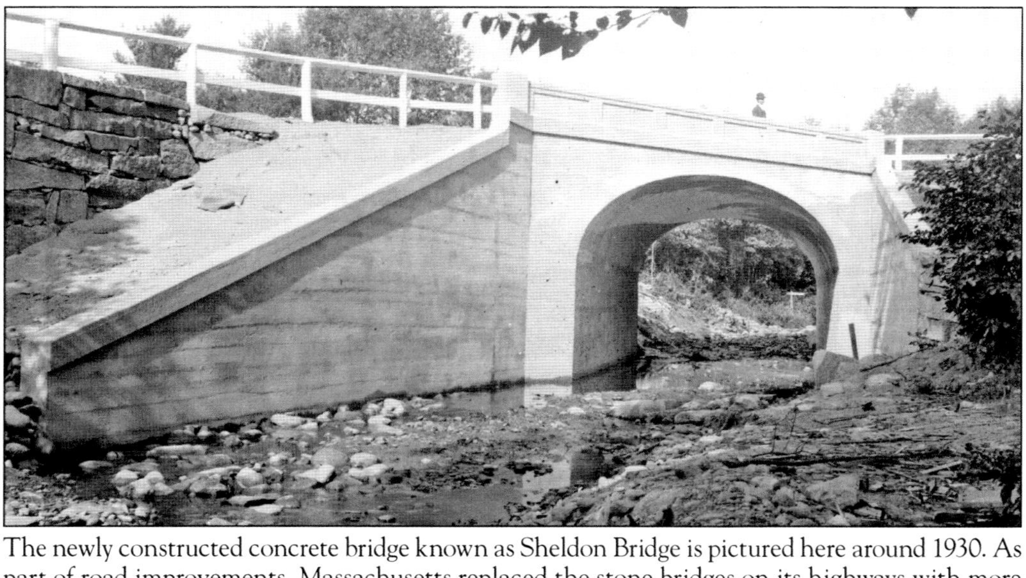

The newly constructed concrete bridge known as Sheldon Bridge is pictured here around 1930. As part of road improvements, Massachusetts replaced the stone bridges on its highways with more stable structures. This was a major improvement over the previous stone structure.

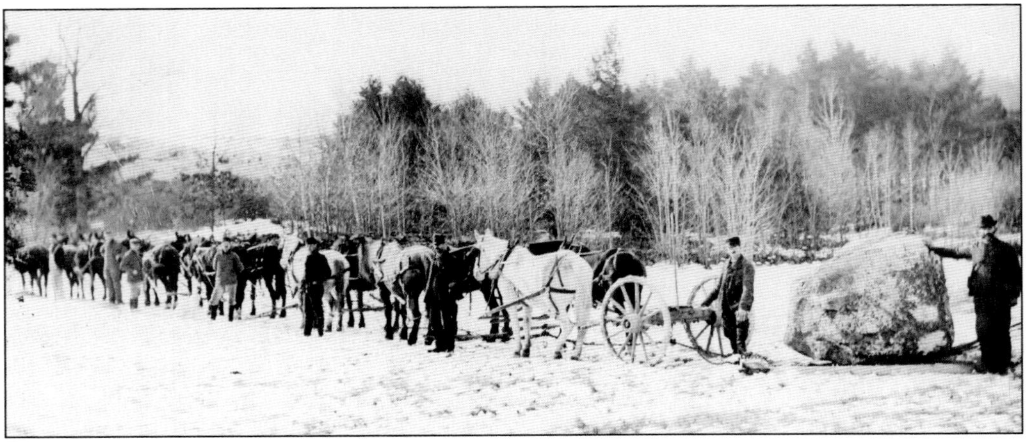

A 14-horse team is moving a rock to Glenwood Cemetery to serve as a grave monument. Moving heavy stones took cooperation among neighbors, bringing animals, people, and equipment together to accomplish the job. Here, the crew takes advantage of a light snow cover to allow the stone boat to slide more easily.

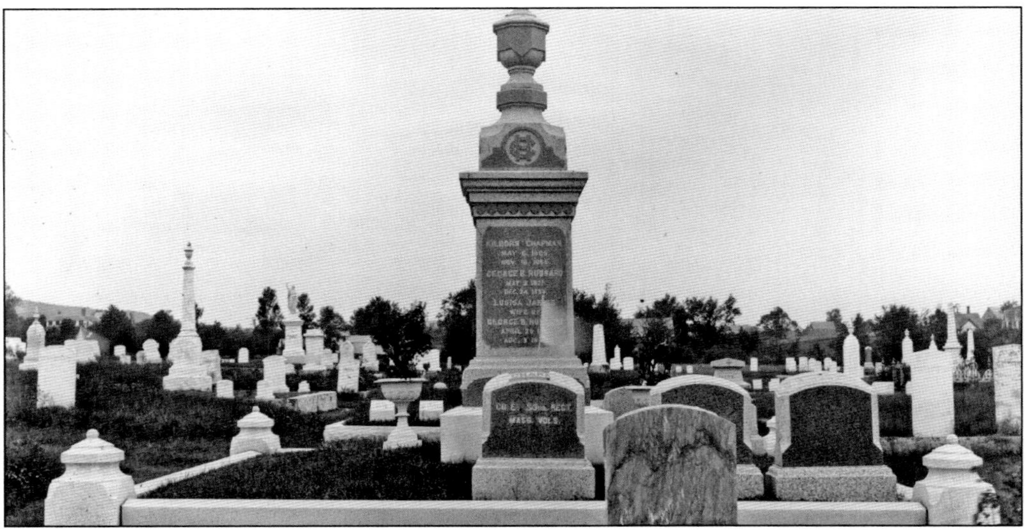

Glenwood Cemetery was dedicated in 1851. This view of the cemetery from around 1895 shows the extensive use of marble monuments popular in the second half of the 19th century. Unfortunately, marble does not weather well, and much of the delicate carving has eroded or broken over the years.

Four

Education

THE SECOND REUNION OF

ASHBY SCHOOL DISTRICT No. 5

IS TO BE AT THE

Pearly Gates Farm, Thursday, June 24, 1915

Ashby, Mass.

11 a. m. Social Intercourse. 12 to 1.30 p. m. Basket Lunch

1.30 p. m. Literary and Musical Program

"Come, dear old comrade, you and I
Will steal an hour from days gone by,
The shining days when life was new,
And all was bright with morning dew,
The lusty days of long ago,
When you were Bill and I was Joe."

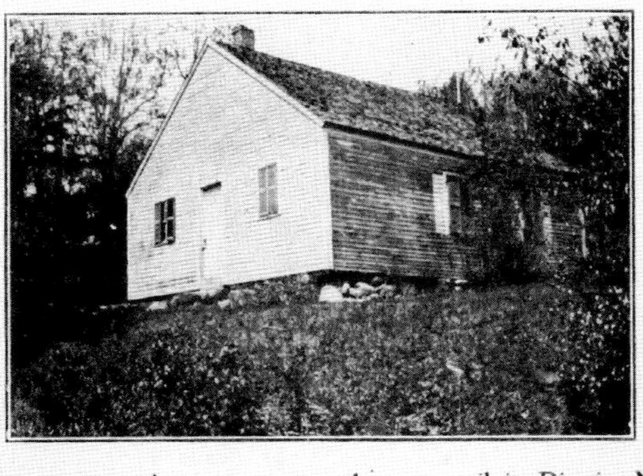

We want everyone who ever was teacher or pupil in District No. 5, to come and bring their families and friends. We would also like to have you extend this notice for we are anxious none be omitted.

Nearly every year, one or more of the nine schoolhouses in town would have a reunion of pupils and teachers. This leaflet invites alumni of Schoolhouse No. 5 to a reunion in 1915.

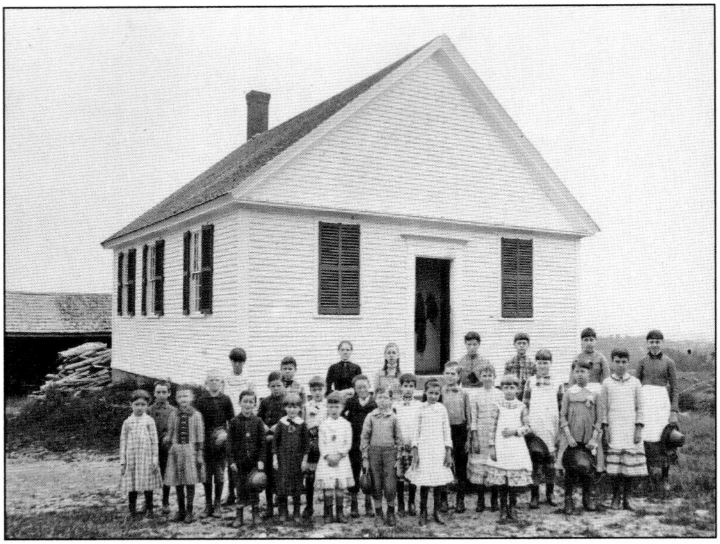

The children and teacher of Schoolhouse No. 1 pose for a photograph about 1900. Teacher Annie Billings instructed 26 students in the first through eighth grades. There were eight similar schoolhouses throughout Ashby. In the eighth grade, students had to decide whether to go on to high school or go to work, as education was not compulsory after eighth grade.

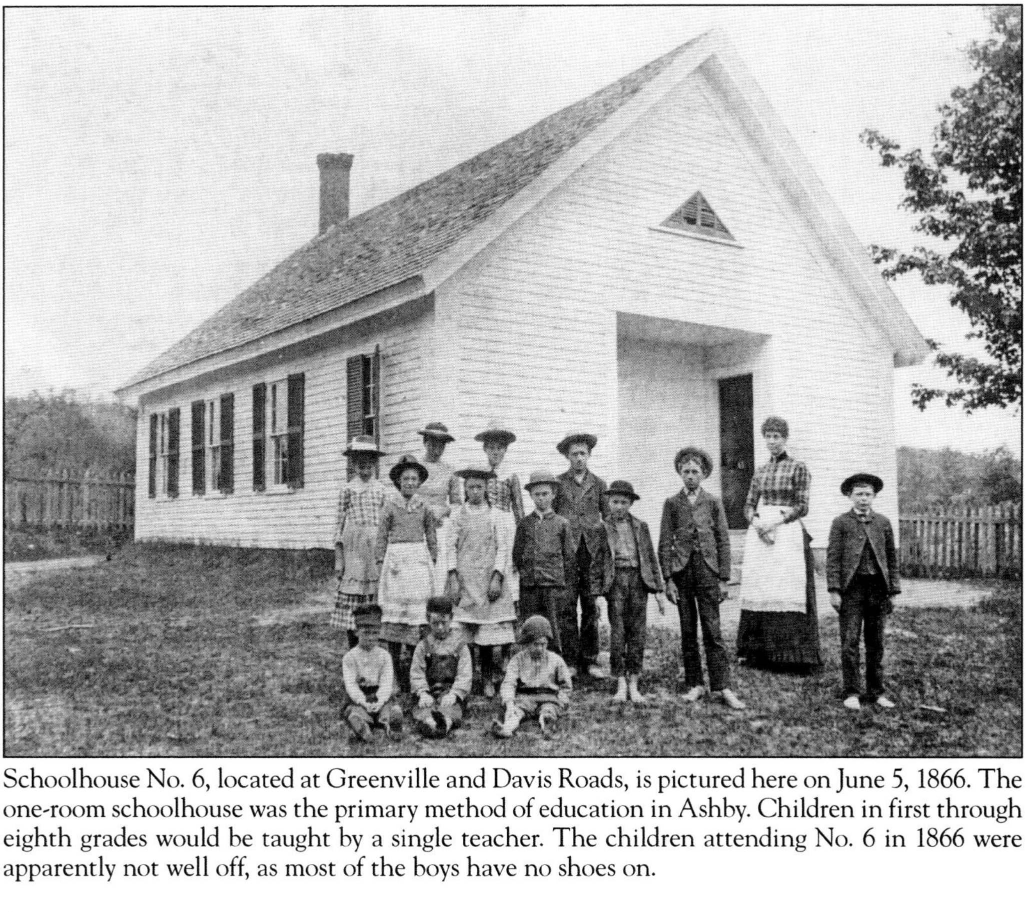

Schoolhouse No. 6, located at Greenville and Davis Roads, is pictured here on June 5, 1866. The one-room schoolhouse was the primary method of education in Ashby. Children in first through eighth grades would be taught by a single teacher. The children attending No. 6 in 1866 were apparently not well off, as most of the boys have no shoes on.

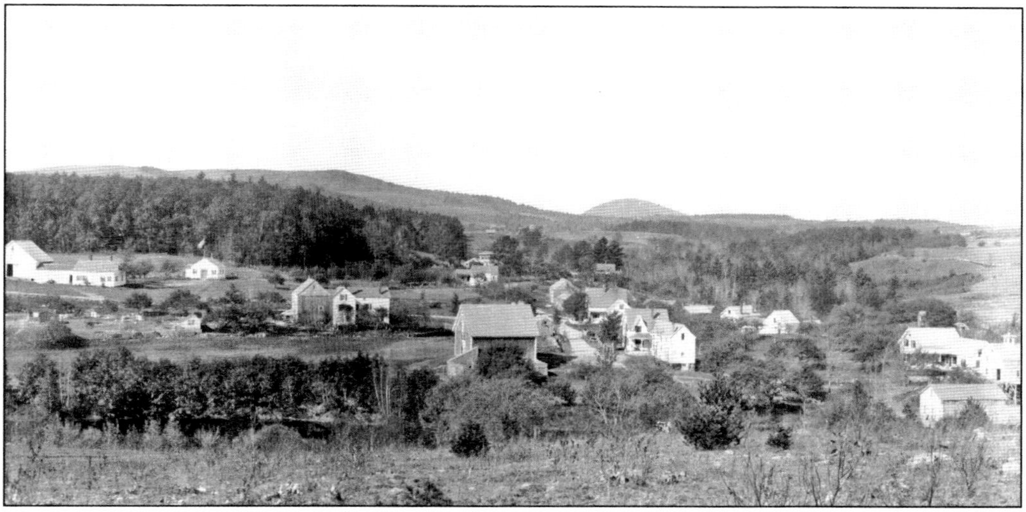

This view of South Village at the corner of Erickson and South Roads was taken about 1900. South Village grew up around the mills along this section of Willard Brook. In this photograph, Loveland's Saw and Gristmill can be seen at the lower right and Schoolhouse No. 8 is the second building from the left. The building on the far left is now on the Pernaa farm.

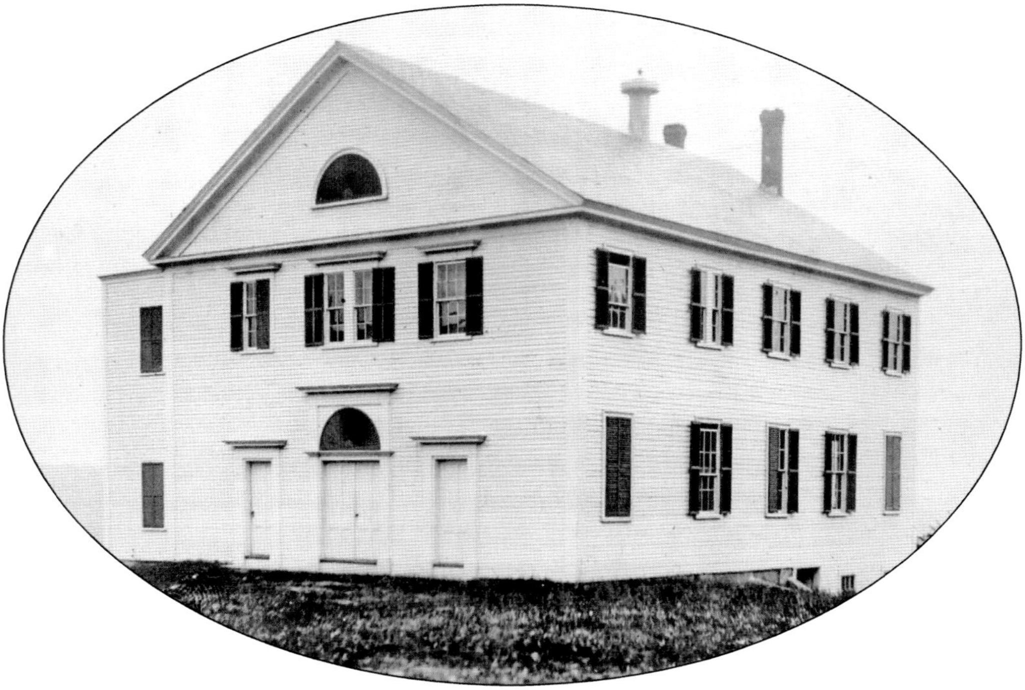

Pictured here around 1905, the town hall was used primarily as a function hall and gymnasium with the town government offices in the basement. This building was originally constructed as the Calvinistic Congregational Church on the site of what is now the library. When the Congregational church built a new sanctuary, this building was moved to its present location next to the church and became Watatic Academy. The academy served those who could afford it and desired an education beyond eighth grade. When the academy failed and the building was taken over by the town, it served as the high school until the Lyman School was built in 1902. (Courtesy of William and Katherine Stanwood.)

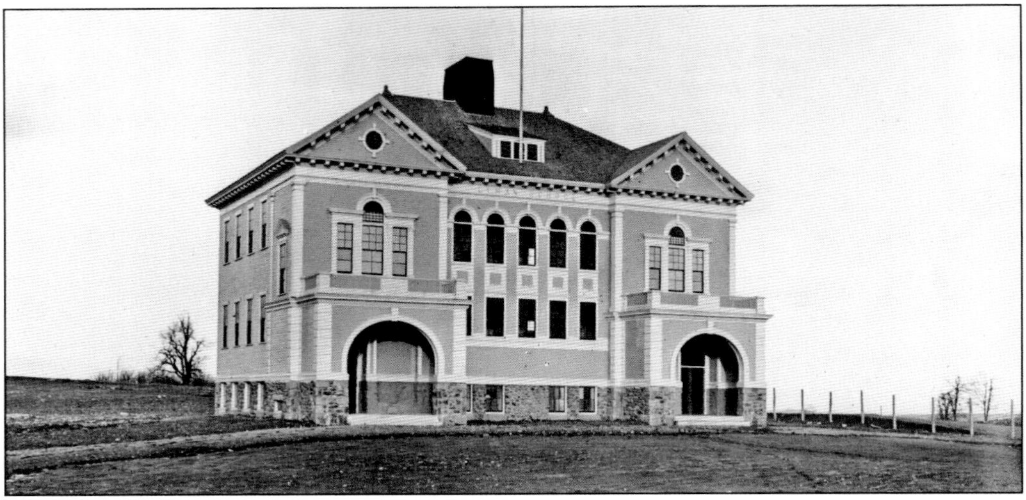

The Lyman School opened in 1903 and is pictured here shortly after its completion. It was built to replace Watatic School, which was too small for a growing population. The new school was named for Jesse Lyman, who donated the land upon which it was built. The cost to build the schoolhouse was $13,580, of which $4,000 was donated.

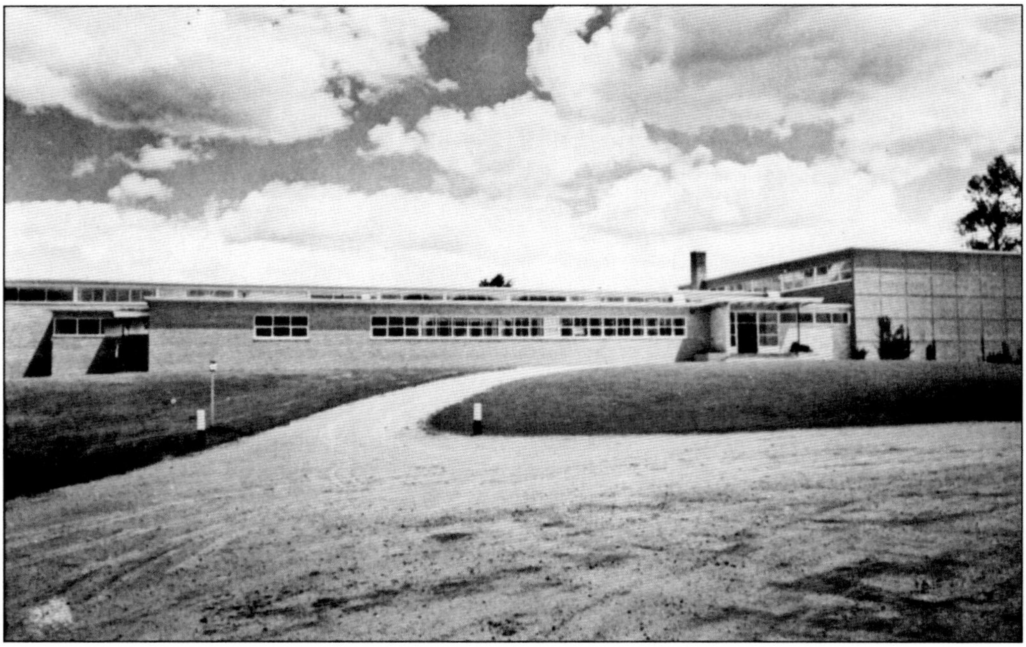

The new Ashby Elementary School is pictured here after it was completed in 1952. The new school was built to handle the growing population of children that would later be known as the baby boomers. (Courtesy of William and Katherine Stanwood.)

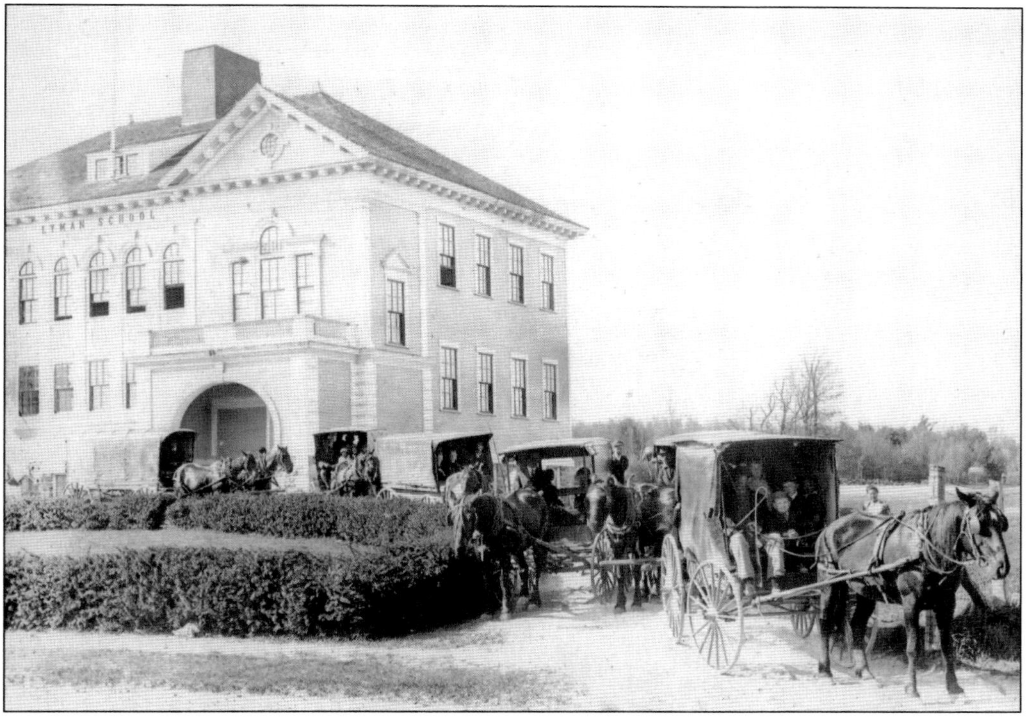

With the advent of a centralized school, transportation was provided to students. Massachusetts was the first state to provide public funds to assist with the cost of transportation. The school would provide the wagons, and local farmers would bid to provide the horses and drivers. Students sat on benches facing one another, and entry and exit was from the rear of the wagon so as not to startle the horses. (Courtesy of Richard and Nancy Catalini.)

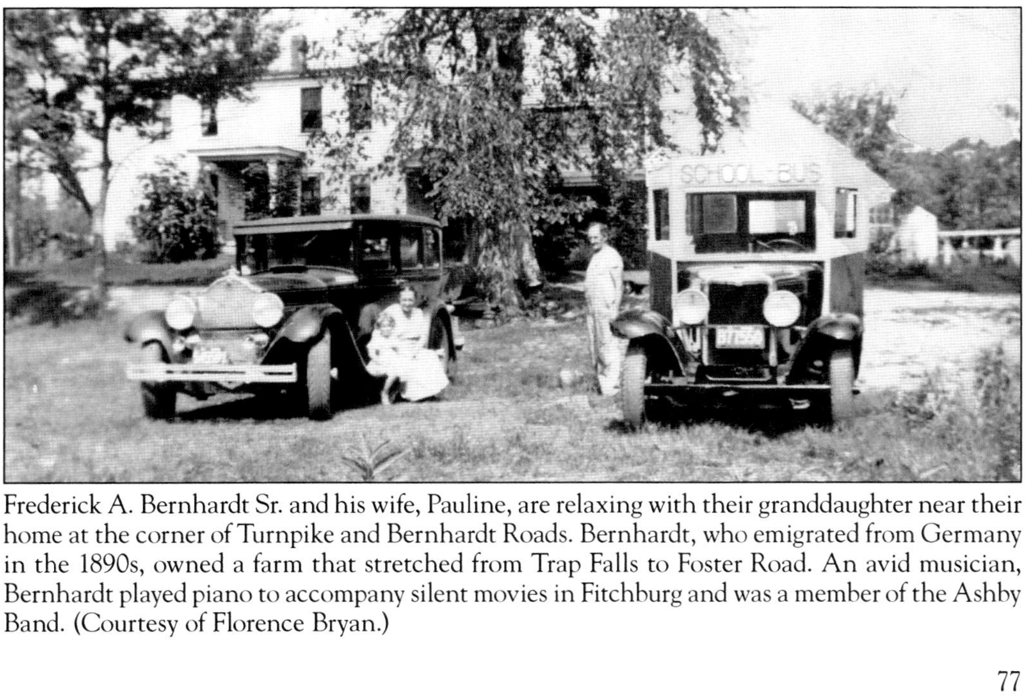

Frederick A. Bernhardt Sr. and his wife, Pauline, are relaxing with their granddaughter near their home at the corner of Turnpike and Bernhardt Roads. Bernhardt, who emigrated from Germany in the 1890s, owned a farm that stretched from Trap Falls to Foster Road. An avid musician, Bernhardt played piano to accompany silent movies in Fitchburg and was a member of the Ashby Band. (Courtesy of Florence Bryan.)

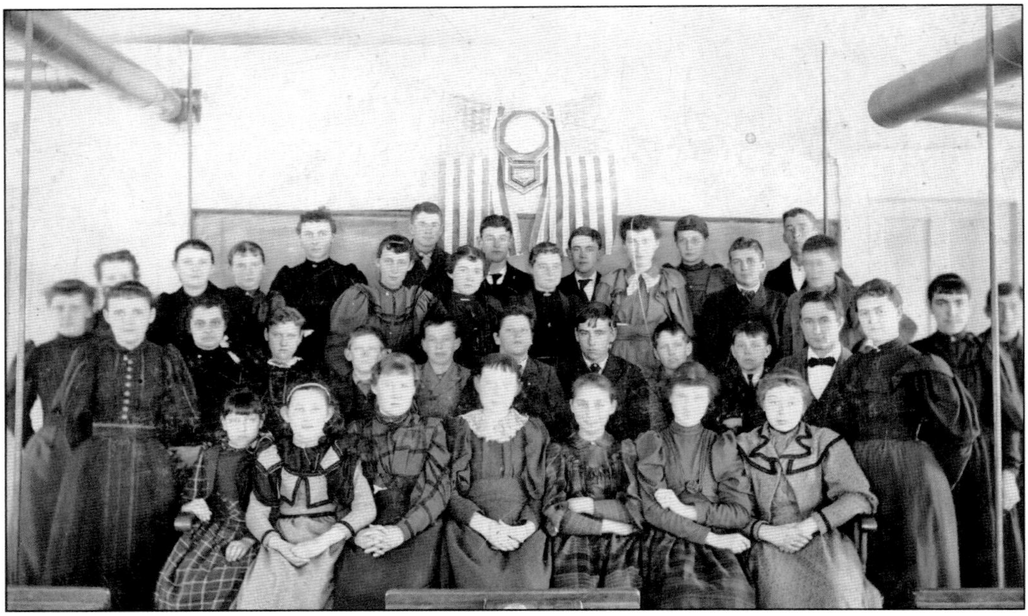

The Watatic School was started as a private academy in 1836. The town later took it over, and it served as Ashby's high school for many years prior to the construction of the Lyman School. The 45-star flags on the wall indicate the photograph was taken after 1896, but it dates from before construction of the Lyman School, which opened in 1902.

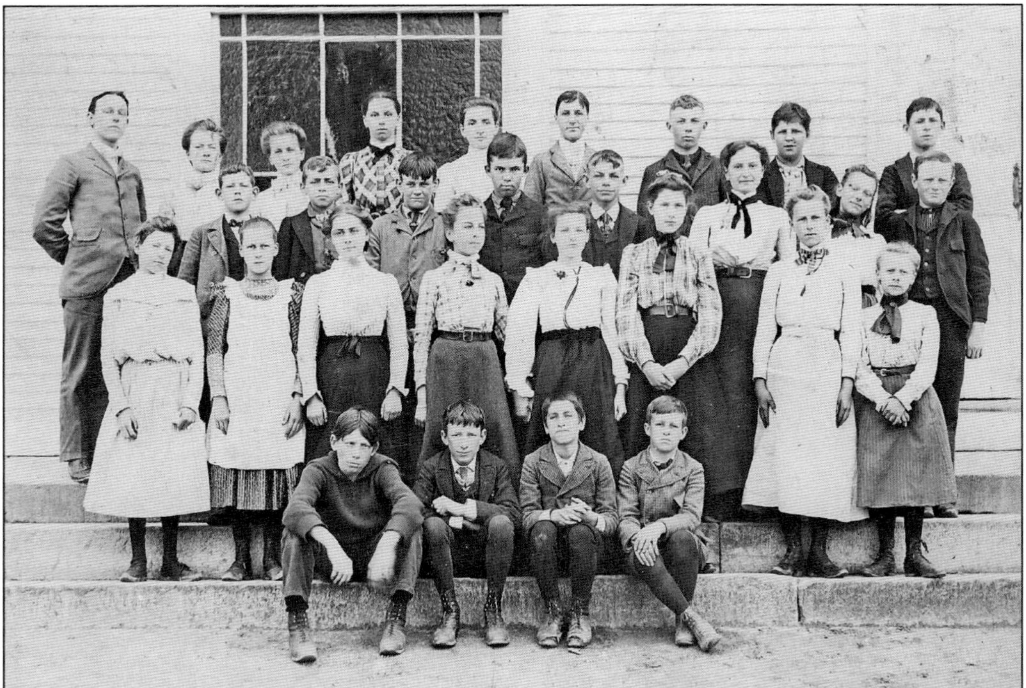

These Ashby students and teachers are dressed for a special occasion in front of Ashby Congregational Church in the late 19th century. Due to limited space in the school, the church was used as an assembly hall on special occasions. (Courtesy of Carol Bennett Lielasus.)

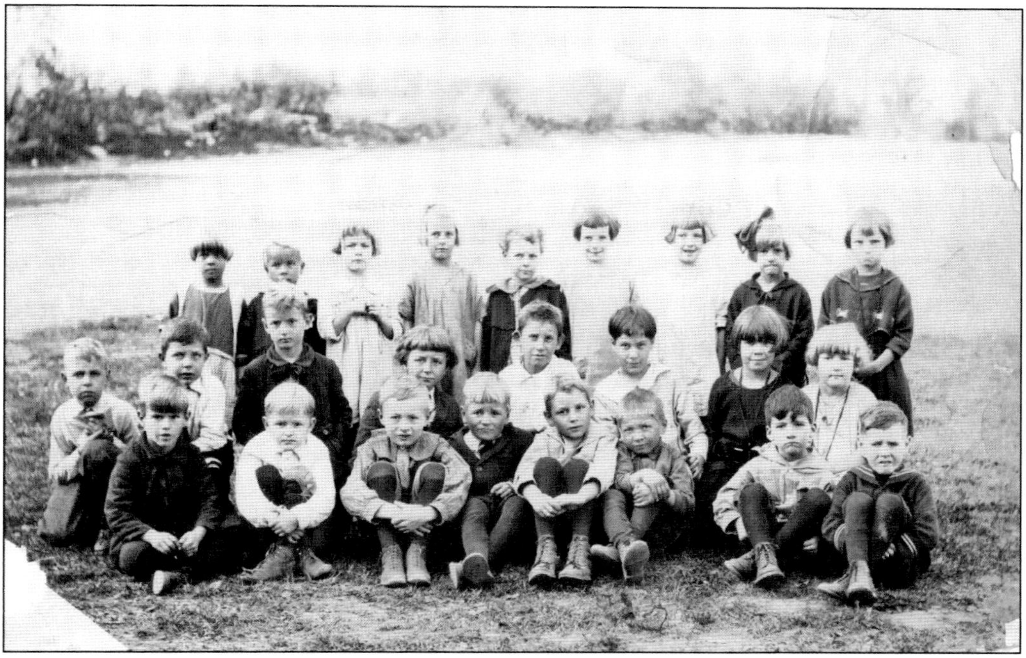

Ashby schoolchildren are assembled on the athletic field for a special event in the late 1920s. The school lacked a gymnasium, so students had athletic activities outdoors.

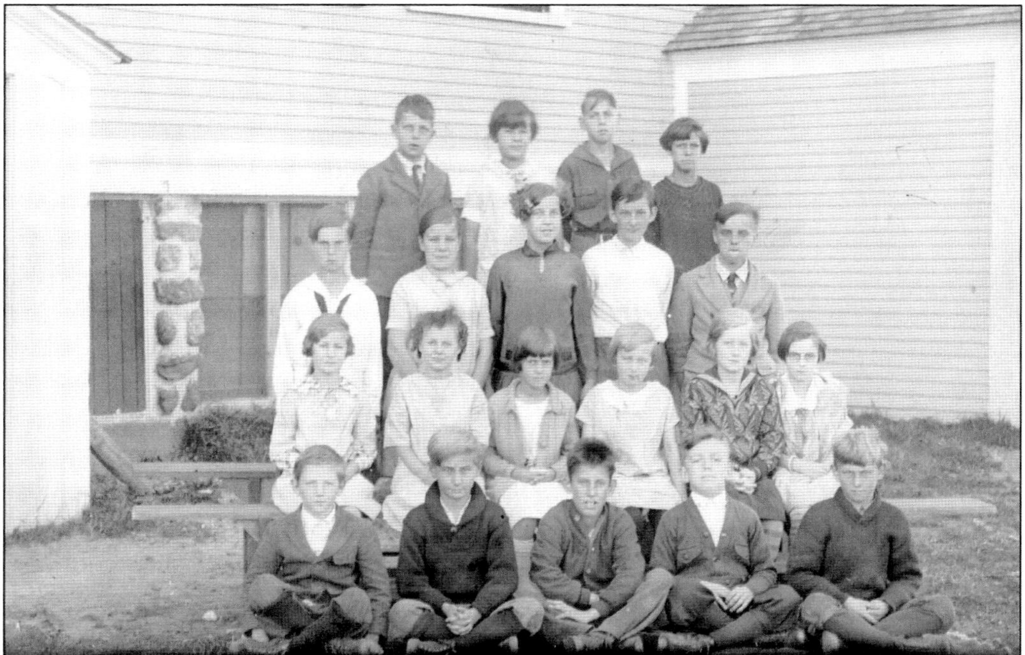

Ashby seventh-grade schoolchildren assemble behind the Lyman School. The Lyman School housed both elementary and high school grades. Each grade had its own room.

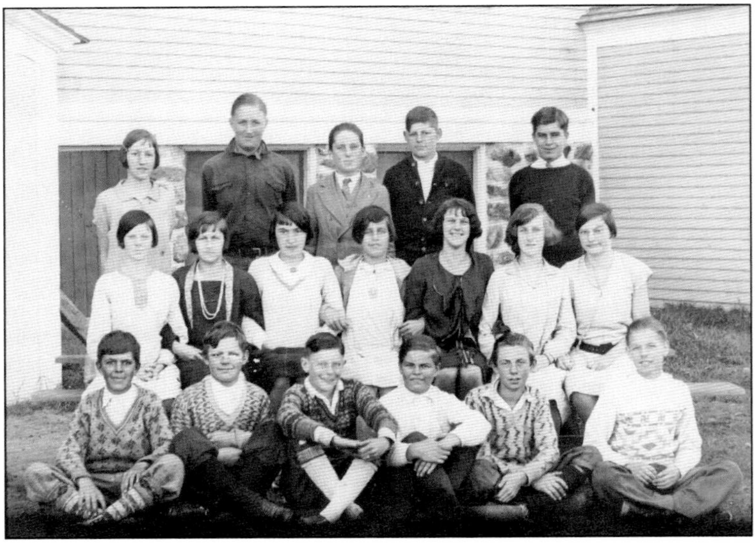

Pictured here are some Ashby students in the 1930s. They are, from left to right, (first row) Ralph B., Huye E., Alpo L., Ero J., Uuno L., and Eino P.; (second row) Rachael H., Doris K., Muriel B., Helen Hopkins, unidentified, Kate, and Elizabeth W.; (third row) Esther B., Irami S., Harold W., Uunto L., and Edwin J.

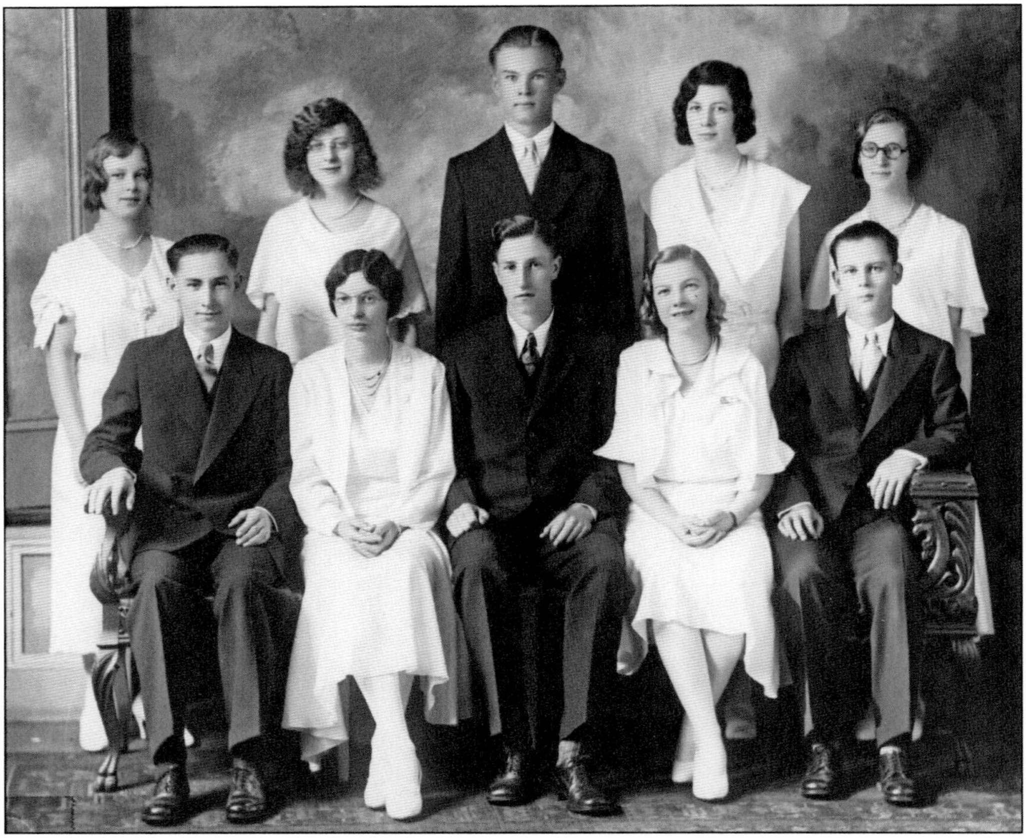

The class of 1933 had 10 graduates. Pictured here are, from left to right, (first row) Francis Bennett, Irma Holmes, Wilbur Loveland, Aura Louhi, and Everett Treworgy; (second row) Wilma Ekola, Elizabeth Piper, Olavi Ojamaki, Virginia Robbins, and Mary Pillsbury. (Courtesy of Richard and Nancy Catalini.)

Rebecca Elliott (left), Elizabeth Piper (right), and Helen Hopkins (kneeling) pose for a photograph in front of the school in September 1929. With it being a small school, Ashby High School students formed close ties with their schoolmates. Even today, some 40 years after the school closed, Ashby High class reunions attract a large percentage of each class.

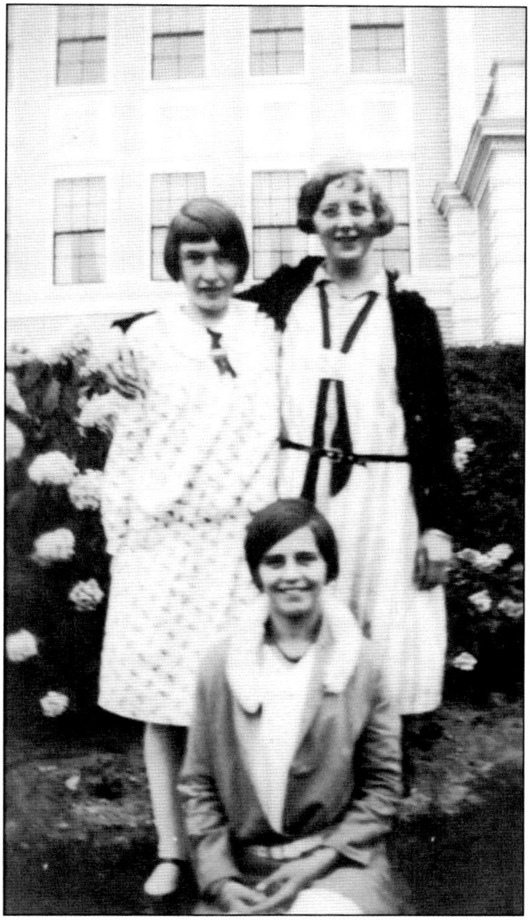

Pictured here is a student field day spent at Breed's Field in 1931. The field is now known as Allen Field after Asa Allen, who donated it to Ashby in the 1940s. (Courtesy of Richard and Nancy Catalini.)

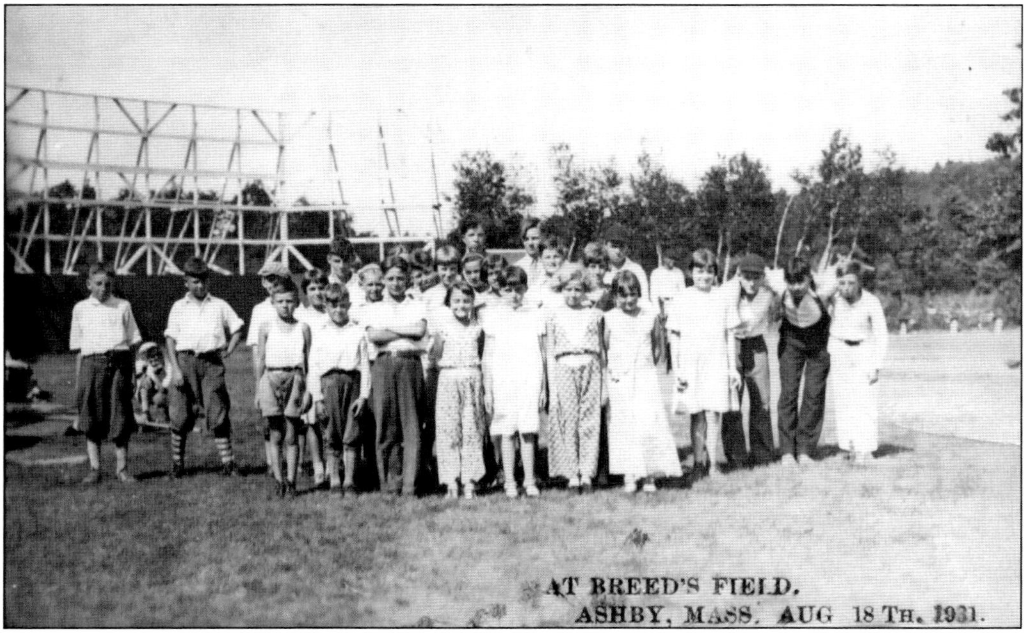

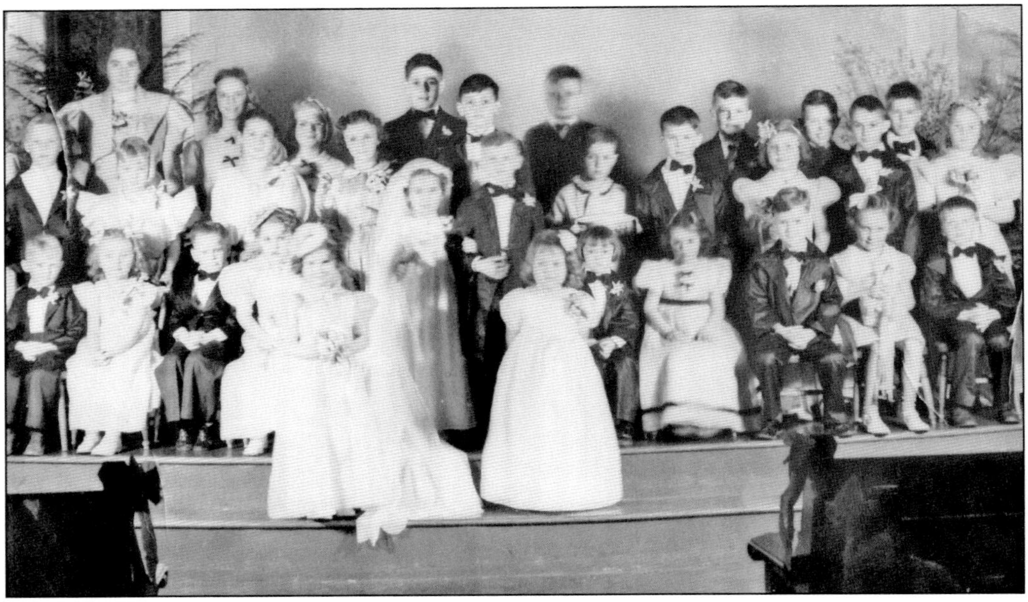

A Tom Thumb wedding is a mock wedding of a child bride and groom. The children dress as if for a real wedding, walk down the aisle, and exchange "vows." The events were often held to raise money for a cause, and in the process the children learned about formal attire, manners, and ceremony. At this Tom Thumb wedding, Janice Hopkins and William Seymour Sr. are the bride and groom, with Florence Reynolds (left) and Nancy Sivula (right) standing just in front of them. (Courtesy of Florence Bryan.)

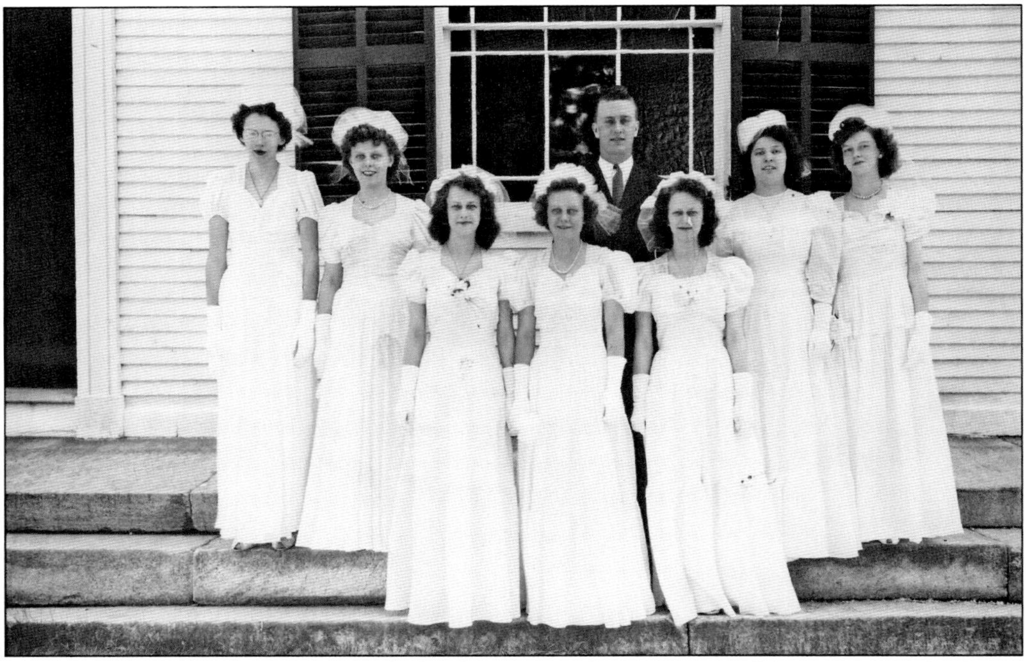

The Ashby graduating class of 1944 had only one man, because most of the young men had gone off to war. Members of the class are, from left to right, (first row) Rena Bennett, Joan Bailey, and Renice Bennett; (second row) Jane Simonds, Richard Gooley, and Bertha Johnson; (third row) Mary Damon and Gladys Brewer. (Courtesy of Carol Bennett Lielasus.)

Five

Service to Community and Country

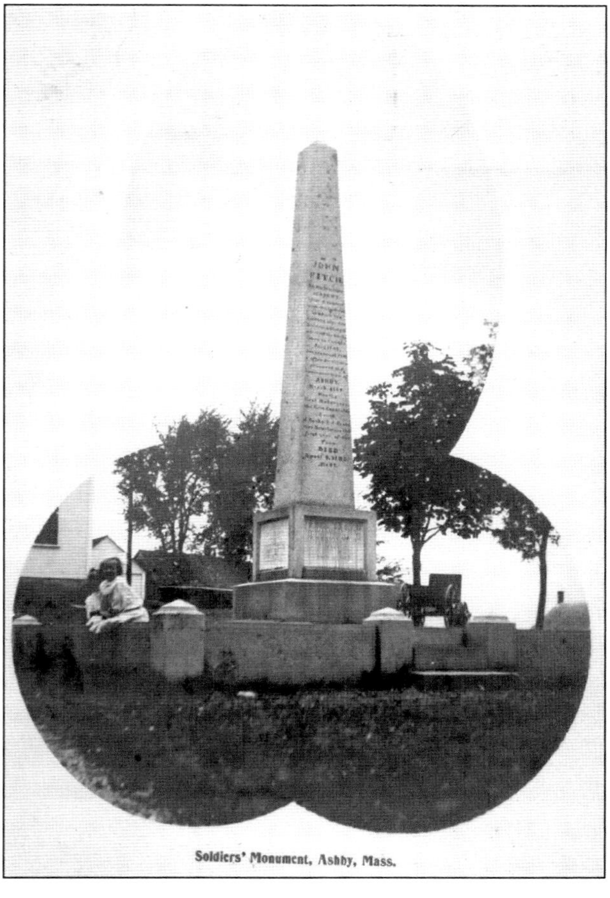

The Soldiers Monument was erected after the Civil War to pay tribute to those soldiers who fought in the Revolutionary and the Civil Wars. The face of the monument honors John Fitch, who fought and was taken captive along with his family in the French and Indian War. The monument still stands near the center of the town common, though the lettering has faded with time. Since this photograph was taken about 1900, the town has added monuments on the common to those who fought in World War I, World War II, Korea, and Vietnam. (Courtesy of William and Katherine Stanwood.)

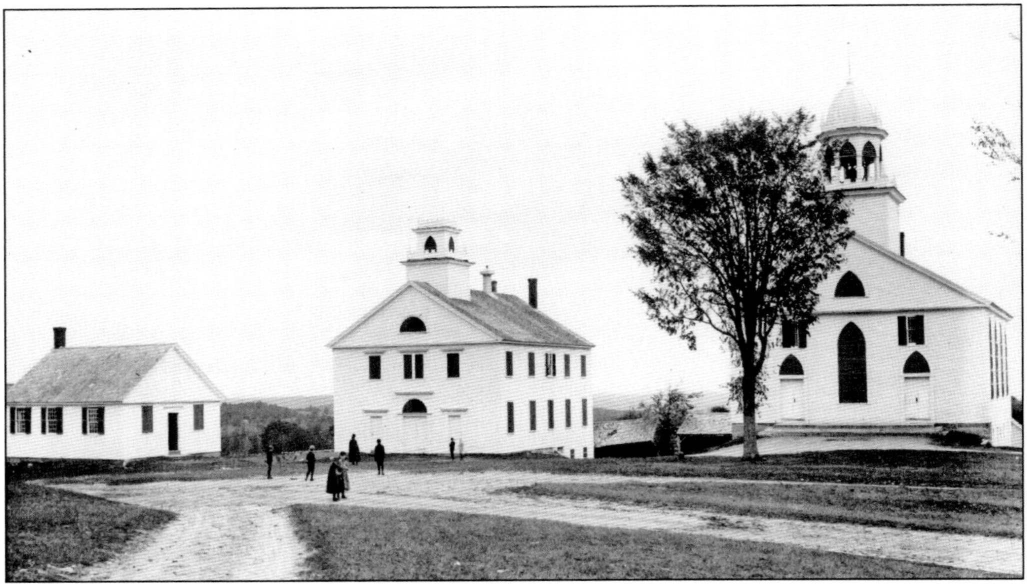

This view from the common across New Ipswich Road shows Schoolhouse No. 1, Ashby High School (later Ashby Town Hall), and the Ashby Congregational Church as they looked in 1895. Some children have gathered in front of the high school, perhaps waiting for it to open.

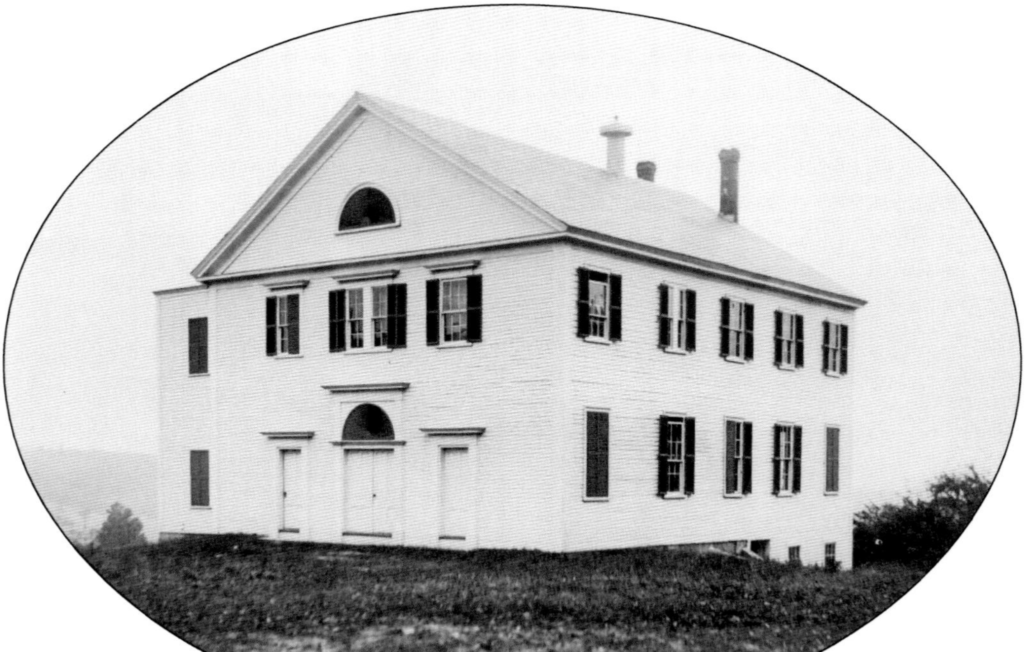

Town Hall, Ashby, Mass.

Ashby Town Hall, which had been Ashby High School in the latter part of the 19th century, housed the town offices in the basement in 1910. The upper floors were used as a meeting hall and gymnasium, as the new Lyman School did not have these facilities. (Courtesy of Richard and Nancy Catalini.)

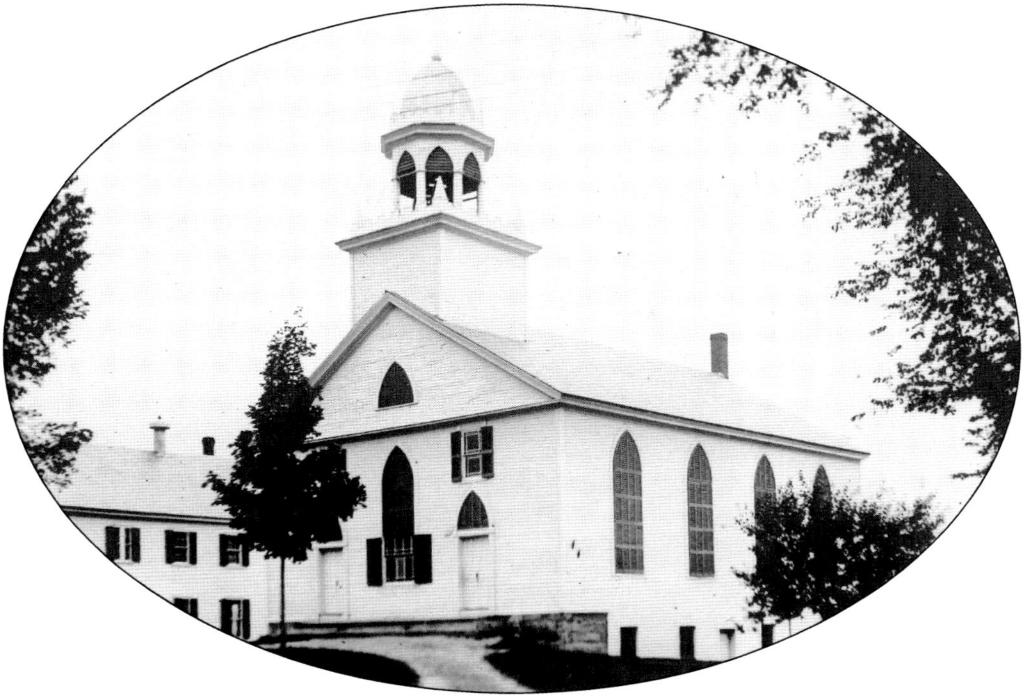

Ashby Congregational Church was built in 1835 on the east side of Ashby Town Common. It was the second church building of the Calvinistic Congregational Society. The first church building was on the south side of the common, where the library stands now. Upon completion of the new church, the original building was sold and moved next to the church to serve as an academy. It is partially visible on the left side of the photograph. (Courtesy of Joyce Hopkins.)

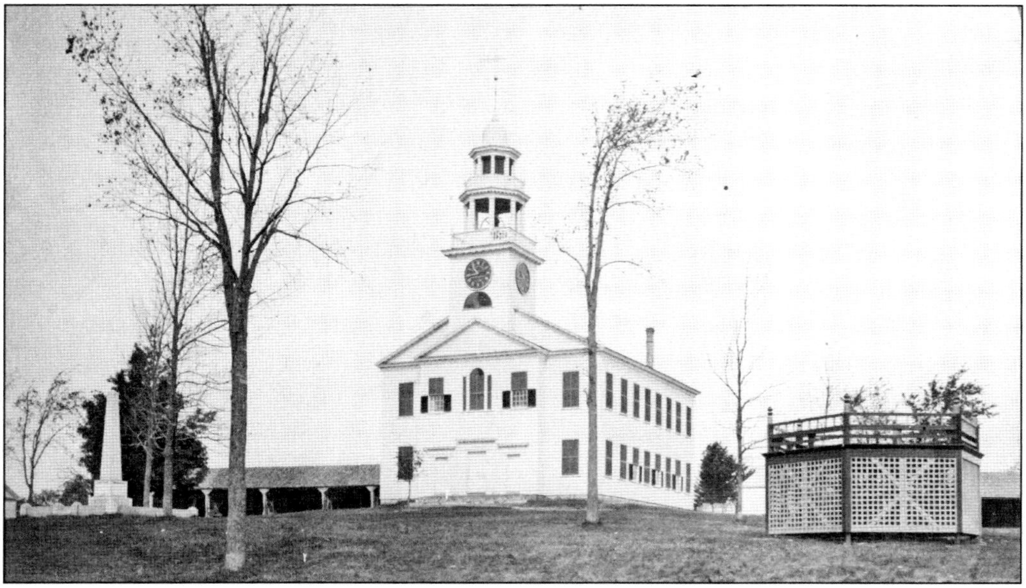

This is one of the earliest photographs of the Ashby Town Common, likely from the 1880s. In it, one can see the bandstand is somewhat higher than it is today and has yet to acquire its roof. Two of the railing newel posts from this bandstand are incorporated into the handrails on the existing bandstand.

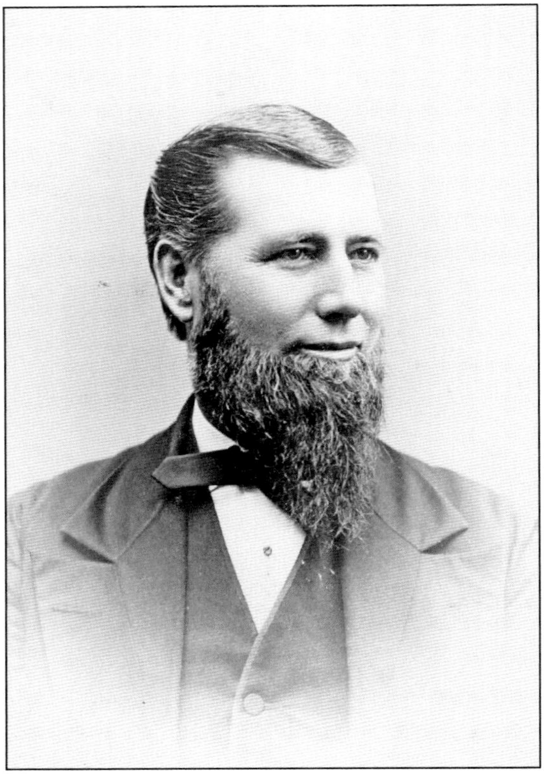

Rev. George Shaw served as minister of the First Parish Church from 1868 to 1909. During his 41-year tenure, he preached over 3,100 sermons. He was also active in civic affairs as a charter member of the Ashby Grange, the Ashby Farmer's Club, the Chemical Fire Engine Company, and the Ashby Historical Society.

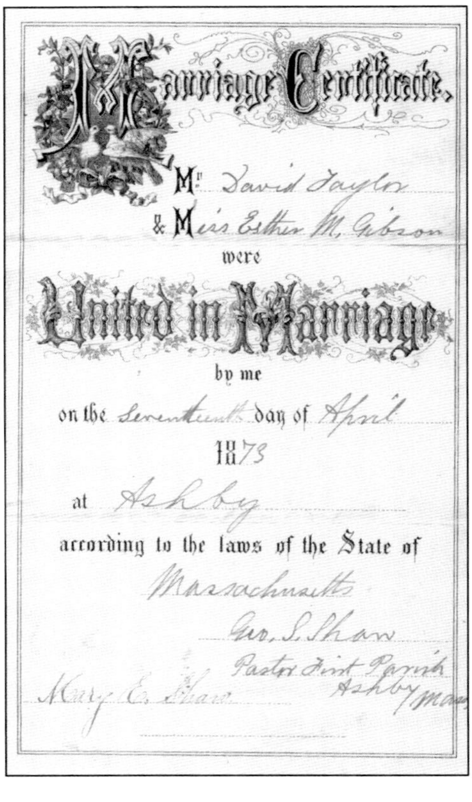

Marriage Certificate

Mr David Taylor
& Miss Esther M. Gibson
were
United in Marriage
by me
on the Seventeenth day of April
1873
at Ashby
according to the laws of the State of
Massachusetts

Geo. S. Shaw
Pastor First Parish
Ashby / Mass

Mary E. Shaw

This marriage certificate was signed by Reverend Shaw in 1875. During his ministry in Ashby, Reverend Shaw officiated at more than 250 weddings.

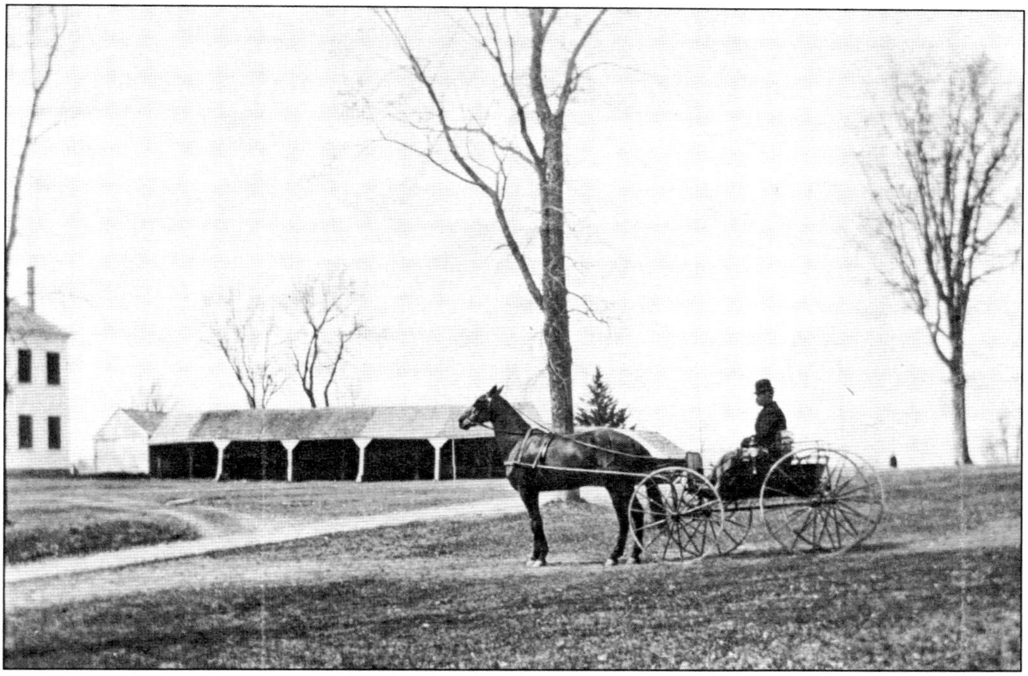

A man in a four-wheel buggy approaches the common about 1895. In the background are the carriage sheds where parishioners would leave their buggies while attending church services. The individual sheds were assigned to those who owned a pew in the church. The sheds shown here have been torn down, but those on the other side of the church were preserved through local efforts.

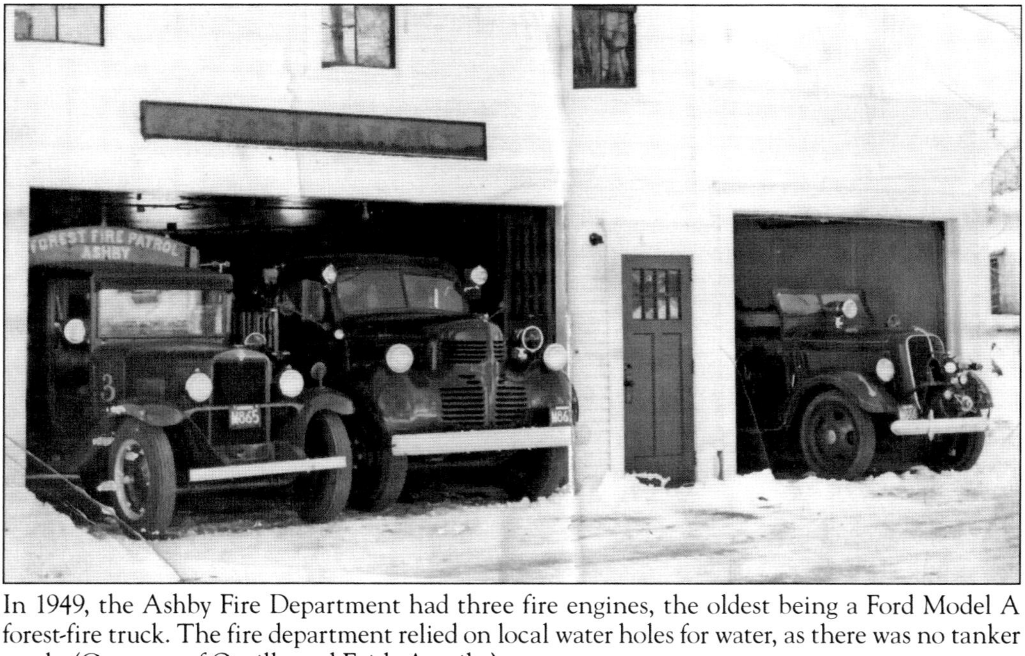

In 1949, the Ashby Fire Department had three fire engines, the oldest being a Ford Model A forest-fire truck. The fire department relied on local water holes for water, as there was no tanker truck. (Courtesy of Orville and Faith Anttila.)

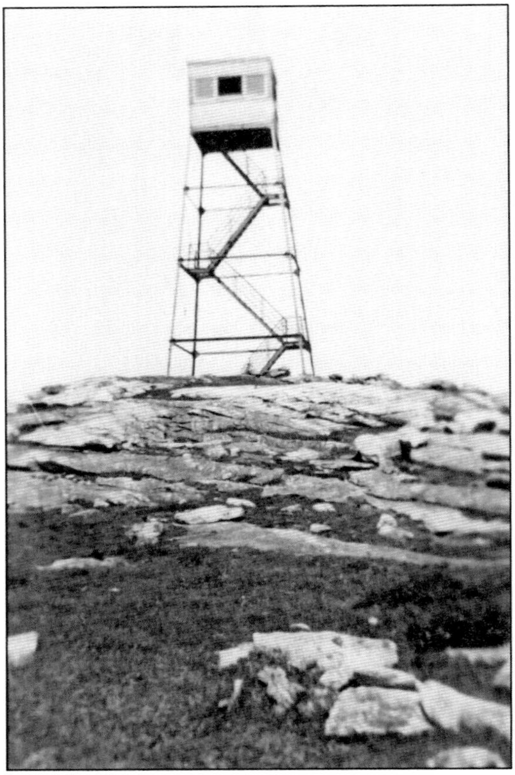

The watchtower on Mount Watatic has been a landmark since the late 19th century. It kept watch over a wide area of Massachusetts' forests. The tower was blown over in the 1938 hurricane and again in 1952. Each time it was rebuilt. In 1985, the state decided it was no longer needed, and the tower was removed. (Courtesy of Richard and Nancy Catalini.)

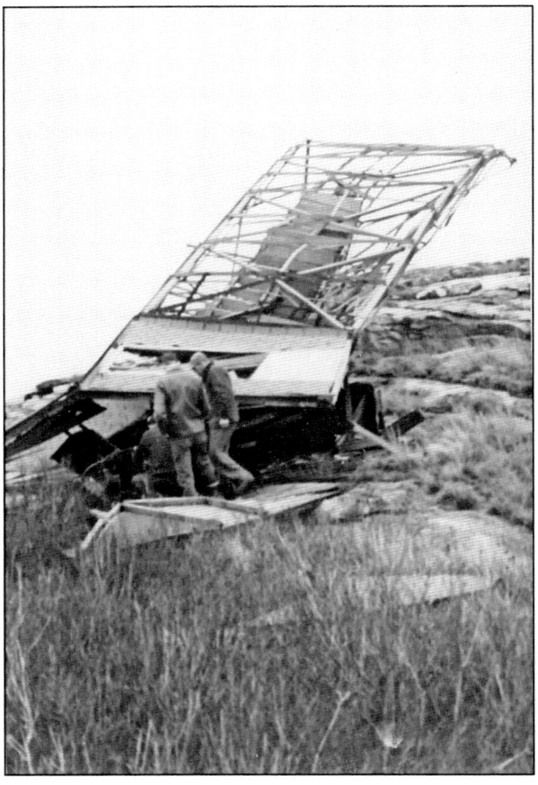

Workmen recover what they can from the fire tower on Mount Watatic. In 1952, strong winds took the fire lookout tower down for a second time, the first time being in the 1938 hurricane. Fortunately, it was not occupied when it fell. (Courtesy of the Stacy family.)

Lina Pernaa stands here with the captain and sailors of the USS *Constitution*, "Old Ironsides." For 25 years, Pernaa donated the large Christmas tree that stood on the deck of the historic ship.

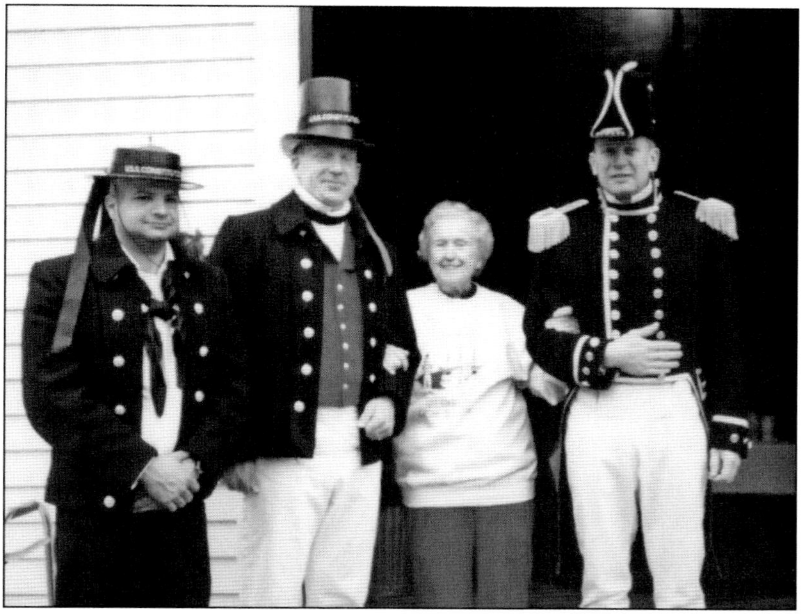

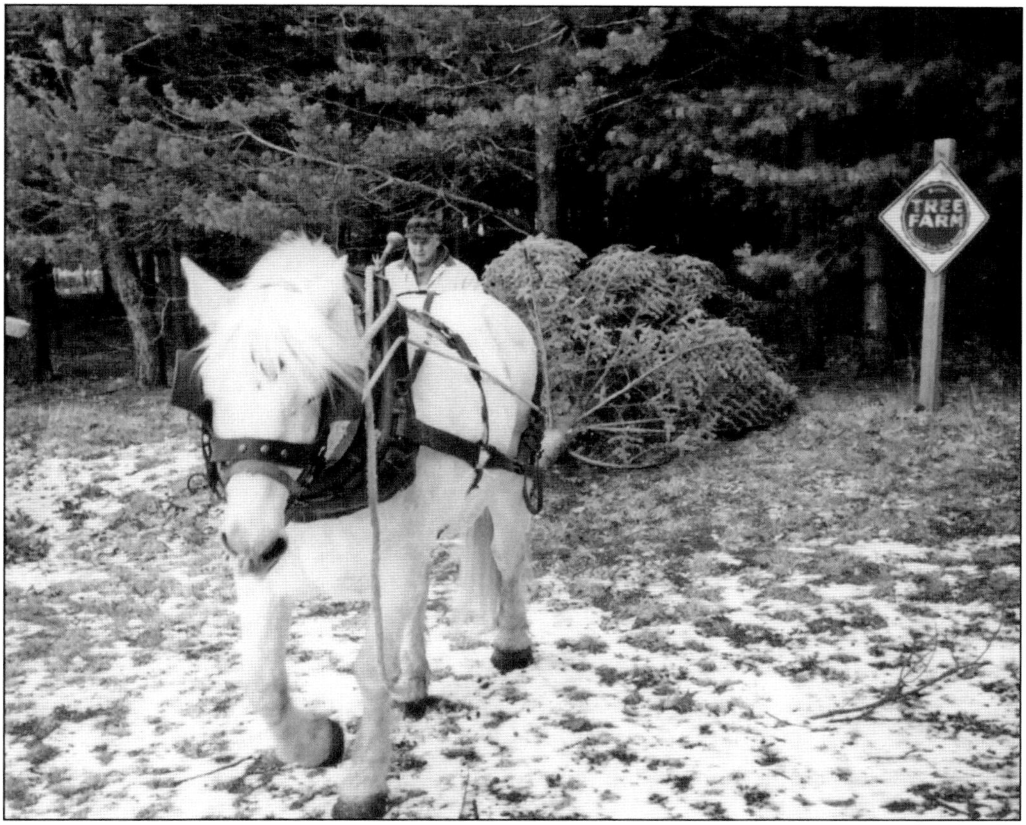

For 20 years, starting in 1986, Lina Pernaa donated the Christmas tree for the USS *Constitution*. Each year, a cutting party from Old Ironsides would be dispatched to Ashby to cut a tree. The 20-foot-tall trees were brought out of the woods by horse and sent to Boston to be placed on the historic ship for the holiday season. (Courtesy of Richard and Nancy Catalini)

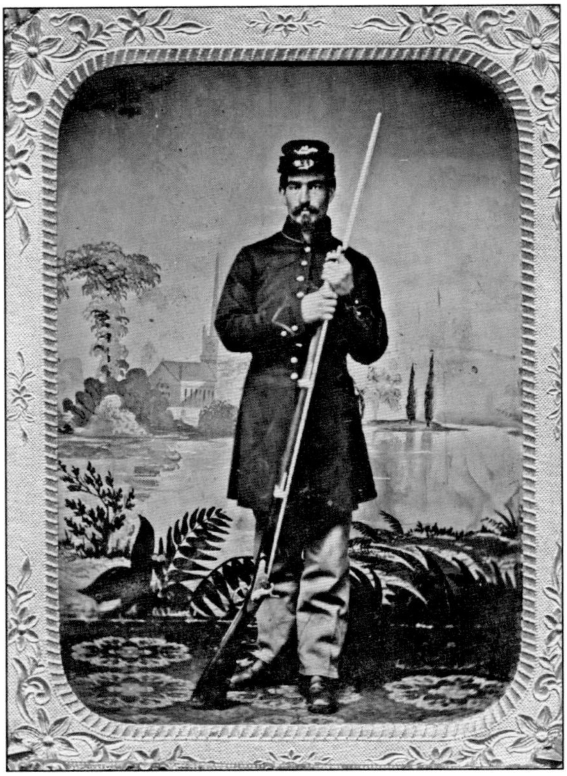

Herbert Willard was born in Ashby and joined the Union army in 1863. At the end of the war, he returned to Ashby, married, and fathered two children. He is buried at Glenwood Cemetery.

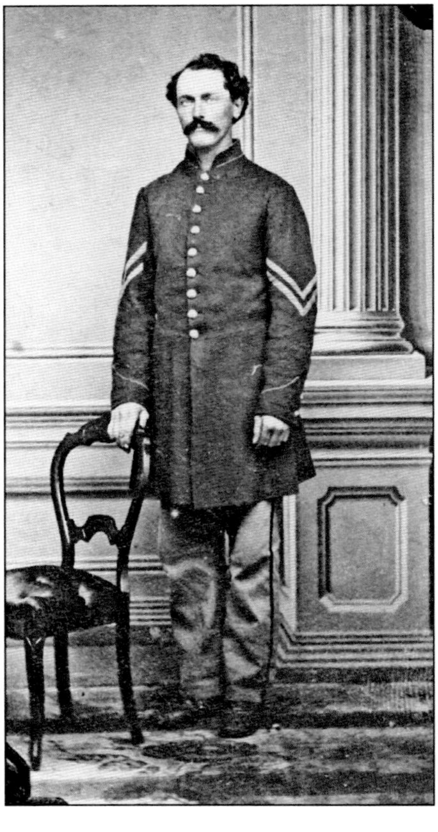

Stephen Hosmer was in the 4th Regiment of Massachusetts Heavy Artillery during the Civil War. He was fortunate enough to survive the war.

Eliab Churchill was a member of the 33rd Regiment of the Massachusetts Infantry. The 33rd saw action from Pennsylvania to Georgia. Churchill was one of three Ashby soldiers killed in the Battle of Lookout Mountain, near Chattanooga, Tennessee.

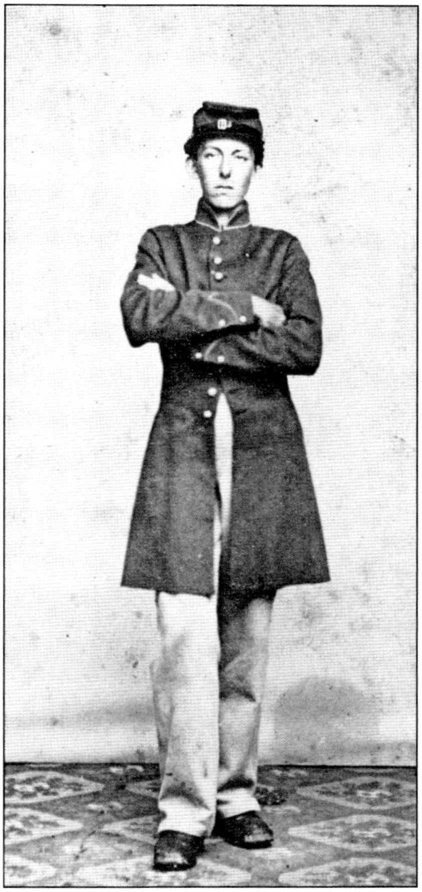

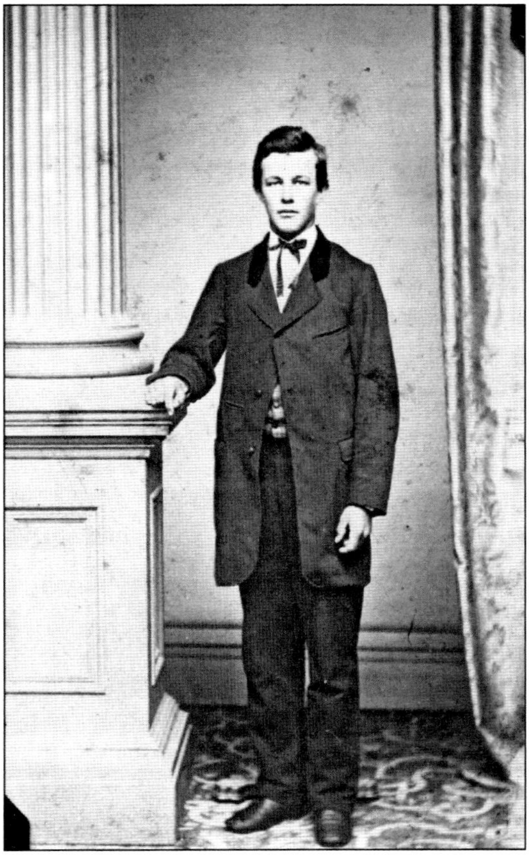

John Mayo was a member of the 33rd Regiment of the Massachusetts Infantry. He died in the Battle of Lookout Mountain. In all, 18 Ashby men perished in the Civil War.

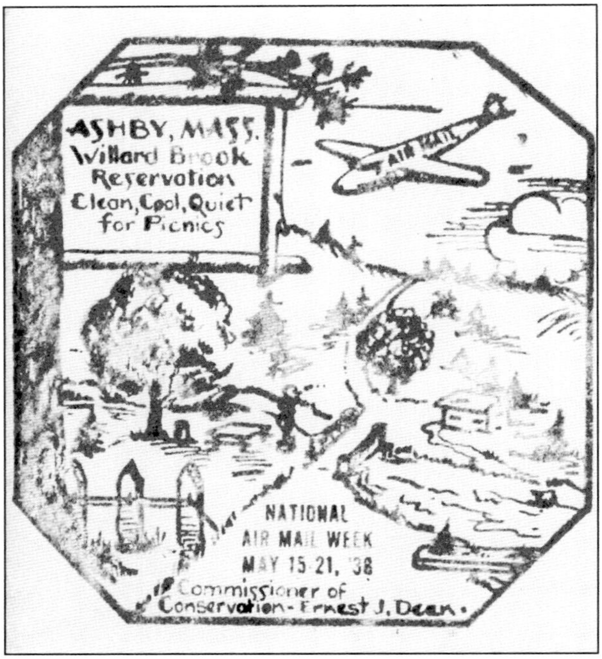

In 1938, Postmaster General James Farley organized a weeklong event to celebrate the 20th anniversary of airmail in the United States. Every town in the country was encouraged to create an envelope with its own cachet, a commemorative design to mark the event. Citizens were encouraged to participate by sending airmail letters with their local cachet. The post office recruited amateur and professional pilots to be sworn in for 24 hours and carry the mail by air to as many towns as possible. As far as is known, no airplane delivered the mail to Ashby, perhaps due to the lack of a level area to land. The photograph is of an envelope with Ashby's cachet for the 1938 airmail celebration. (Courtesy of William and Katherine Stanwood.)

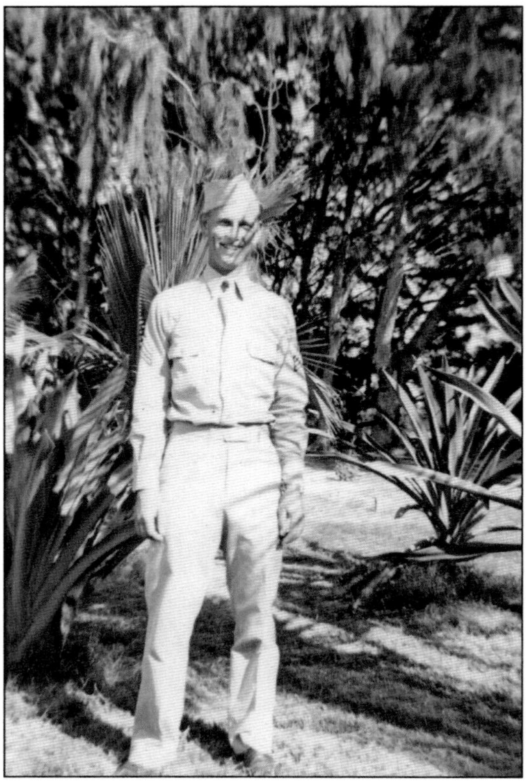

Richard A. Bennett is seen here in the Pacific theater in 1943. He was a staff sergeant with the 419th Night Fighter Squadron, 18th Fighter Group of the US Army Air Forces. He died on January 8, 1944, at Guadalcanal. (Courtesy of Carol Bennett Lielasus.)

Dorothy Bernhardt, youngest child of Frederick and Pauline Bernhardt, graduated from Ashby High School in 1939 and went on to study nursing at Burbank Hospital. After graduating from nursing school, she enlisted in the US Army Nursing Corps and was sent to England on the ocean liner *Queen Mary*. She was assigned to a medical group that crossed the English Channel and followed General Patton's Third Division in the drive to Germany. She achieved the rank of lieutenant and married Capt. Otto Zeman shortly after the end of the war. This photograph was taken in England or France about 1944.

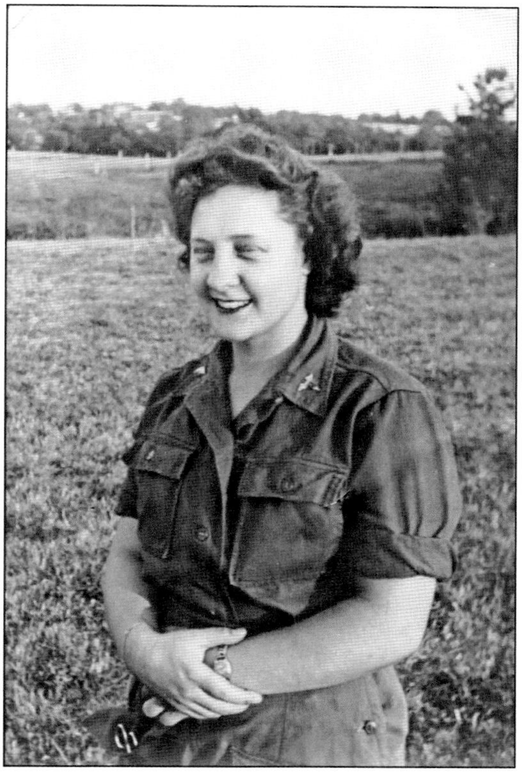

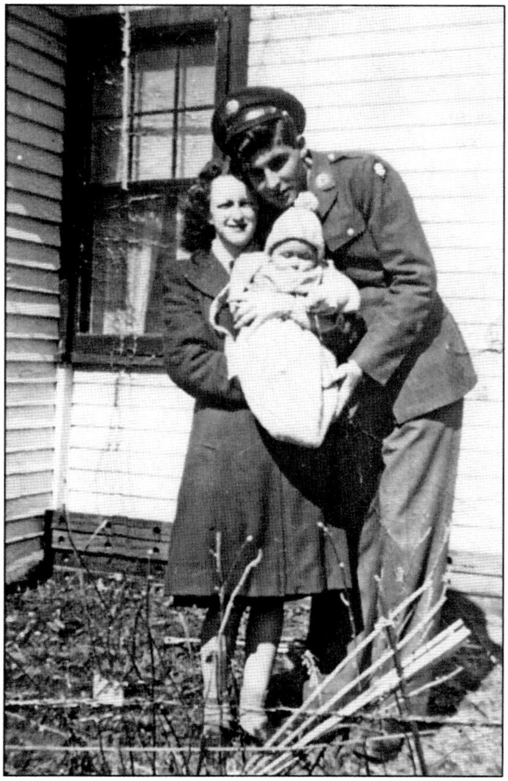

SSgt. Charles W. Bennett of Battery B 557th Field Artillery battalion is pictured here with his wife, Rena, and son Richard before leaving for duty in Europe during World War II. Sergeant Bennett would receive the American Theater Campaign Ribbon, Victory Medal, and Army of Occupation Medal among others. He served until 1946. (Courtesy of Carol Bennett Lielasus.)

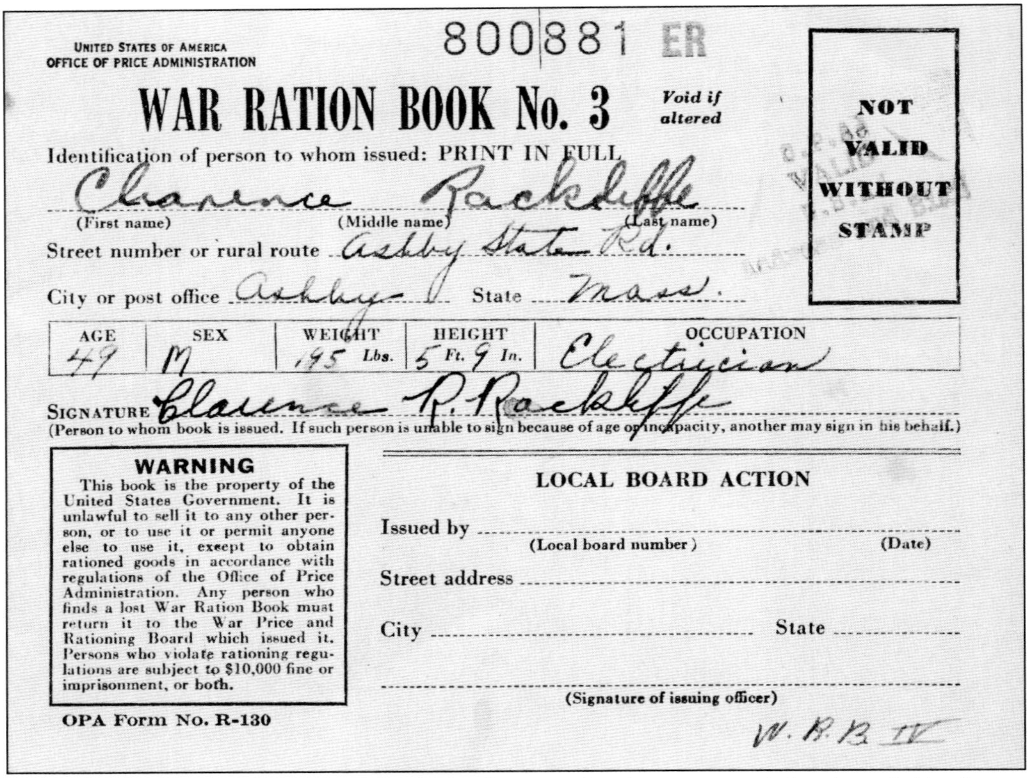

UNITED STATES OF AMERICA
OFFICE OF PRICE ADMINISTRATION

800881 ER

WAR RATION BOOK No. 3

Void if altered

NOT VALID WITHOUT STAMP

Identification of person to whom issued: PRINT IN FULL

Clarence Rackliffe

(First name) (Middle name) (Last name)

Street number or rural route Ashby State Rd.

City or post office Ashby State Mass.

AGE	SEX	WEIGHT	HEIGHT	OCCUPATION
49	M	195 Lbs.	5 Ft. 9 In.	Electrician

SIGNATURE Clarence R. Rackliffe

(Person to whom book is issued. If such person is unable to sign because of age or incapacity, another may sign in his behalf.)

WARNING

This book is the property of the United States Government. It is unlawful to sell it to any other person, or to use it or permit anyone else to use it, except to obtain rationed goods in accordance with regulations of the Office of Price Administration. Any person who finds a lost War Ration Book must return it to the War Price and Rationing Board which issued it. Persons who violate rationing regulations are subject to $10,000 fine or imprisonment, or both.

OPA Form No. R-130

LOCAL BOARD ACTION

Issued by .... (Local board number) (Date)

Street address ....

City .... State ....

.... (Signature of issuing officer)

W. B. B. IV

This World War II ration book was similar to the ration book given to each family in Ashby during the war. One needed the book to buy food and clothing, as the amount one could purchase was restricted. Sugar was in particularly short supply, and Ashby mothers came up with new recipes to cut back on sugar or use local honey or maple syrup. (Courtesy of Barbara Despres.)

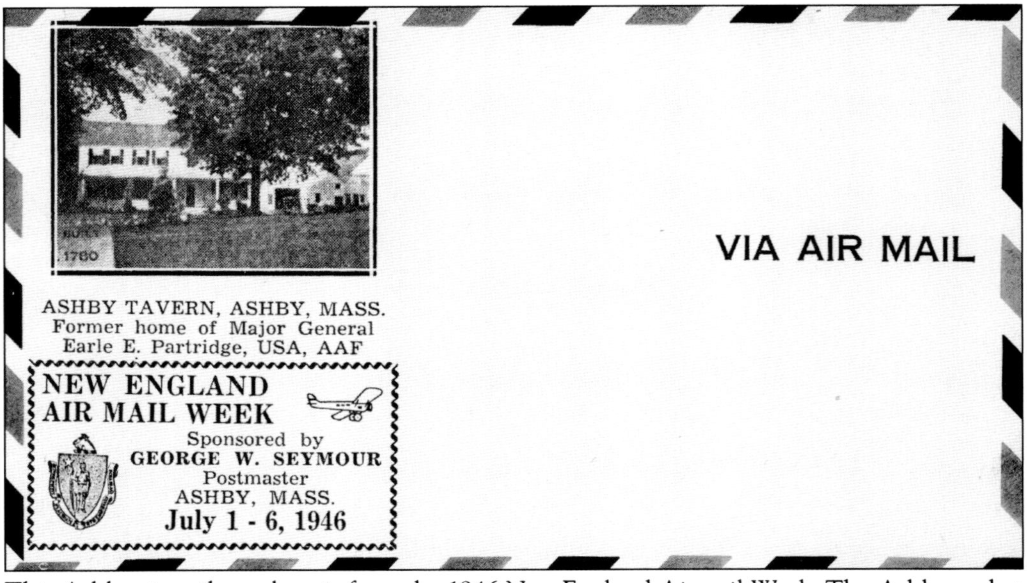

This Ashby airmail envelope is from the 1946 New England Airmail Week. The Ashby cachet celebrates the Ashby Tavern, former home of Gen. Earl Partridge. (Courtesy of William and Katherine Stanwood.)

Six

Celebrations and Recreation

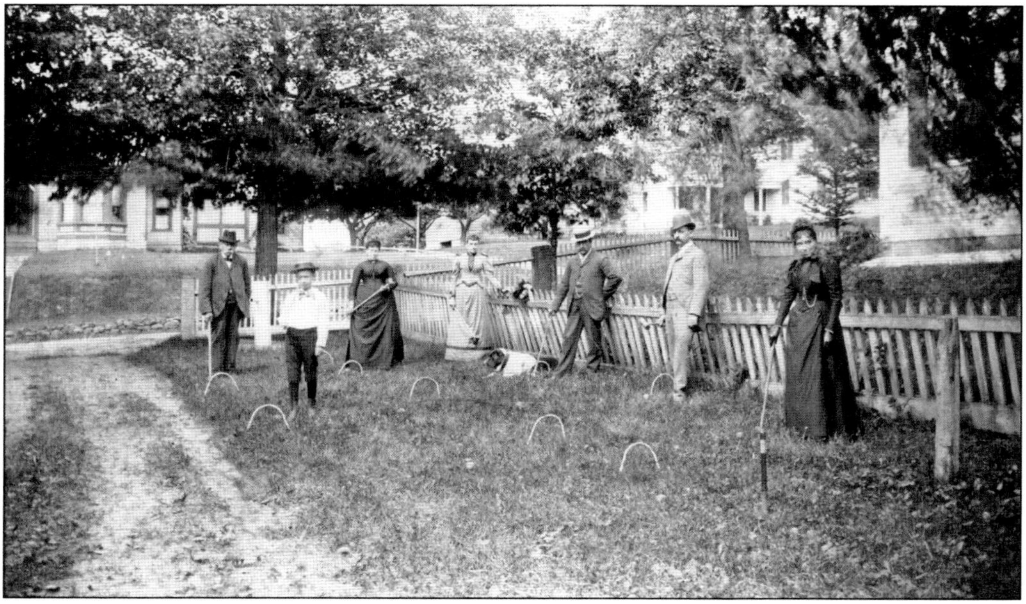

Croquet is being played on the front lawn of the Estabrook home on Main Street. From left to right are William Estabrook, Emery Willard, Etta Estabrook Willard, Ella Estabrook Lawrence, Arthur Willard, Ed Lawrence, and Mrs. William Estabrook.

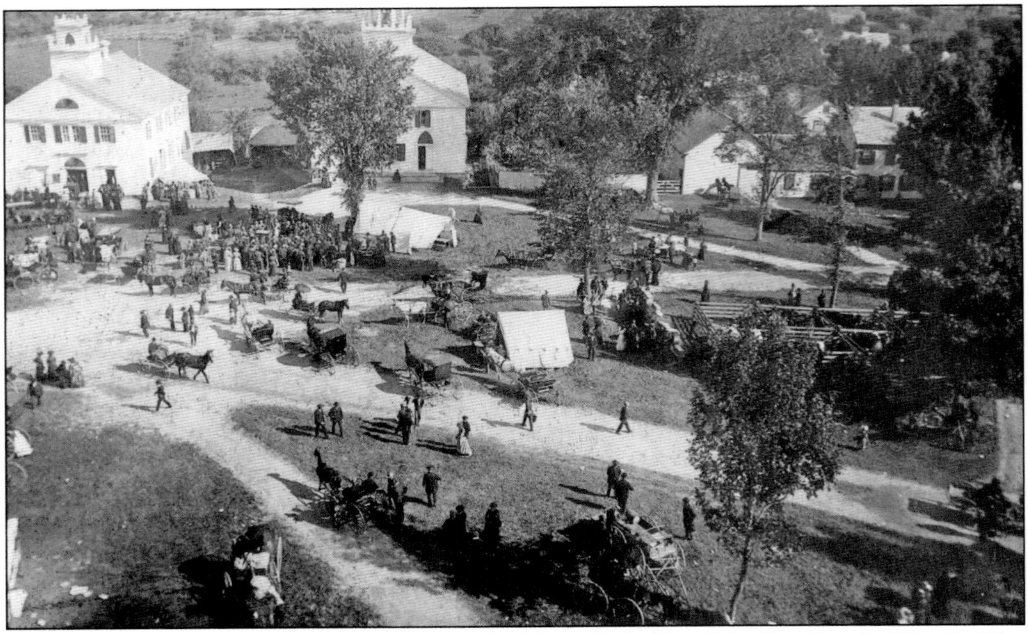

This 1892 fair on the common was photographed from the belfry of the First Parish Church. The fair was both a social event and an agricultural one. The pens on the right hold various breeds of cattle, while on the left a crowd has gathered around an orator. (Courtesy of Charles Parlee and William Duffy.)

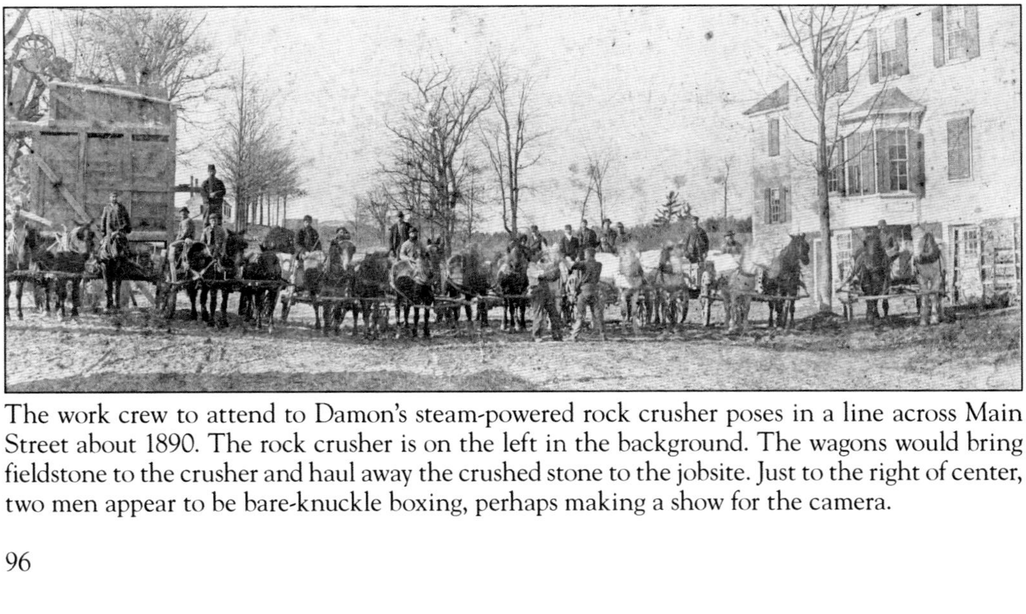

The work crew to attend to Damon's steam-powered rock crusher poses in a line across Main Street about 1890. The rock crusher is on the left in the background. The wagons would bring fieldstone to the crusher and haul away the crushed stone to the jobsite. Just to the right of center, two men appear to be bare-knuckle boxing, perhaps making a show for the camera.

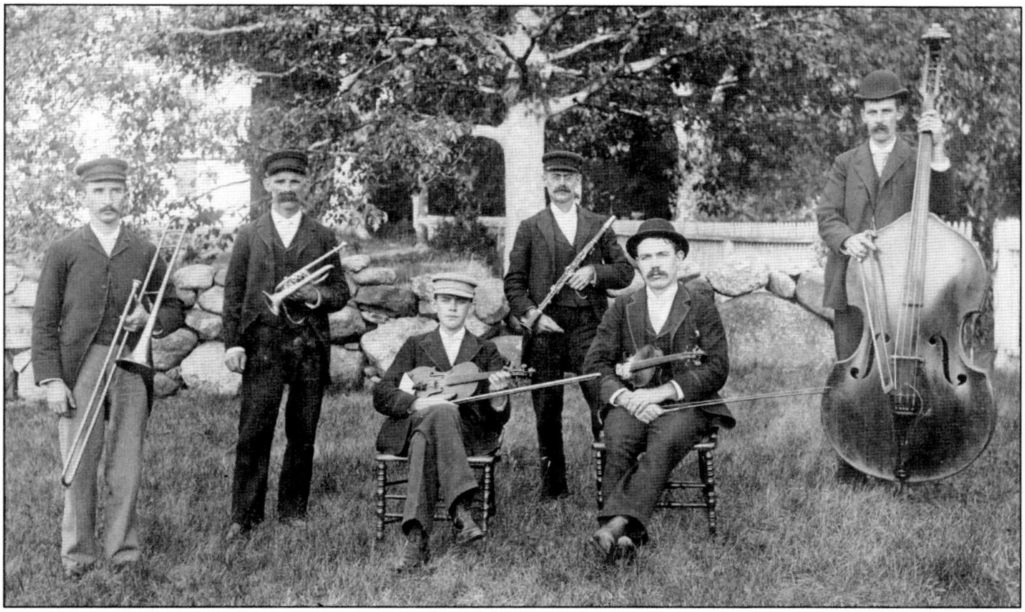

In this November 11, 1895, image, the Ashby Orchestra consists of, from left to right, W.G. Spaulding, Fred Willard, Fred Piper, Dell Foresman, John Willard, and Charles Blanchard. Before recorded music was commonplace, live performances were in demand, and locals with the skill found becoming a musician a way to make needed cash.

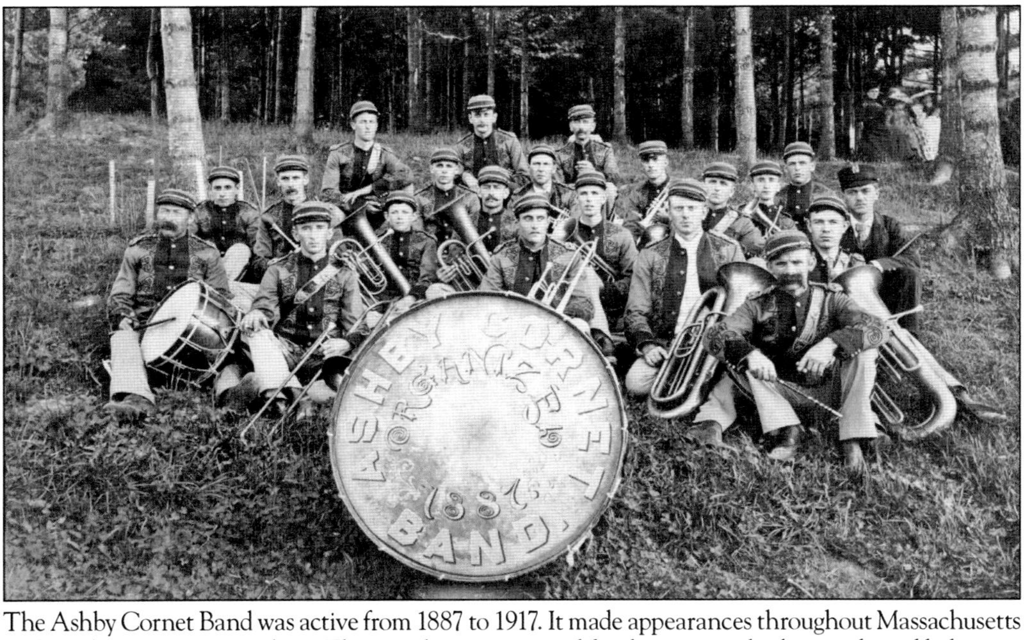

The Ashby Cornet Band was active from 1887 to 1917. It made appearances throughout Massachusetts and southern New Hampshire. The members were noted for their musical talent and good behavior, as the band forbade alcohol during practice and performance.

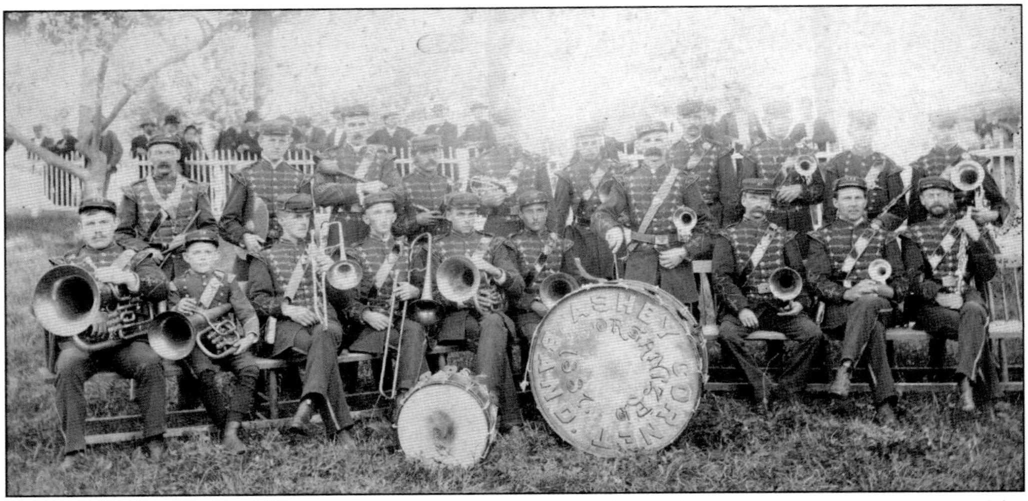

Before the advent of recorded music, bands were in great demand. In the late 19th century, Ashby had a band and an orchestra. The Ashby Cornet Band, organized in 1887, is composed almost entirely of brass and percussion, with the addition of two flutes seen on the right. It is likely flutes were added to play the popular marches of new composer John Philip Sousa.

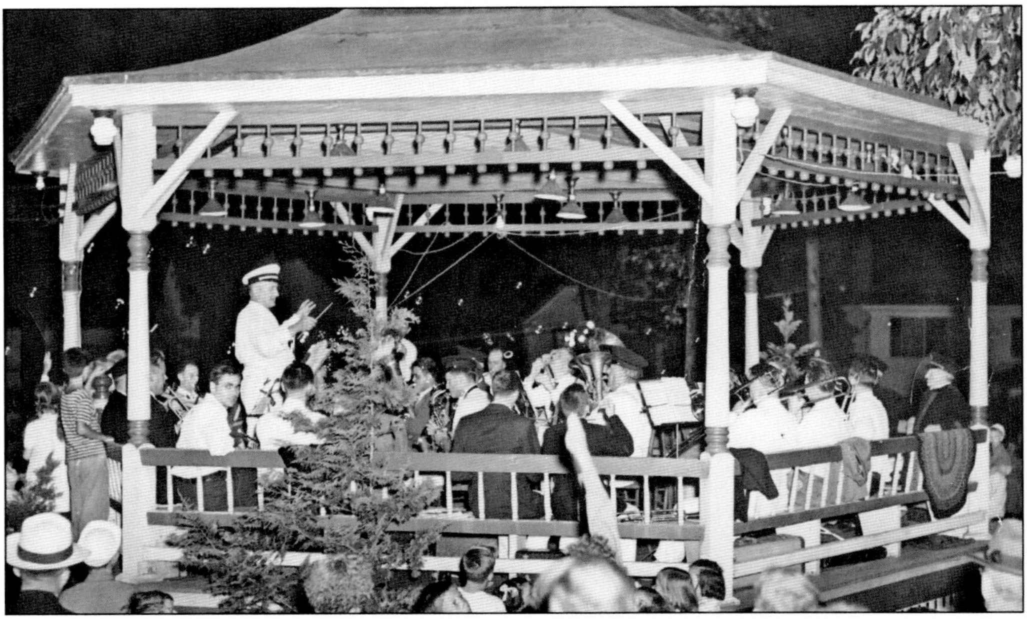

The Ashby Band has been playing concerts on the common on Wednesday evenings since 1932. This photograph of the band playing "I'm Forever Blowing Bubbles" is from about 1950. Fred Bernhardt, the bandleader for more than 20 years, is conducting. The Ashby Band attracted talented performers, some of whom went on to play professionally for major orchestras and bands. (Courtesy of Florence Bryan.)

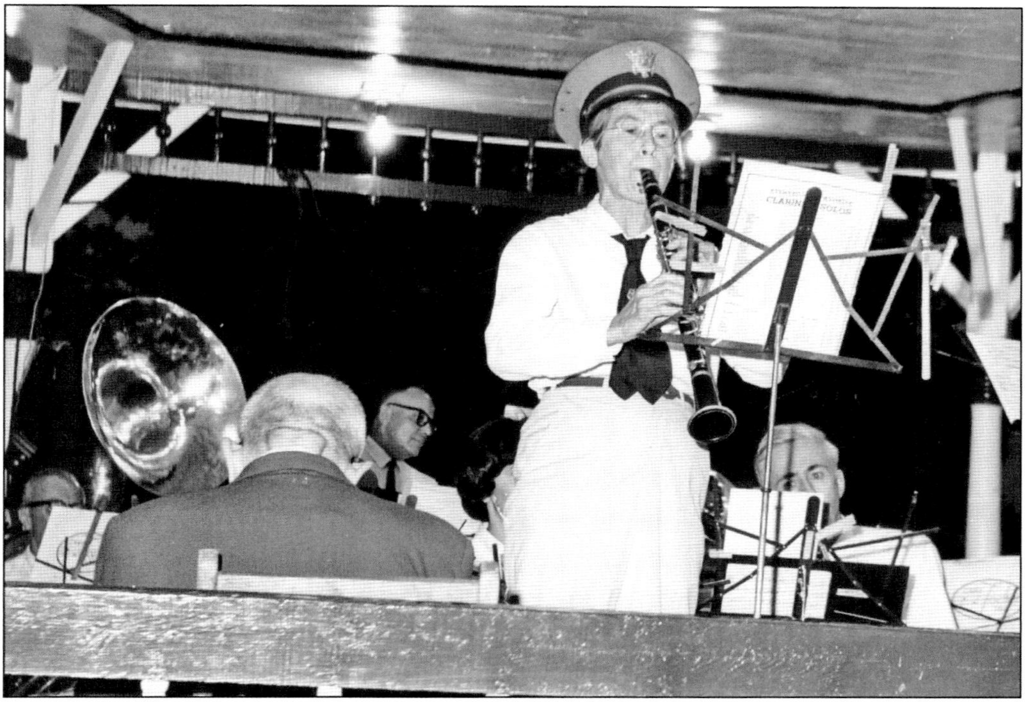

Dorothy Wilder is seen performing a clarinet solo with the Ashby Band in the 1960s. Wilder was among the pool of talented musicians that Ashby could draw from to play in the Wednesday night concerts.

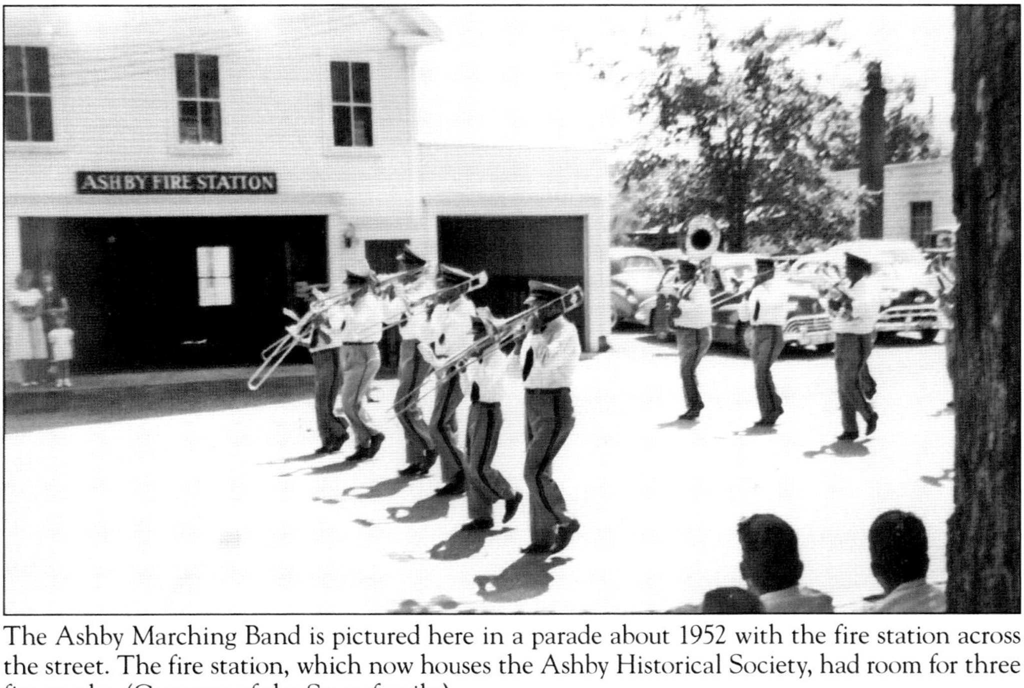

The Ashby Marching Band is pictured here in a parade about 1952 with the fire station across the street. The fire station, which now houses the Ashby Historical Society, had room for three fire trucks. (Courtesy of the Stacy family.)

GRAND CONCERT.

TUFTS COLLEGE GLEE AND MANDOLIN CLUBS,

FIRST PARISH HALL, ASHBY,

JANUARY 15, 1904. EIGHT O'CLOCK.

BENEFIT ASHBY HIGH SCHOOL.

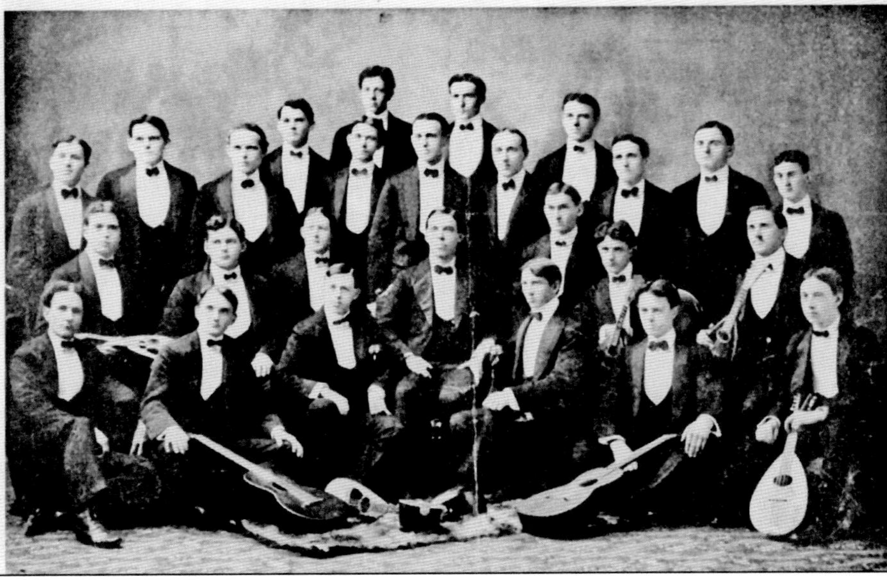

This 1904 advertisement reveals that the early-20th-century citizens of Ashby were interested in both education and cultural improvement. The proceeds of this concert by the Tufts University Glee Club benefited the new high school, which had been built two years earlier.

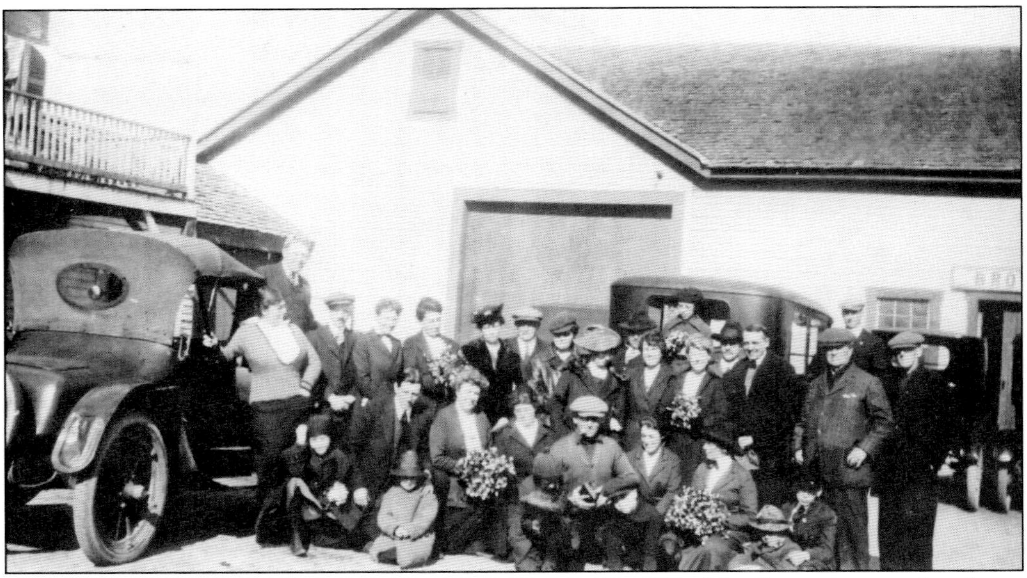

The annual gathering of mayflowers was a family event in the 1920s. The flowers grew in abundance on Spring Hill near the Piper farm. The flower is an early spring flower and provided for a festive gathering before planting started. (Courtesy of Richard and Nancy Catalini.)

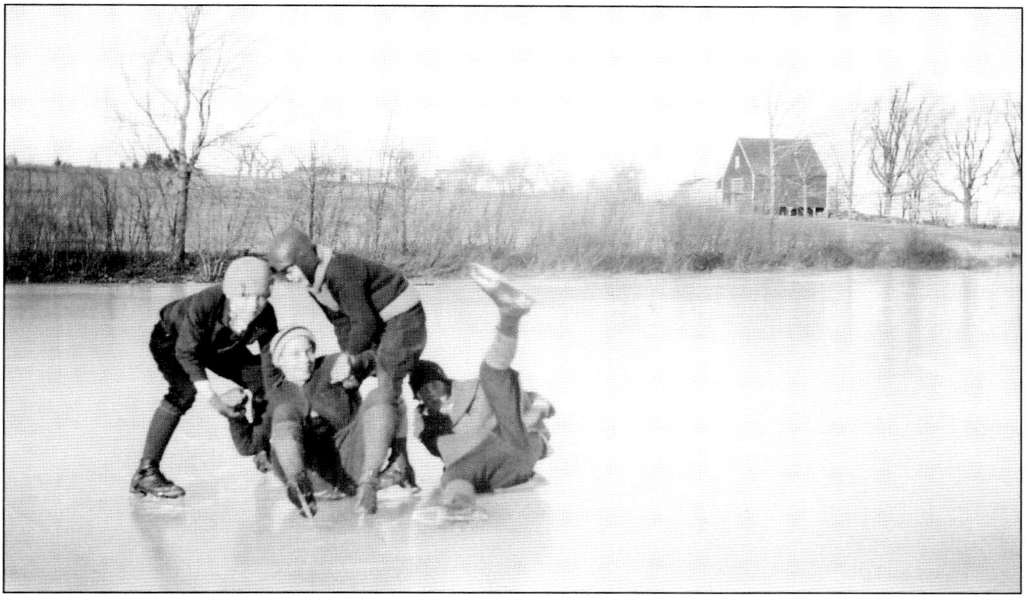

From left to right, Alvah Stacy, Bud Evans, and Verner and Theodore Ketonen are skating on Holt's Mill Pond in 1932. Skating was a favorite winter pastime, and Holt's millpond was a popular spot in northwest Ashby. When the snow came, the adult Stacy would drive his dump truck onto the ice to plow it for the neighborhood boys. (Courtesy of the Stacy family.)

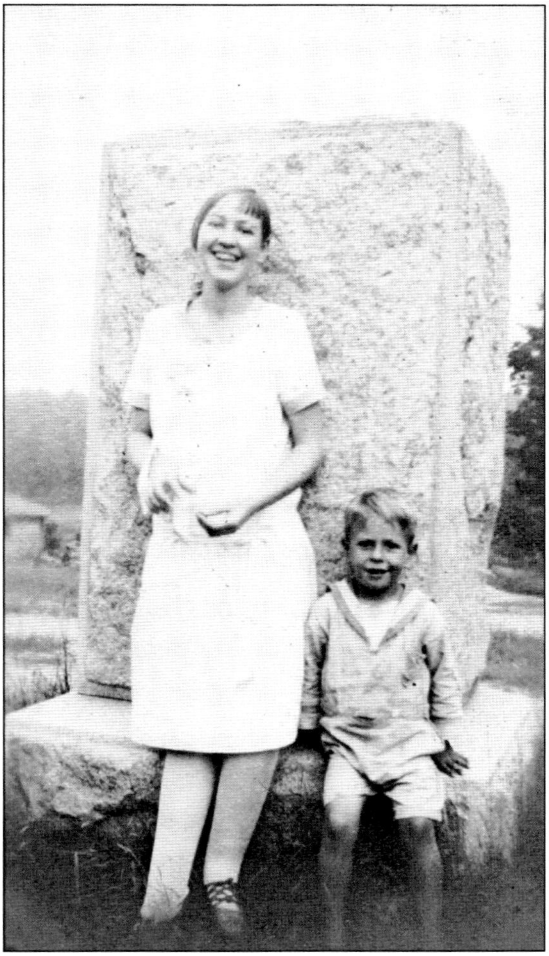

Esther Barrett and her brother Raymond are pictured here at the John Fitch Monument in August 1929. The monument was erected by the Fitchburg Historical Society in 1899 to commemorate the site where Fitch's garrison stood. The garrison was overrun by Indians in 1746 during the French and Indian War. Fitch and his family were taken to Canada and later ransomed.

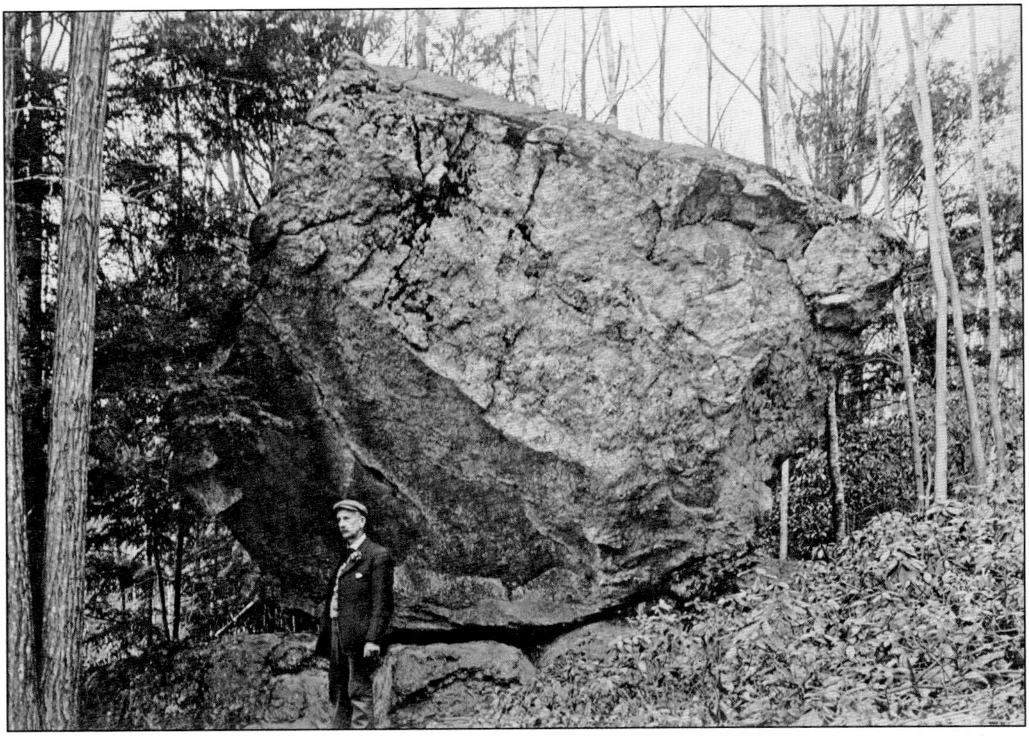

Tilting Rock is another local curiosity that tourists sought out. This large erratic, placed here by retreating glaciers thousands of years ago, is tilted so that it appears to be about to roll down the hill.

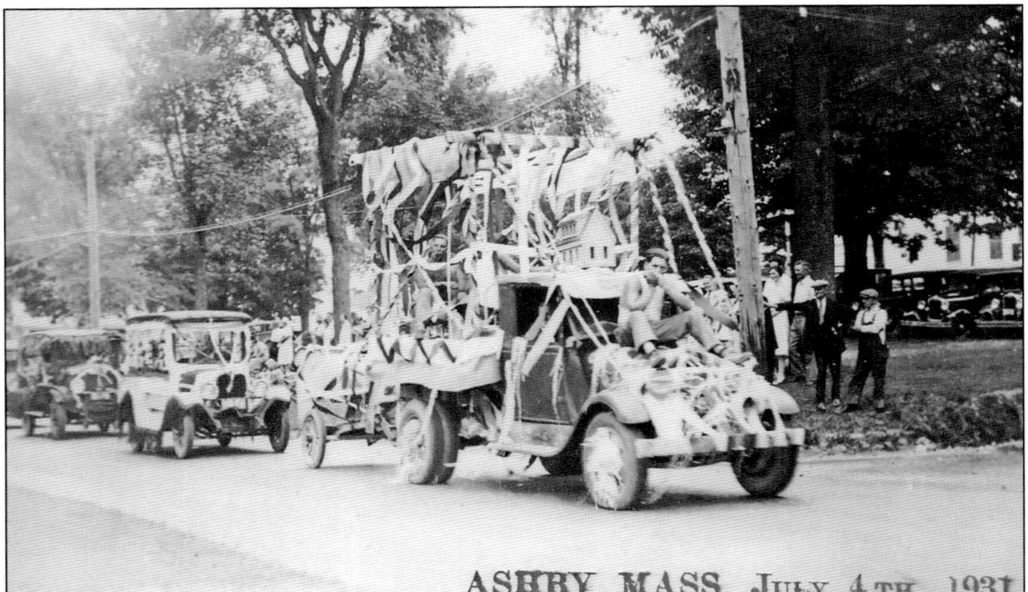

In years past, Ashby had a Fourth of July parade that drew a number of entrants and spectators. This photograph of the parade in 1931 shows several trucks and cars gaily decorated for the parade. (Courtesy of the Stacy family.)

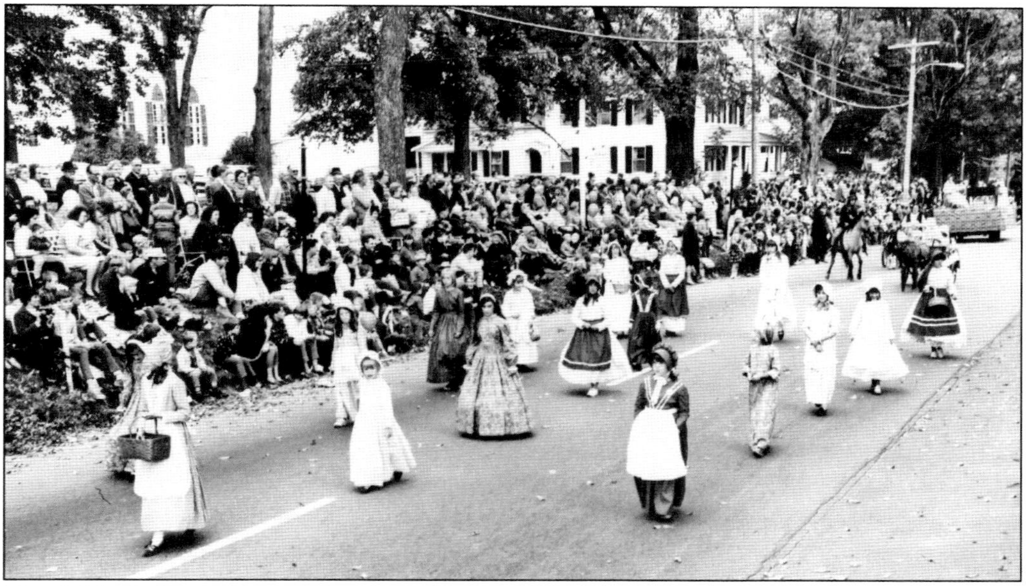

The Ashby Belles wore period gowns and bonnets for the Ashby Bicentennial events. Here, they are seen marching in the bicentennial parade, which attracted thousands of viewers. (Courtesy of Nancy Elliott Rogers.)

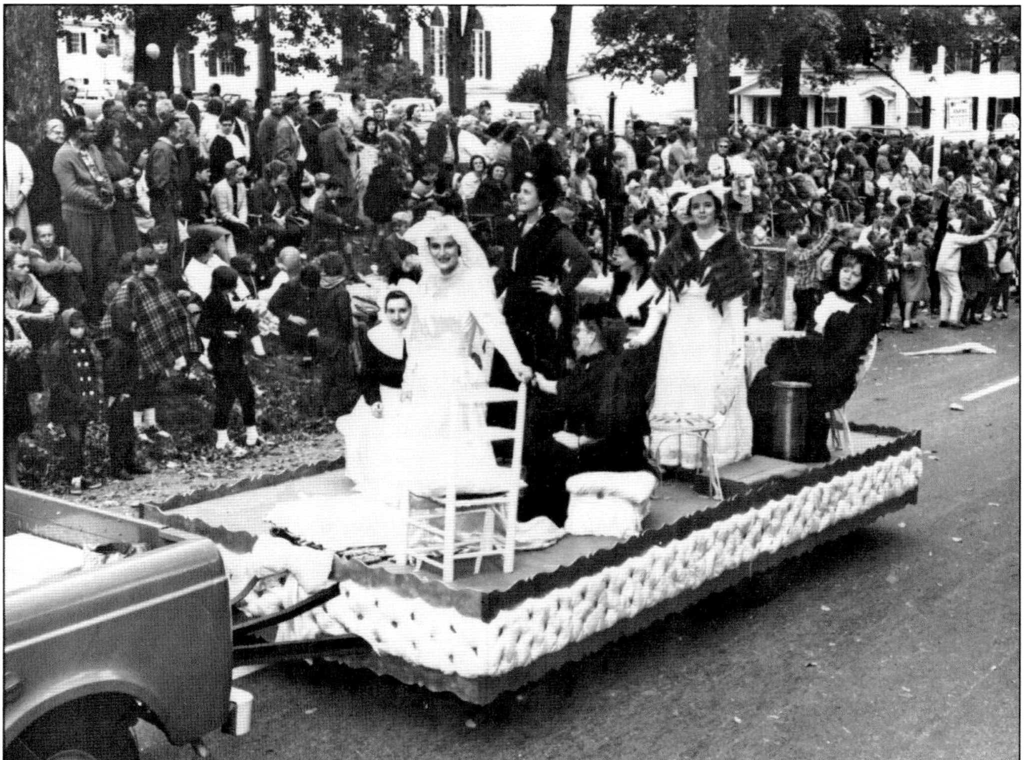

This 1967 photograph is of one of the many floats assembled for the bicentennial parade, which attracted 18,000 viewers. It appears to focus on family life, particularly on the roles of women. (Courtesy of Ashby Free Public Library.)

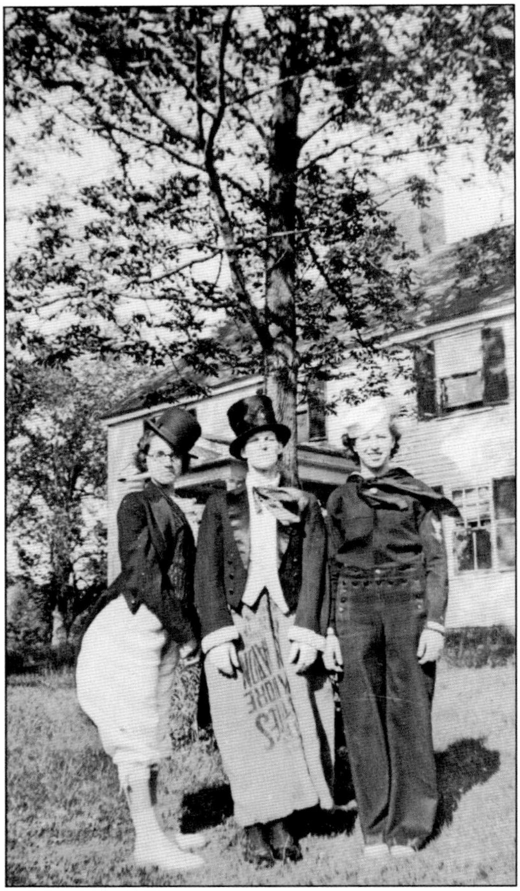

Celebrating Labor Day in the 1930s, some folks dressed in costume to honor or poke fun at various trades and occupations. A couple of industrialists and a sailor are pictured here. (Courtesy of Carol Bennett Lielasus.)

The Finnish Folk Dance Group attracted many Ashby residents of Finnish descent. This photograph from the early 1960s includes, from left to right, (first row) Joel Nash, Donna Halfpenny, Miki Heikkila, Ann Foresman, Eric Jakobowicz, and Debra Flinkstrom; (second row) Anslem Lampi (with accordion), Ritva LaMier, Jean Lemieur, Marla Jakobowicz, Linda Ross, Kathy Graves, and Kari Rantala; (third row) Alan Pernaa, Dwight Anttila, Nancy Jakobowicz, David B. Foresman, Richard Lehtola, and Susan Pernaa.

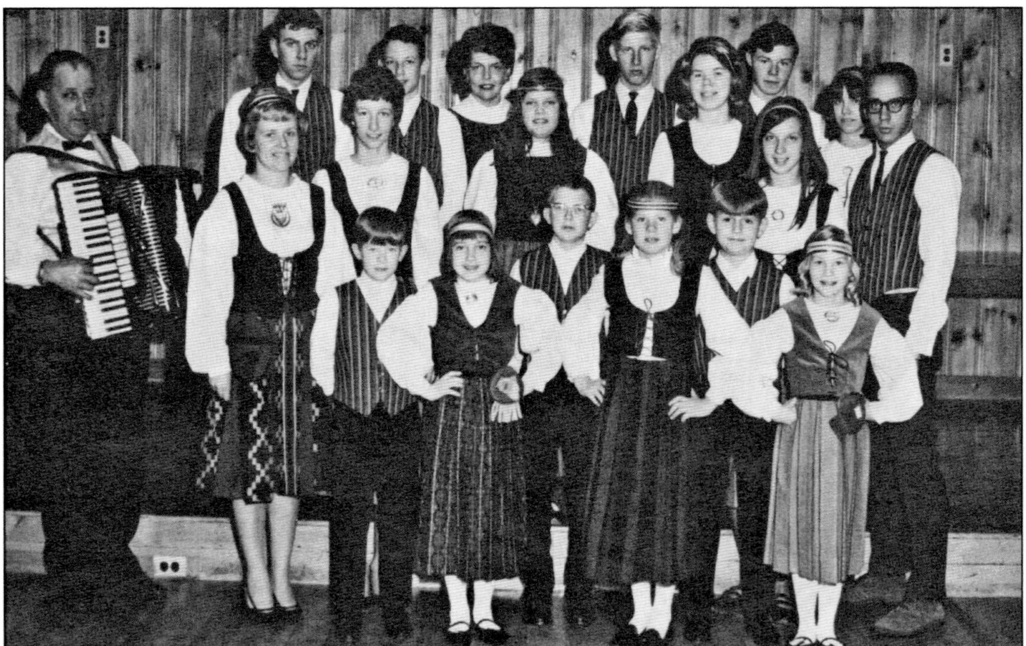

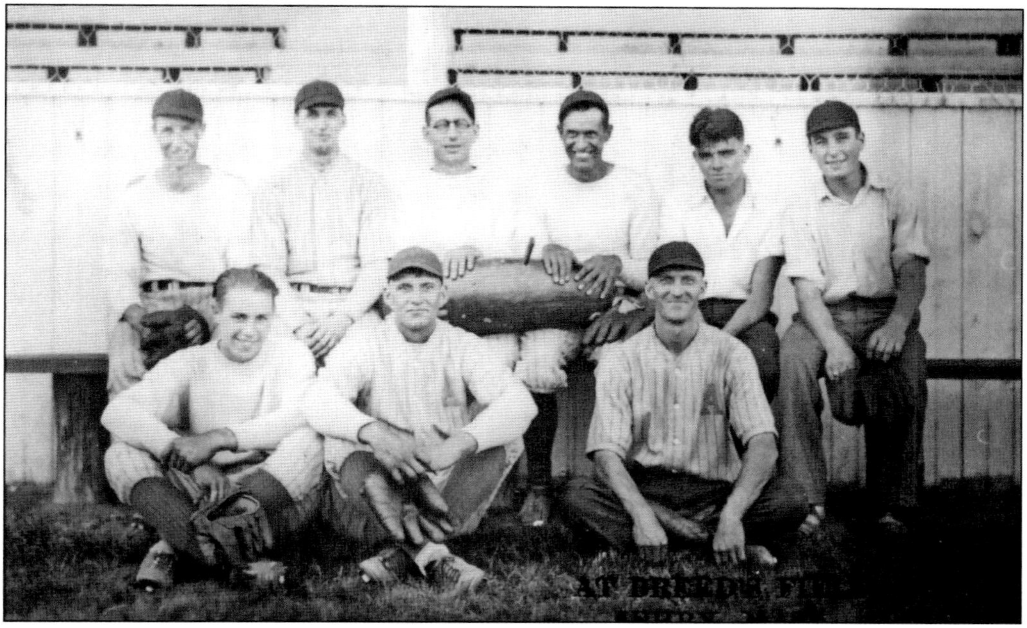

The Ashby baseball team stopped for a photograph about 1931. At that time, each town would have a baseball team, and a regular schedule would be played between neighboring towns, with a championship game at the end of the season. The players shown here are, from left to right, (first row) Albert Damon, Gustave Erickson, and Fred Erickson; (second row) Wilbur Loveland, Richard Robbins, John Brewer, Roland Simonds, Bill Whelan, and Harold Wilkinson. (Courtesy of Richard and Nancy Catalini.)

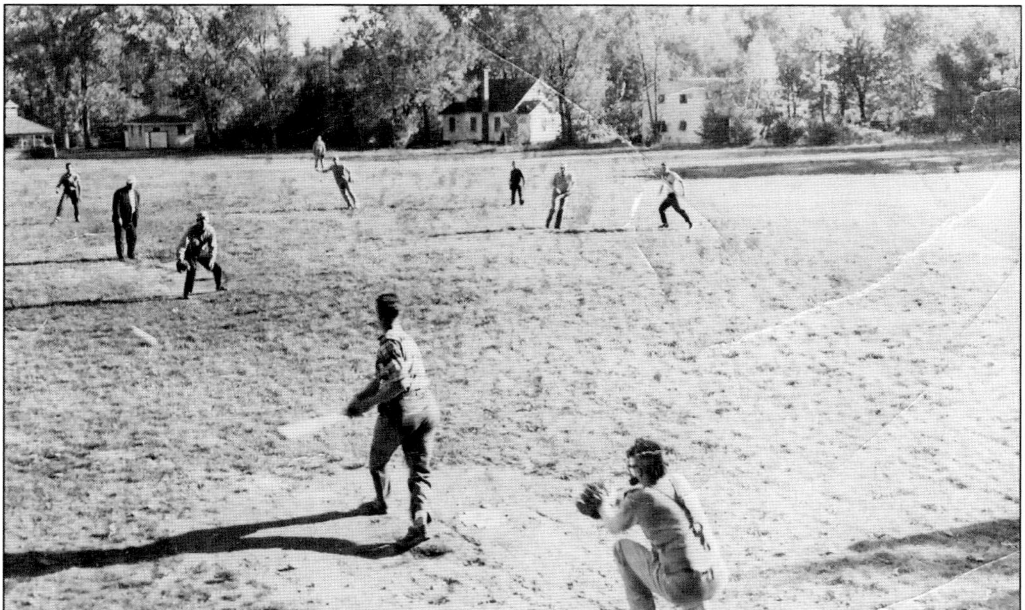

Baseball was a popular summertime sport for young men. Each town would field one or more teams. Alvah Stacy is the batter in this 1930s photograph. The ball can be seen as a streak just in front of and to the left of the pitcher. (Courtesy of the Stacy family.)

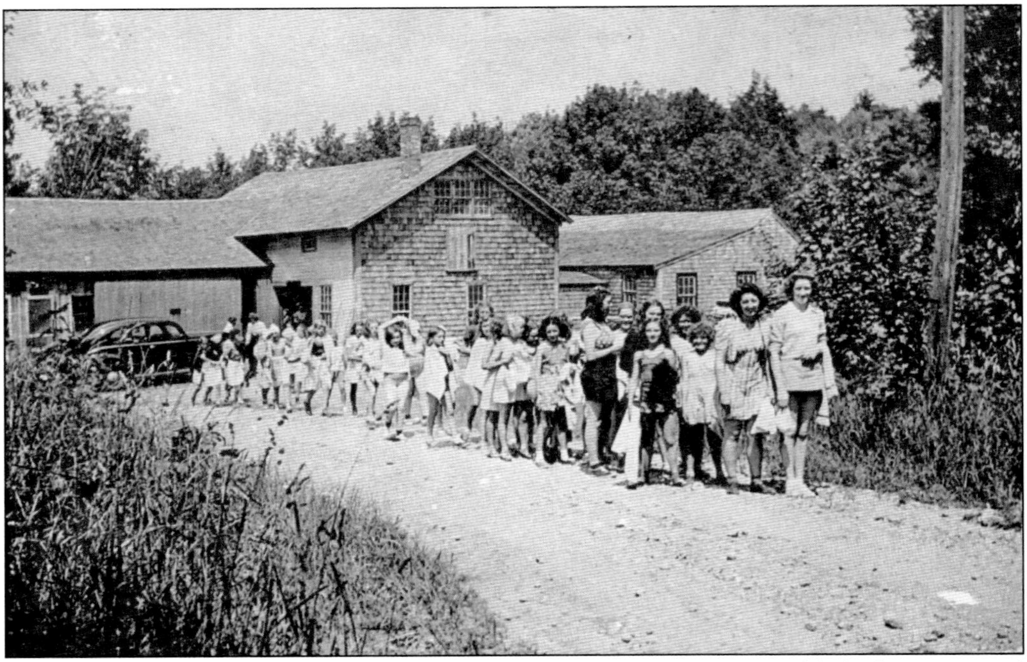

Camp Middlesex was a 4-H summer camp for girls. The camp was established in 1942 and offered instruction in raising crops and animal husbandry. Campers would stay a few weeks and enjoy swimming and hiking in addition to agricultural instruction. (Courtesy of Richard and Nancy Catalini.)

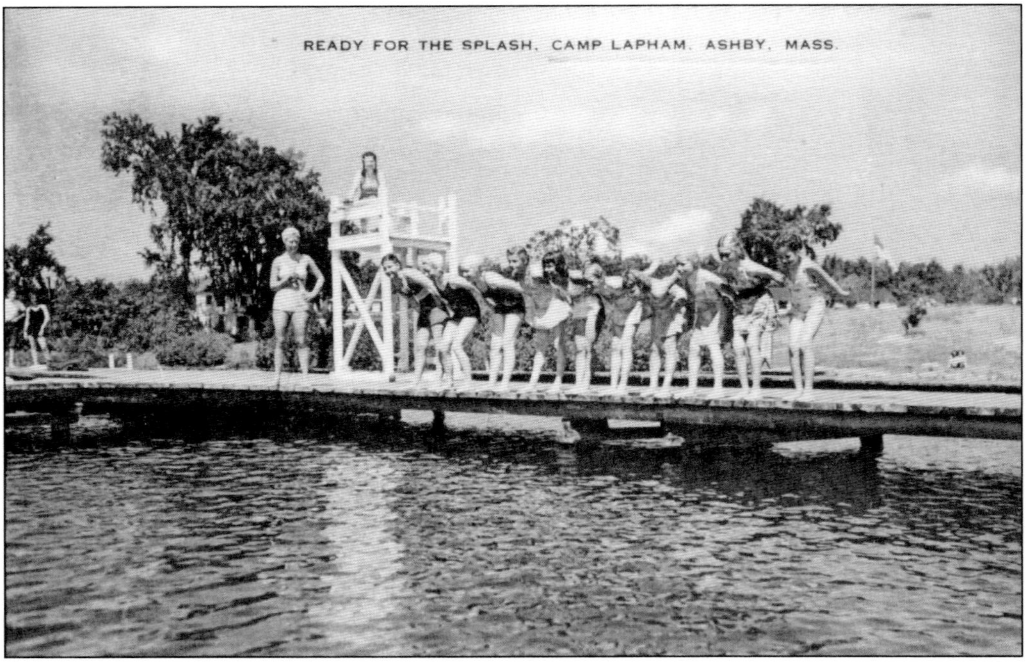

Camp Lapham has been offering summer activities for young campers since the 1940s. This photograph shows enthusiastic youngsters in the mid-1960s ready to dive into the lake. (Courtesy of Richard and Nancy Catalini.)

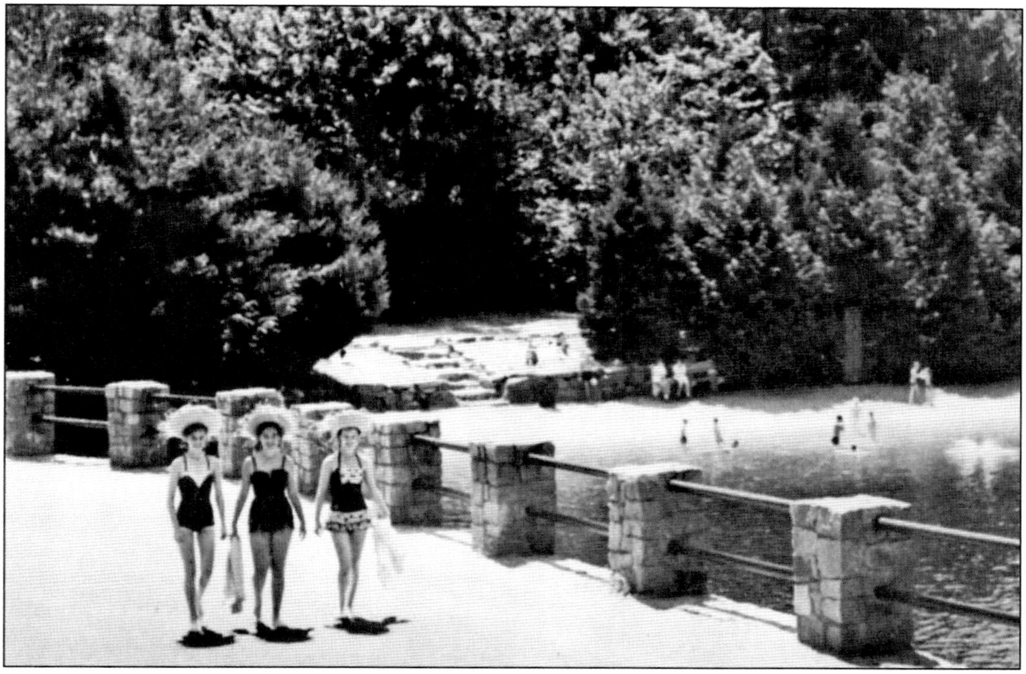

Lois Boudreau (center) and her sisters walk along the bridge at Damon Pond in the 1950s. Damon Pond, in the state forest, is a popular swimming spot. Lois would meet her future husband, Bob Goguen, here. (Courtesy of Richard and Nancy Catalini.)

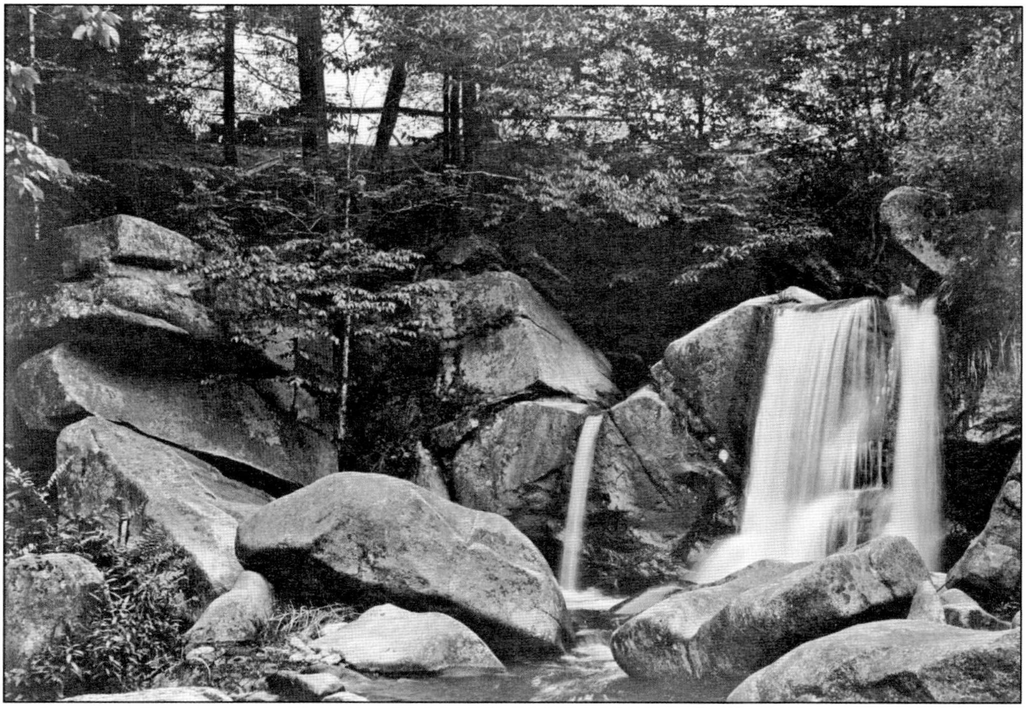

Trap Rock Falls on the Townsend Road is another point of interest that has intrigued visitors for many years. The size of the falls varies with the season—from being a single large waterfall in the spring to three smaller falls in the late summer.

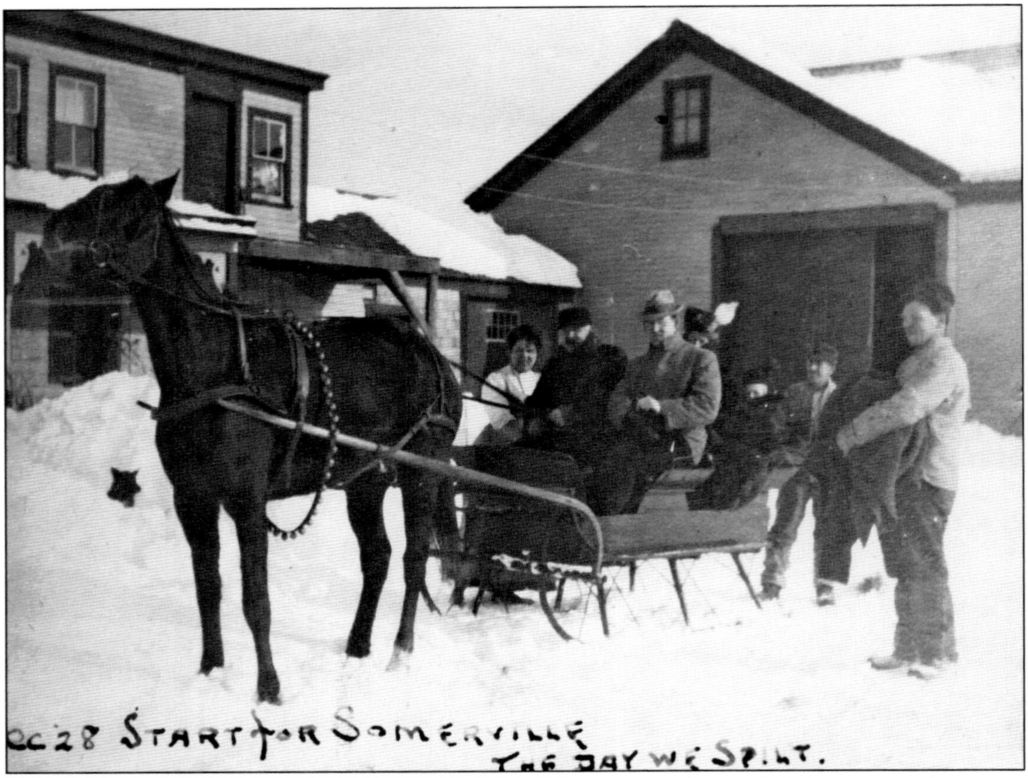

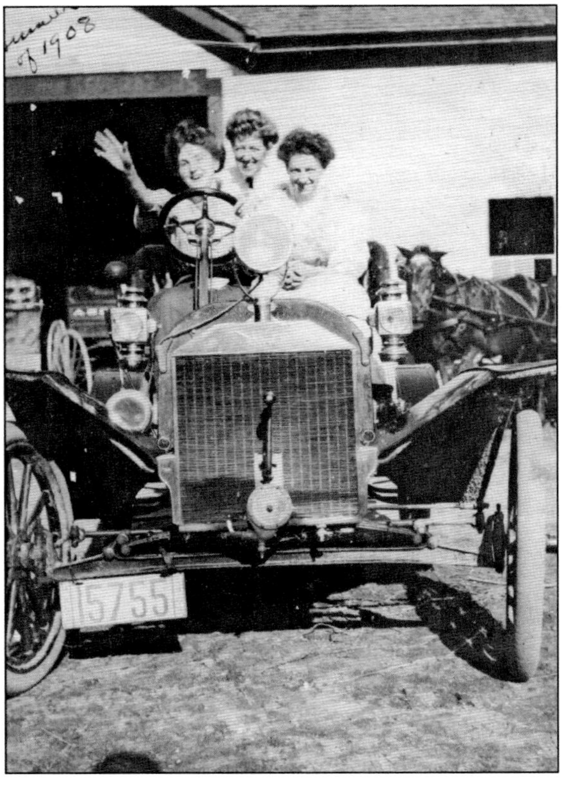

Leaving from a holiday visit with relatives in Ashby in 1909 are Charles (seated right front) and Florence Metchear (seated rear left) and their family in a one-horse open sleigh. The Metchears are returning to Somerville. One of the Ashby relatives is offering robes for the trip. Before roads were plowed, sleighs were a practical means of winter travel. (Courtesy of Richard and Nancy Catalini.)

Lora Piper (left), Florence Piper Metchear (center), and Cora Piper Foresman are having a good time seated in an early Ford in 1908. It is unlikely they were allowed to drive the car, as the first Massachusetts driver's license issued to a woman was in 1908. (Courtesy of Richard and Nancy Catalini.)

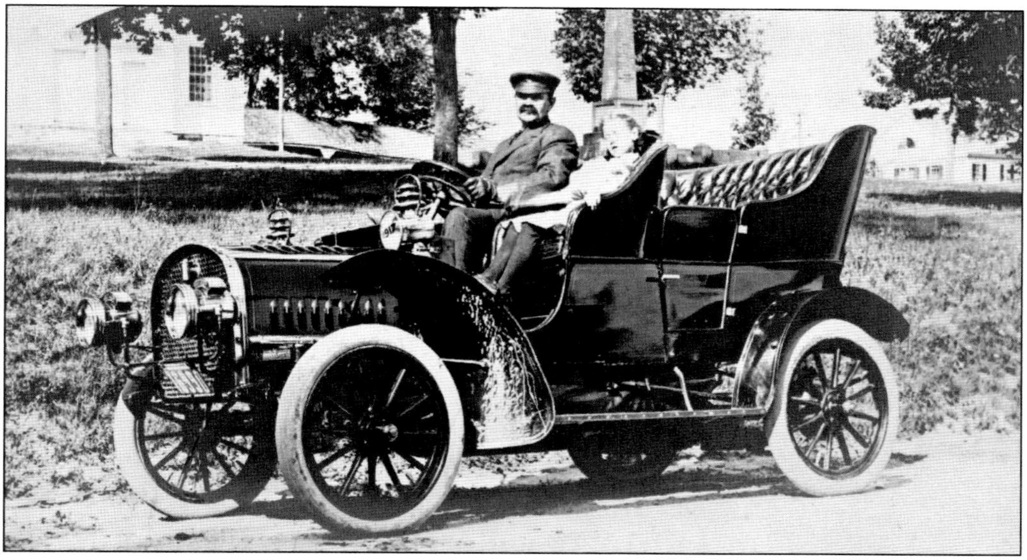

This right-hand drive 1906 Rambler has arrived in Ashby with a young girl apparently asleep in the front seat. Cars like this brought well-to-do people to Ashby. The car was right-hand drive and had no doors in the front so the chauffeur could easily get out to open the door for the passengers in the rear of the vehicle. The idea that people would drive their own automobiles was just coming into vogue in 1906.

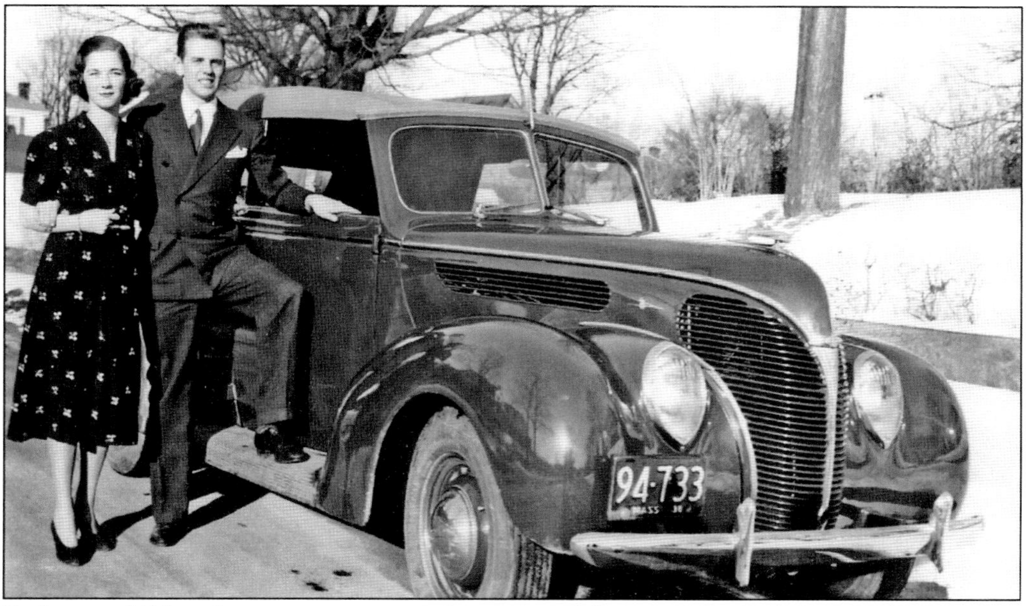

Barbara and Edwin Lyman pose next to their automobile on South Road in 1938, the year they were married. They would purchase Elm Farm on South Road that year and take up residence there. (Courtesy of Warren Lyman.)

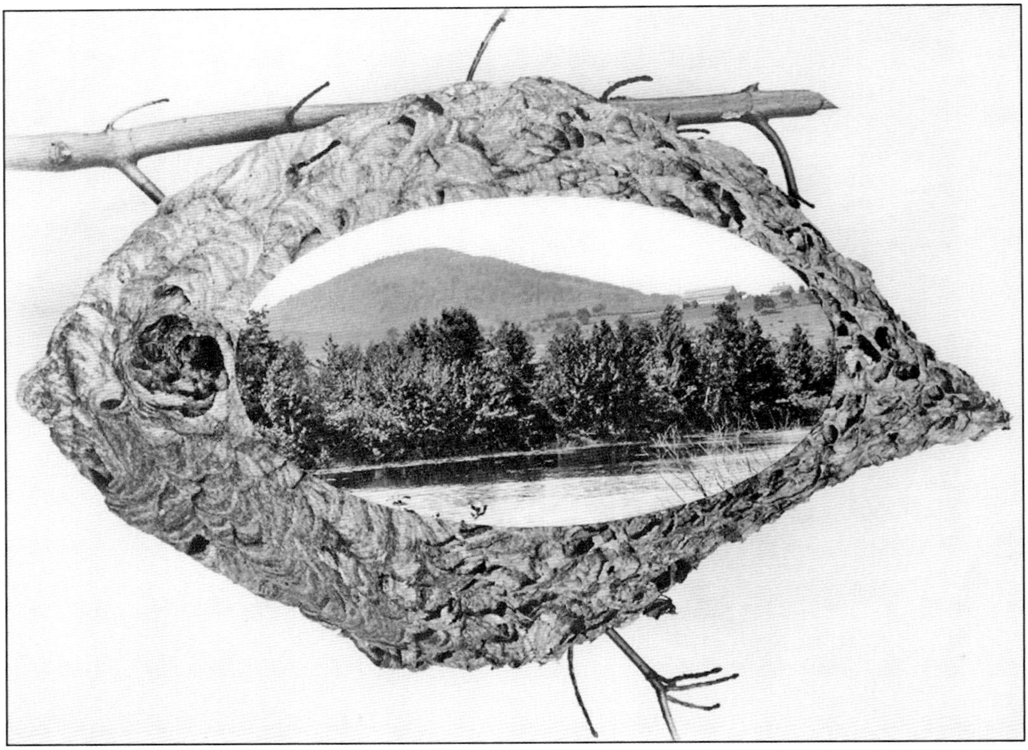

This is one of the most bizarre postcards of Ashby. For some reason, the publisher thought it would be appealing to place Mount Watatic inside a hornet nest. (Courtesy of Carol Bennett Lielasus.)

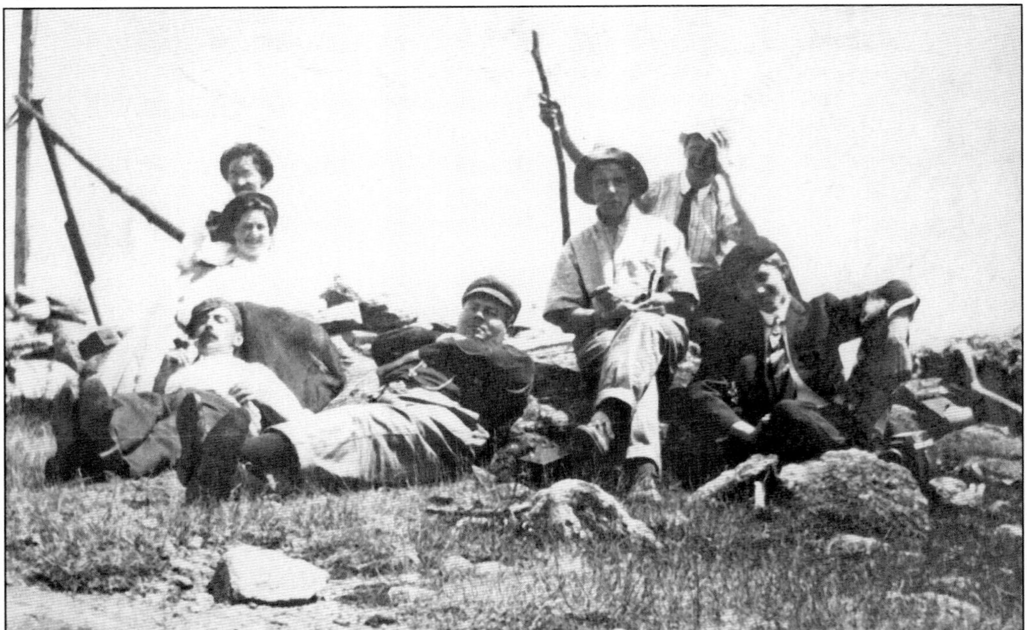

Hiking Mount Watatic was and still is a popular pastime for locals and visitors. One could make the leisurely round-trip from the center of town to the summit in half a day. This photograph of visitors was taken in 1909. (Courtesy of Richard and Nancy Catalini.)

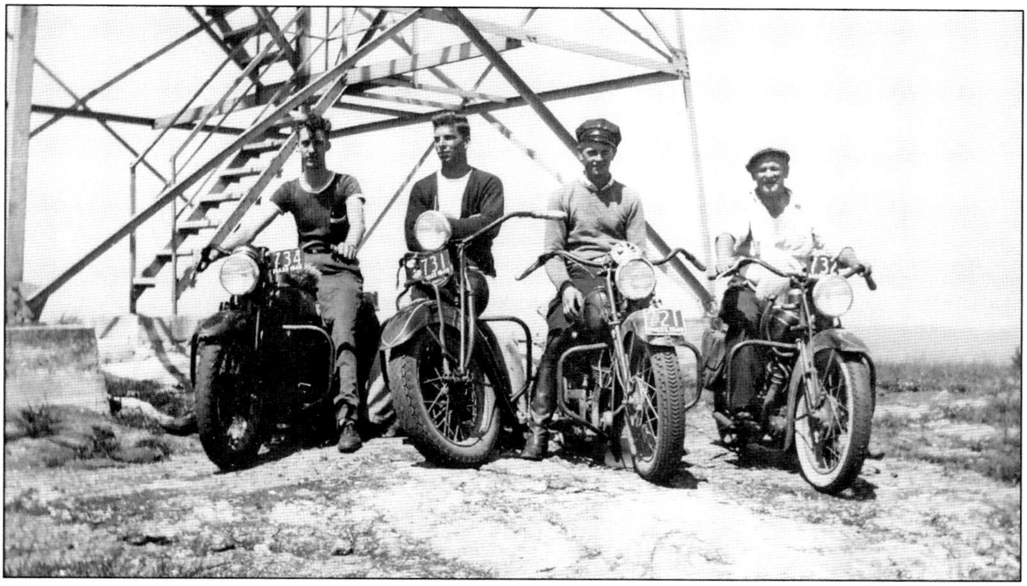

In the summer of 1941, four young men got the idea to ride their motorcycles to the top of Mount Watatic. As they gathered on Mount Watatic Road at the base of the mountain, a local resident handed them a camera and said, "If you boys make it to the top, I want a picture." In this photograph at the summit are Alvah Stacy, Bob Hirsch, Richard Bennett, and Warren "Stub" Bennett. (Courtesy of the Stacy family.)

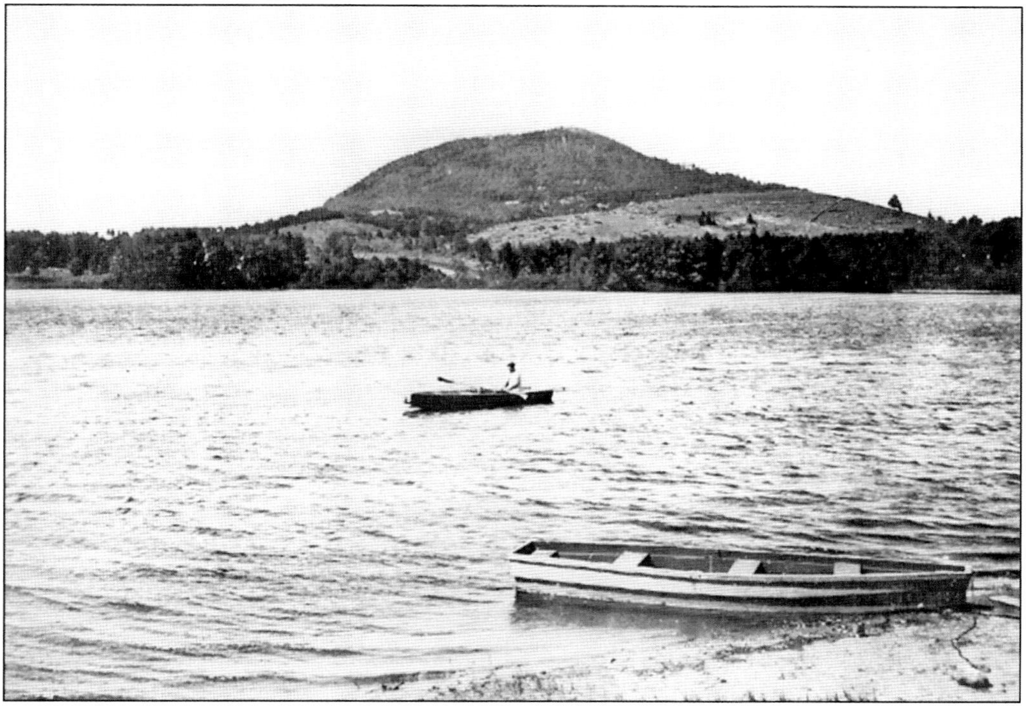

There are several lakes in Ashburnham that were popular day-trip destinations for visitors to Ashby. Enterprising residents on the lakes had small boats to rent to visitors for their enjoyment. This photograph of Mount Watatic with a man in a rowboat was taken from Ward Pond in Ashburnham. (Courtesy of Carol Bennett Lielasus.)

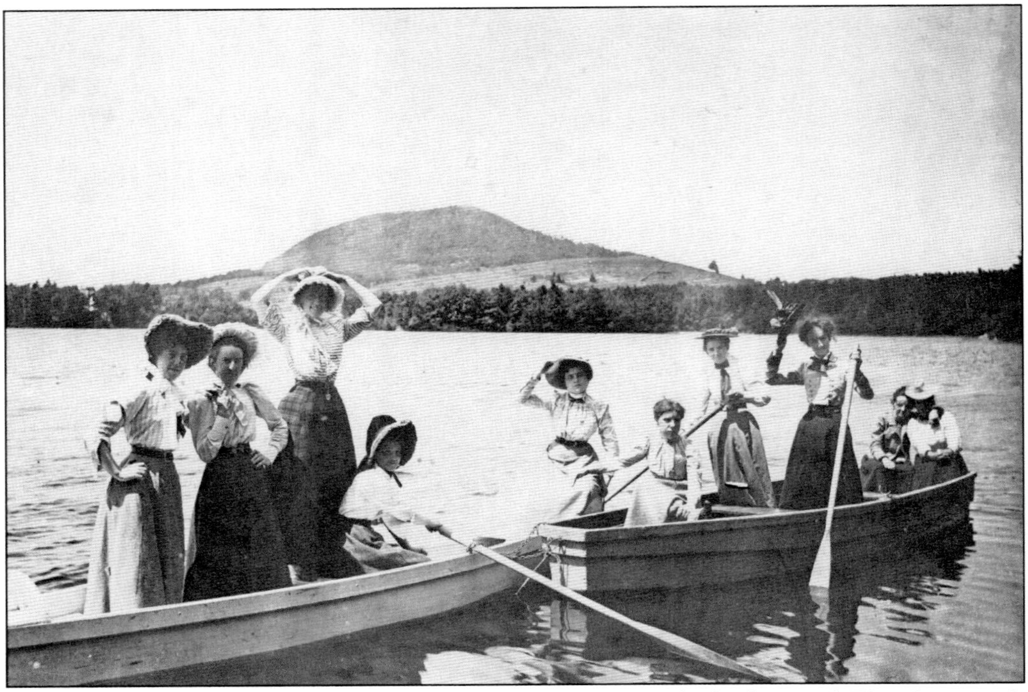

These ladies are having fun on a lake, with Mount Watatic in the background. The photograph was taken at Ward Pond or Winnekeag Lake in Ashburnham. Visitors to Ashby were often taken on outings to the lakes and ponds in Ashburnham for boating excursions.

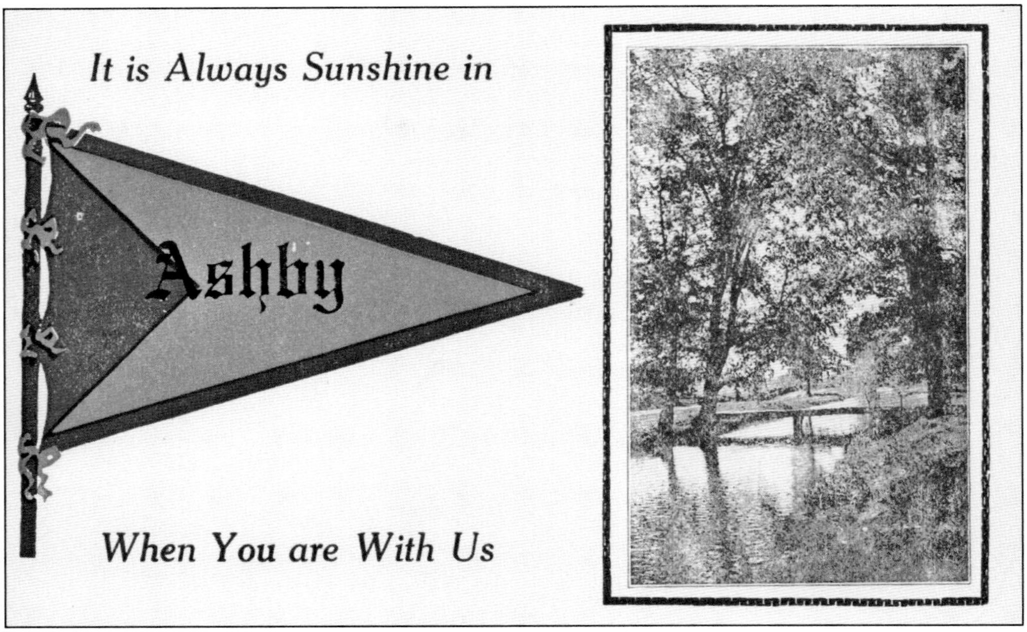

Probably from the 1930s, this promotional postcard places an idyllic image of a place that is nowhere to be found in town next to the text encouraging one to visit. By the 1930s, the automobile had improved to the extent that places like the Berkshires in western Massachusetts and the White Mountains in New Hampshire were accessible to city dwellers. Ashby began to lose out to the competition. (Courtesy of William and Katherine Stanwood.)

Seven

Faces and Places

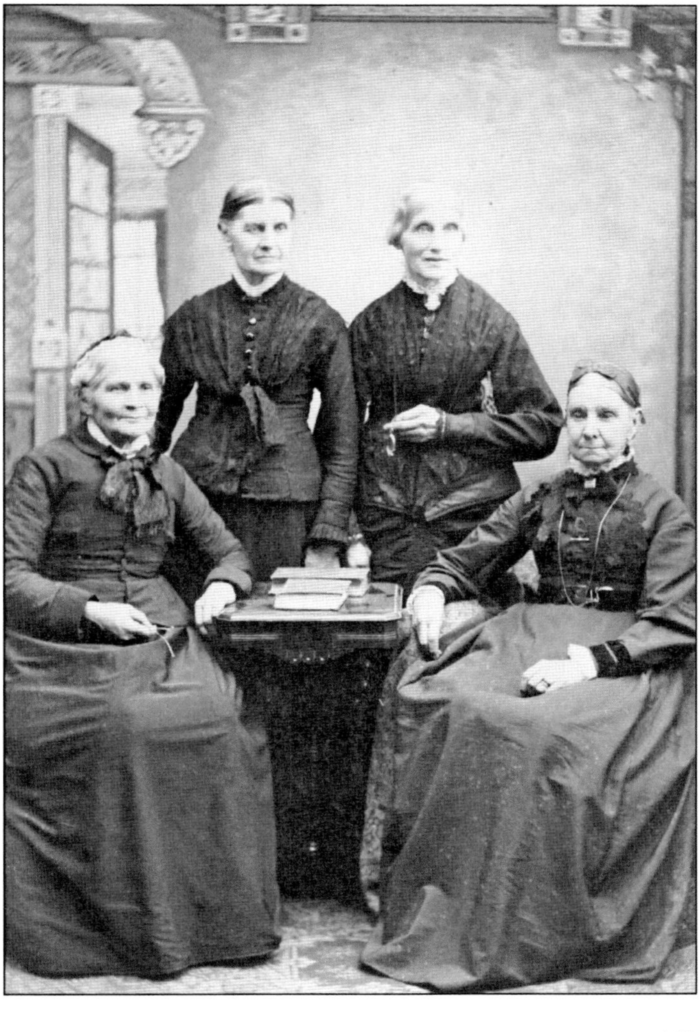

Pictured here in 1884 are, from left to right, Betsy Richardson Waite, Sally Taylor Hayward, Mary Burr Gates, and Charlotte Adams Hodgekins. All were born in Ashby in 1810 and were schoolmates.

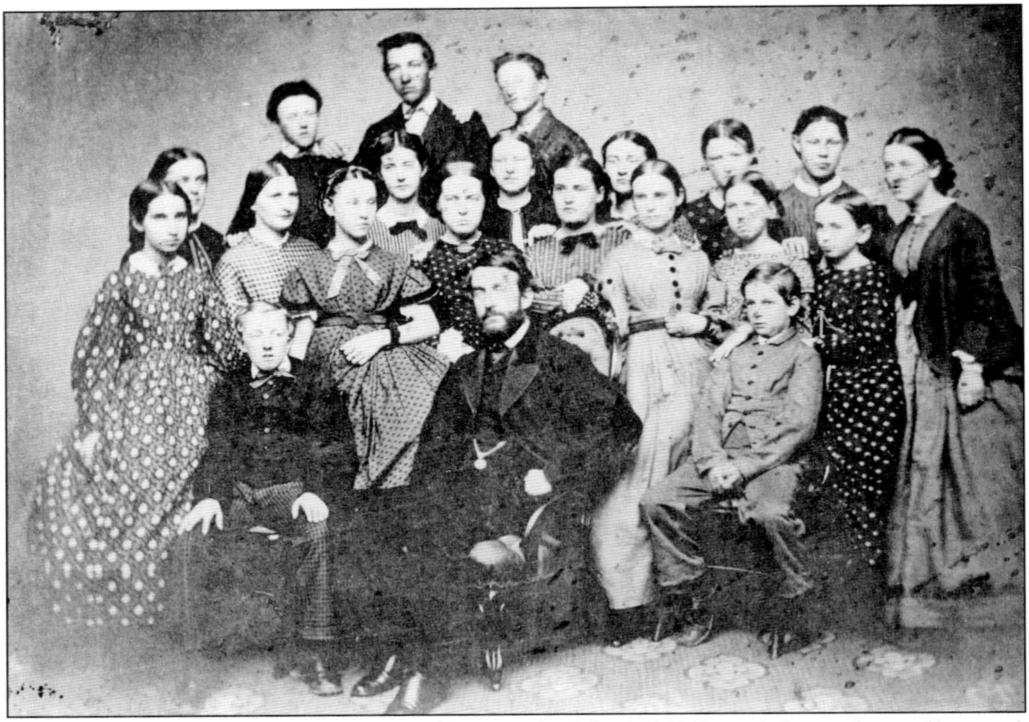

Ashby High School students are pictured here in the fall of 1864. From left to right are (first row) Dascomb Wright, Ashulet Bingham (teacher), and George Adams; (second row) Fannie Damon, Fannie Wyman, Hattie Whitney, L. Clementine Damon, Frances Bennett, Martha Davis, and Mary Davis; (third row) Delice Estabrook, Helen Krugman, Sarah Davis, M. Lizzie Gates, L. Wilder, Hattie Booth, Georgia Hayward, and Lizzie Burr; (fourth row) Joel Davis, Alfred Foster, and Henry Wilder.

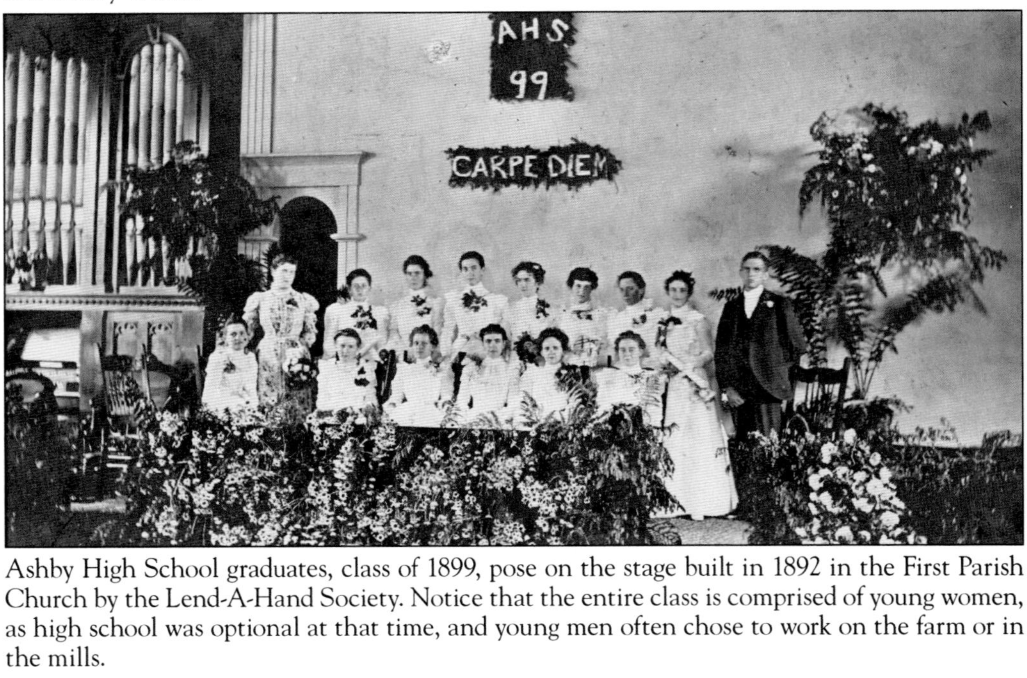

Ashby High School graduates, class of 1899, pose on the stage built in 1892 in the First Parish Church by the Lend-A-Hand Society. Notice that the entire class is comprised of young women, as high school was optional at that time, and young men often chose to work on the farm or in the mills.

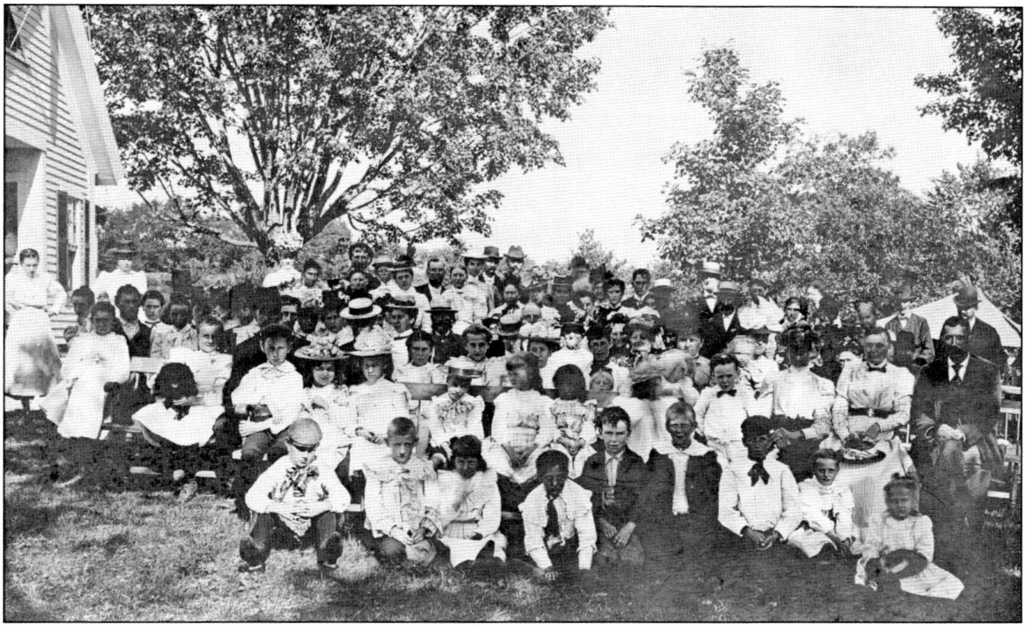

These elementary schoolchildren are all dressed up for picture day. Notice some of the elaborate and quite lovely women's hats and a child's pet on the child's lap.

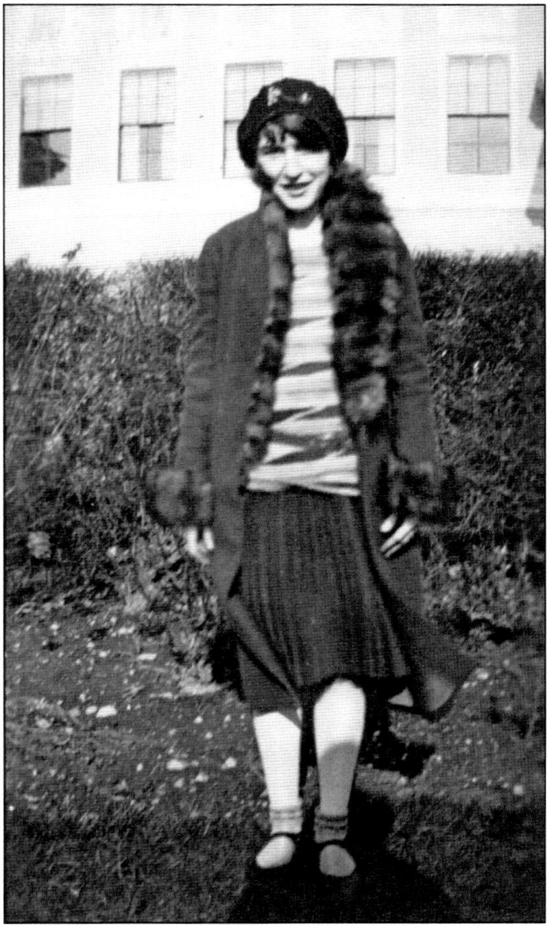

Rebecca Elliott was typical of Ashby students in 1930. Here, she stands in front of the school wearing a pleated skirt and red fox fur–trimmed coat. Even though there is a silver fox farm two miles away, the silver fox pelts were far too valuable for a high school girl.

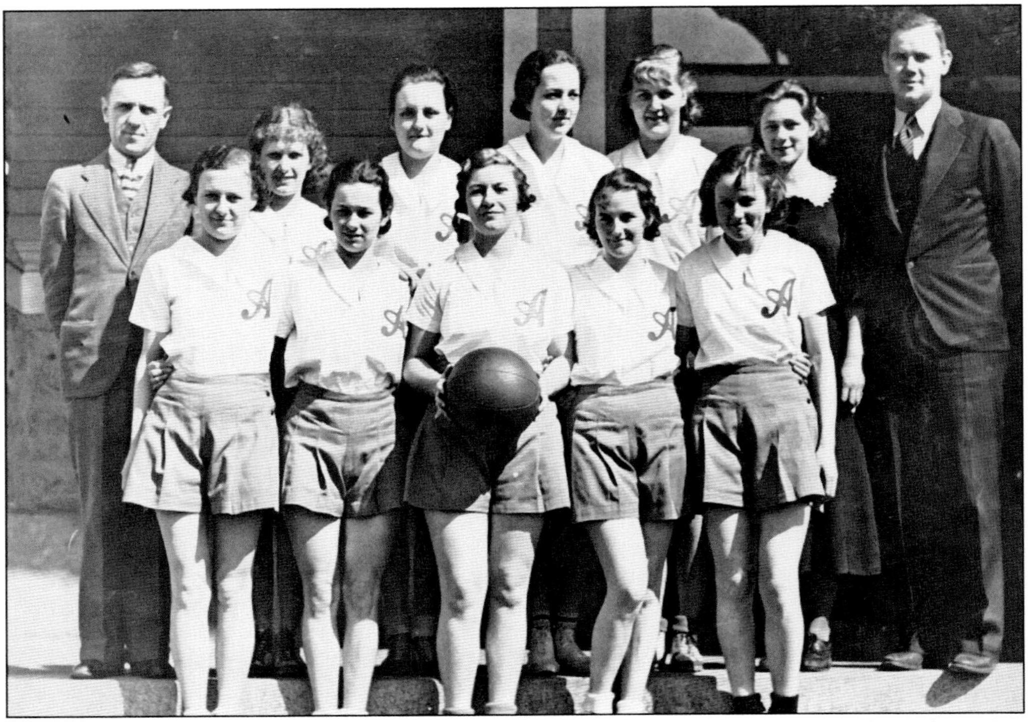

Basketball was a popular sport in Ashby. This Ashby High School girls' team from the 1930s practiced in the Grange Hall gymnasium, and games were held there until the Ashby Elementary School was built in 1953.

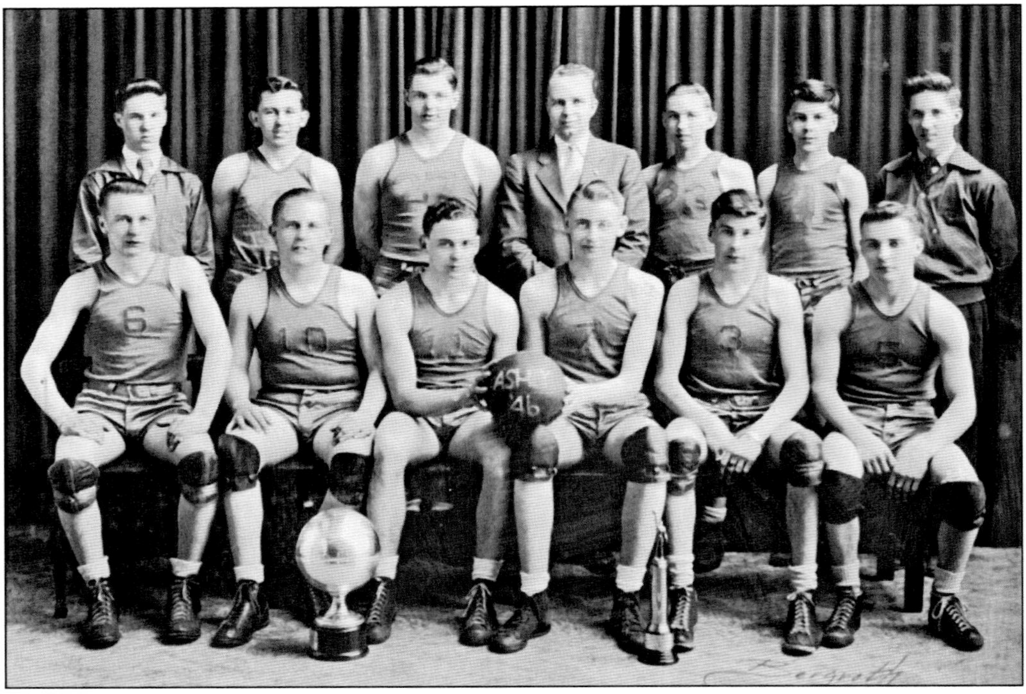

Pictured here are the 1946 Townsend Basketball Tournament Champions. The Ashby Athletic Association was formed in April 1903, and membership to join was 10¢ per month.

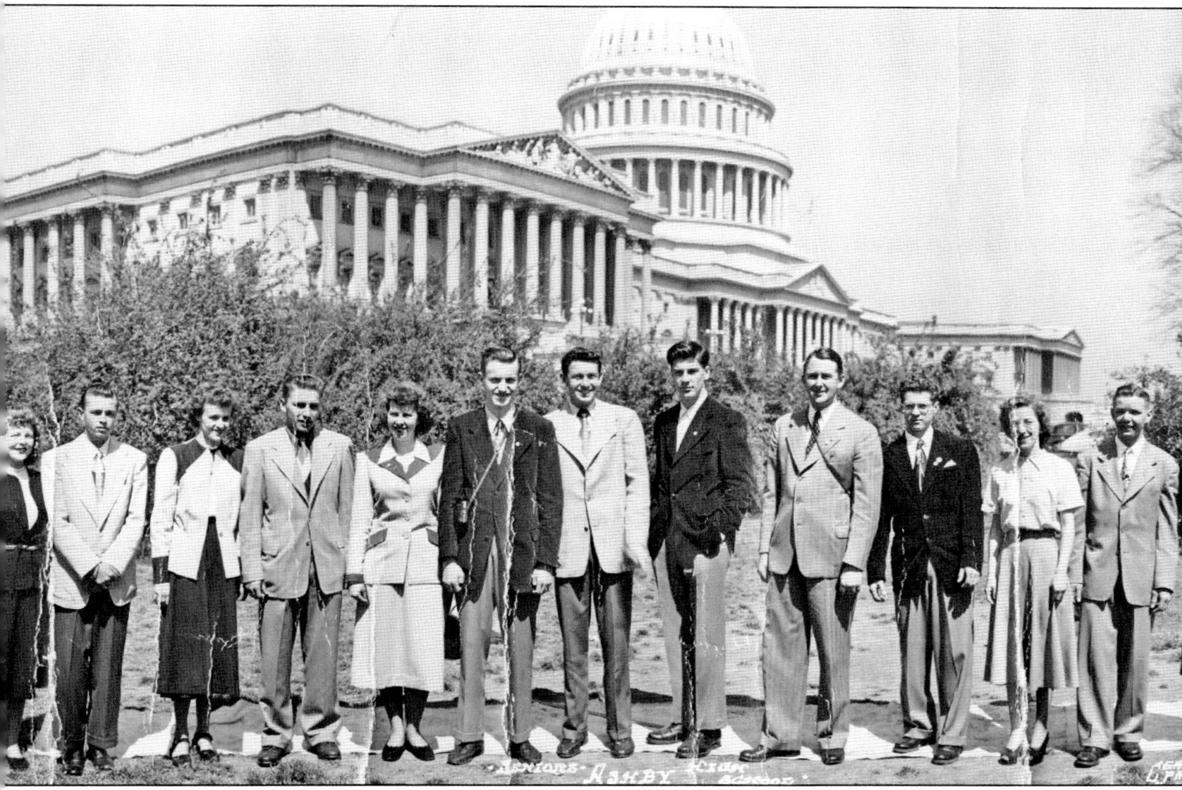

Ashby High School seniors could look forward to a spring trip to Washington, DC, where they toured historic buildings and sites and sometimes met with their local representatives to Congress. This photograph is of the class of 1949 on its class trip that was both educational and a lot of fun. Pictured, from left to right, are Elsie Heikkila, Norman Aho, Joan Mason, Kenneth Lahtinen, Helmi Honkala, Francis Carter, Leonard Shattuck, D. Alan Foresman, Walter Luce (advisor), Alfred Boudreau, Alice Ouellette (class advisor), William Seymour, and Ellen Heikkila. (Courtesy of Florence Bryan.)

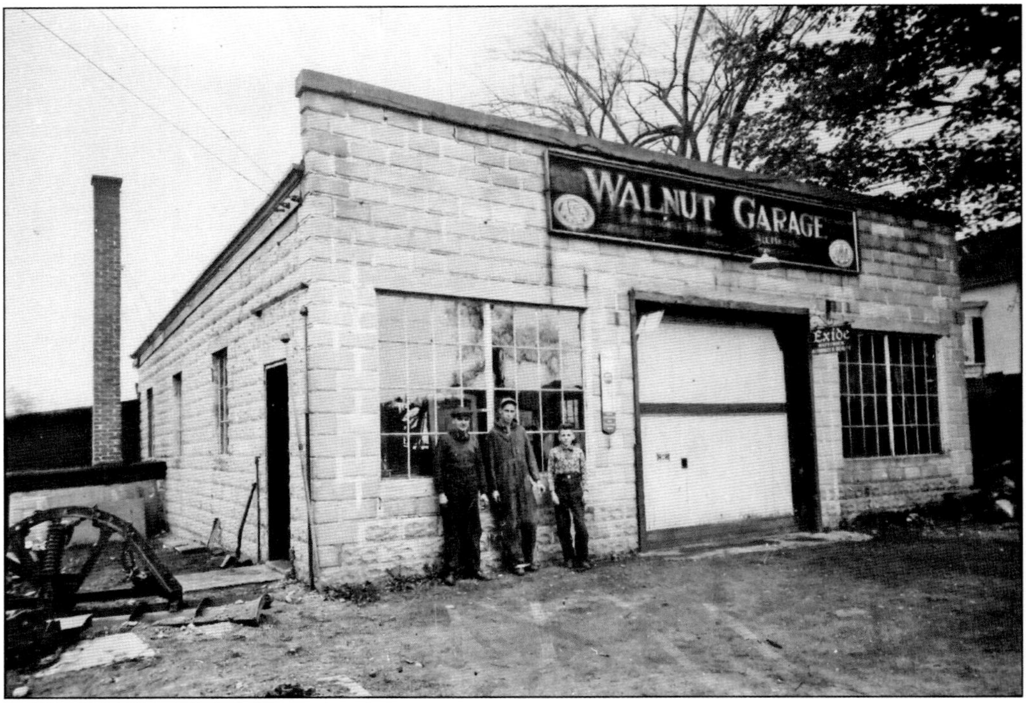

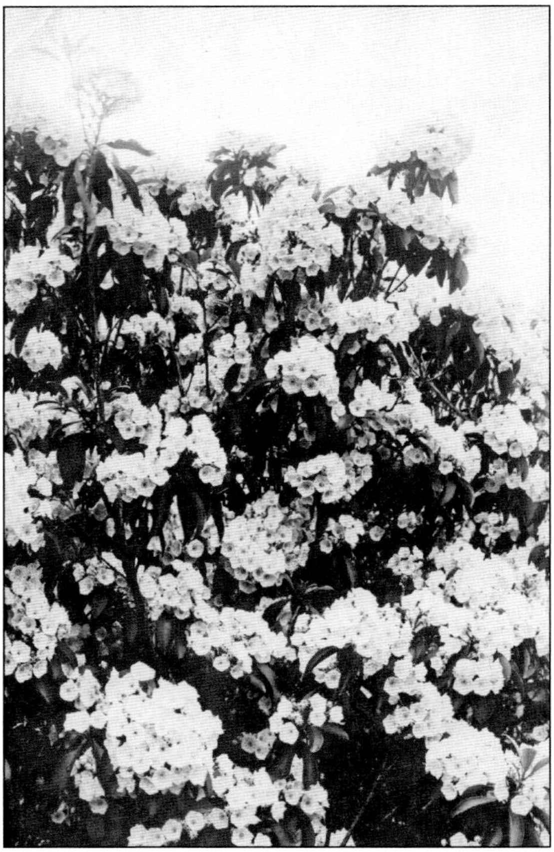

The Walnut Garage was next door to the engine house that housed the Watatic and the Chemical Engine Companies, and there was both professional and social interaction between the garage men and the firemen. The garage was torn down in 1999, and the land was purchased by the town. (Courtesy of Bill Arnold.)

Laurel is Ashby's official town flower. The Massachusetts Horticultural Society recognized Ashby's beautiful banks of laurel with a gold coin in June 1913. (Courtesy of Richard and Nancy Catalini.)

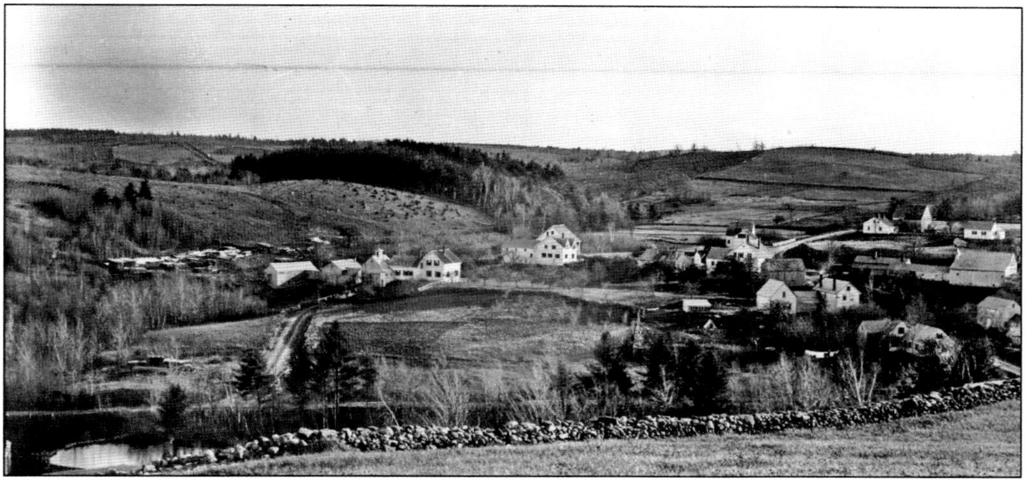

This 1890s photograph shows South Village with Loveland's Tub Mill just to the left of center. To the left of the mill, stacks of lumber that have been set out to dry can be seen. Of particular note is how little land is forested. Fields and orchards dominate the landscape.

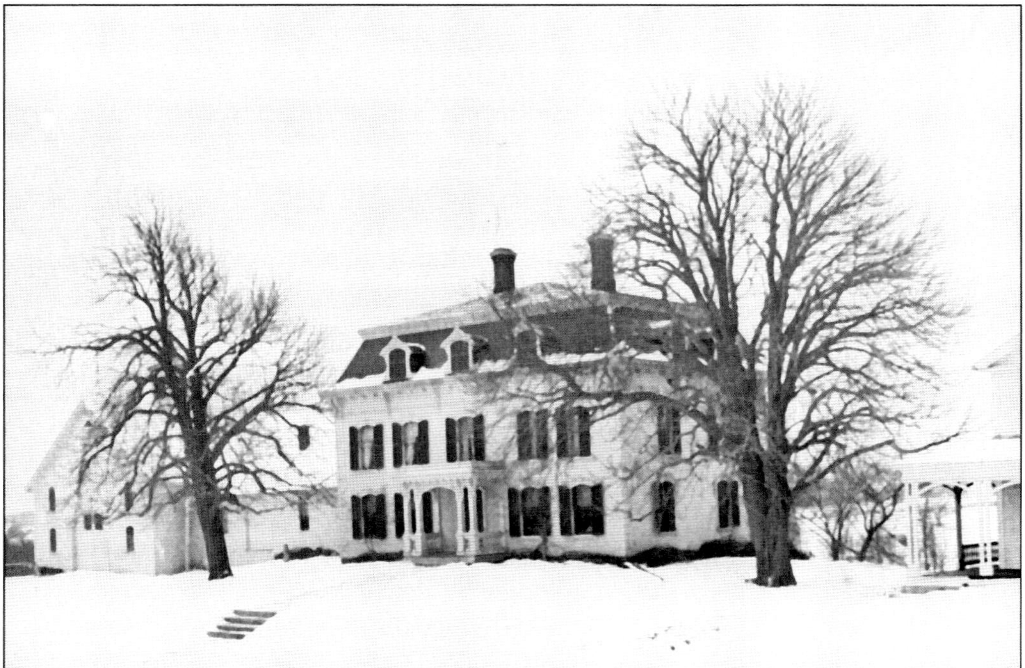

This elegant home with a mansard roof was once the F.W. Wright residence, later owned by George Gilbert. The home is pictured here after the state road was built (note the steps). There were stables where one could board horses or just stable them for the day. (Courtesy of Tom Dorward.)

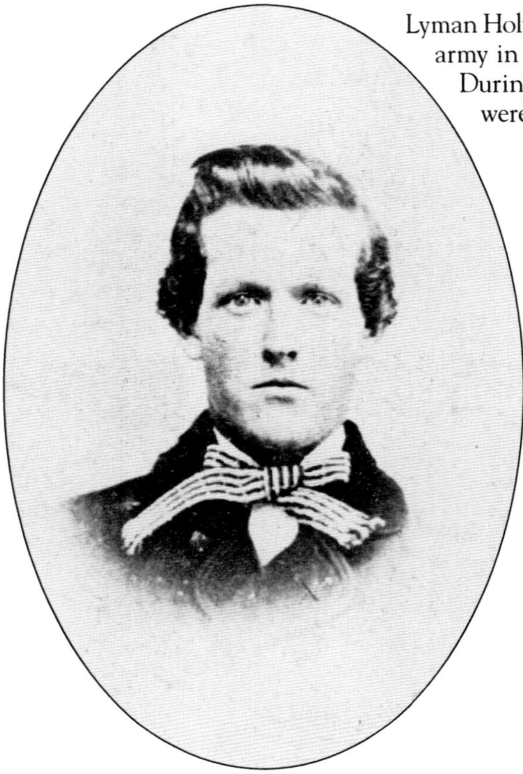

Lyman Holt, an Ashby farmer, was mustered into the Union army in 1862. He died of disease in Louisiana in 1863. During the Civil War, two-thirds of military deaths were due to disease rather than battle.

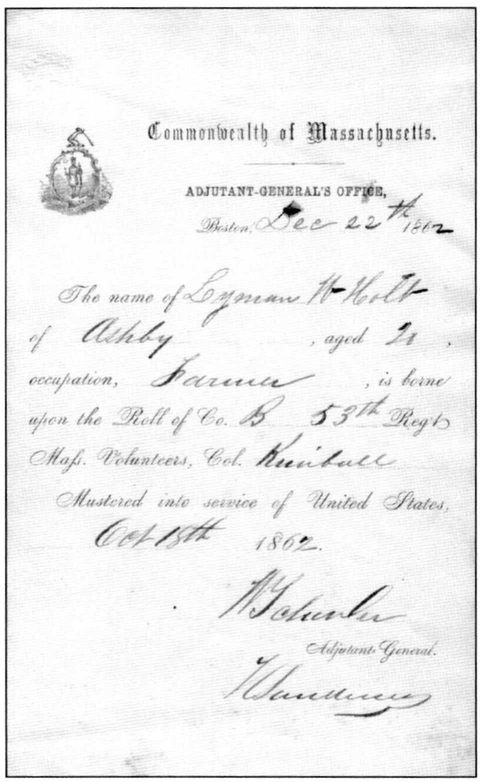

Commonwealth of Massachusetts.

ADJUTANT-GENERAL'S OFFICE,

Boston, Dec 22th 1862

The name of Lyman W Holt
of Ashby , aged 21 ,
occupation, Farmer , is borne
upon the Roll of Co. B 53th Regt
Mass. Volunteers, Col. Kimball
Mustered into service of United States,
Oct 18th 1862.

W Schouler
Adjutant General.

[illegible]

Pictured here are Civil War muster papers for Lyman Holt, marshaling him into the 53rd Regiment of Massachusetts volunteers. The town gave each volunteer $100, a bowie knife, and a Bible. There were 118 men from Ashby serving during the war; 18, including Holt, would perish in the conflict.

Robert W. Holmes was a private first class in the Engineer Corps who died in France on December 19, 1944, as a result of wounds sustained in action. (Courtesy of American Legion Post 361.)

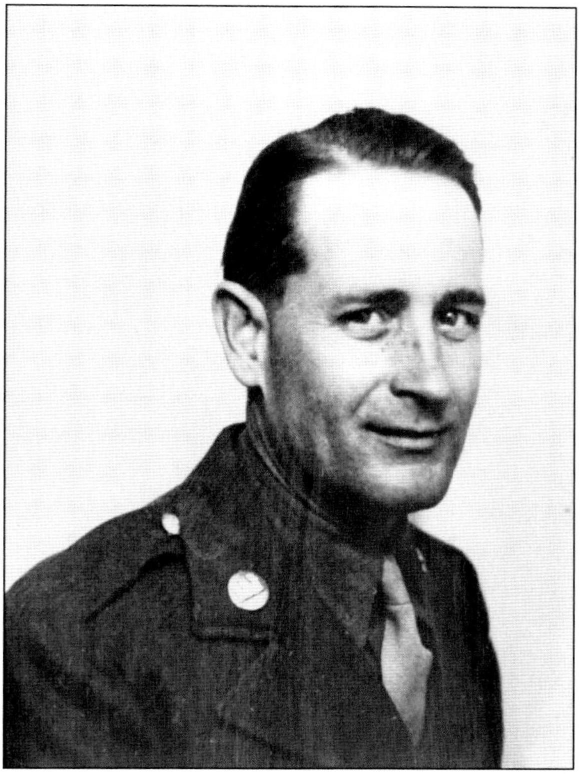

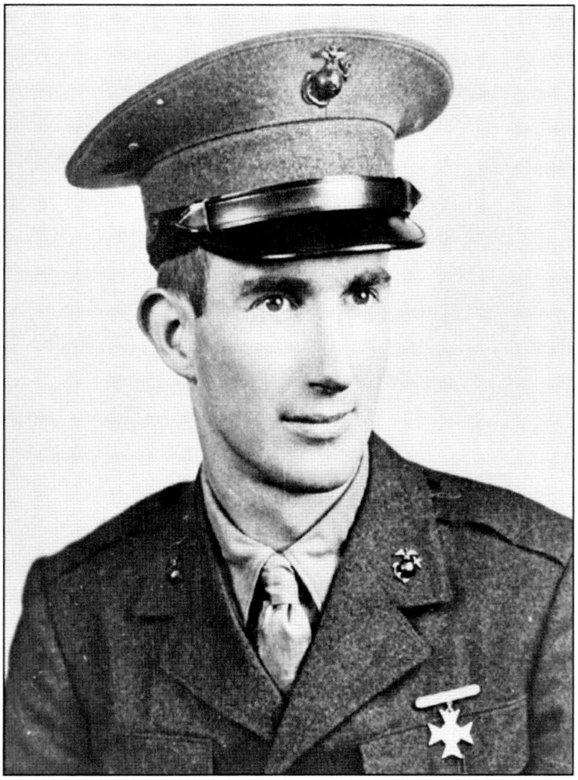

James D. Curran was a US Marine who was killed in action at Saipan, Northern Mariana Islands, on June 15, 1944, at the age of 24. (Courtesy of American Legion Post 361.)

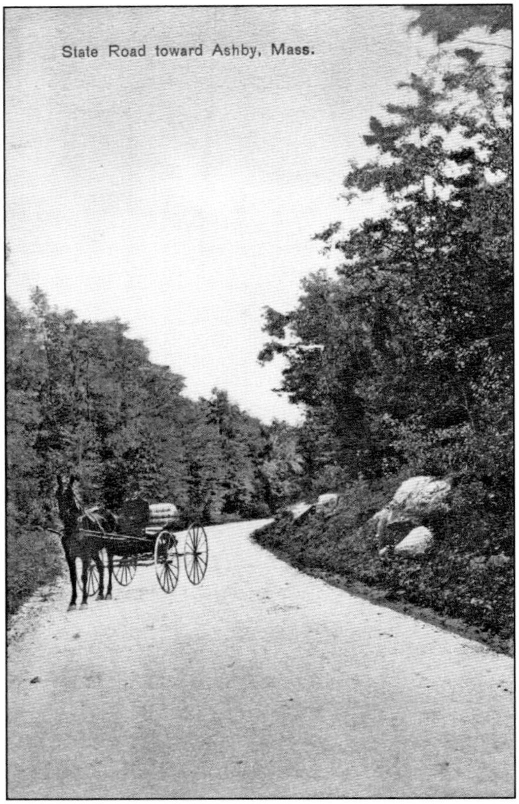

A new state road was cut from the easterly end of Main Street to Sheldon Bridge, making the trip by horse and buggy to and from Fitchburg more direct. (Courtesy of William and Katherine Stanwood.)

This photograph shows Main Street in the late 1960s. The Edwards-Wright house is on the right. A stately elm tree, common along Main Street before succumbing to Dutch elm disease, stands just before the house. The truck on the left side of the street is a Divco milk-delivery truck. (Courtesy of Tom Dorward.)

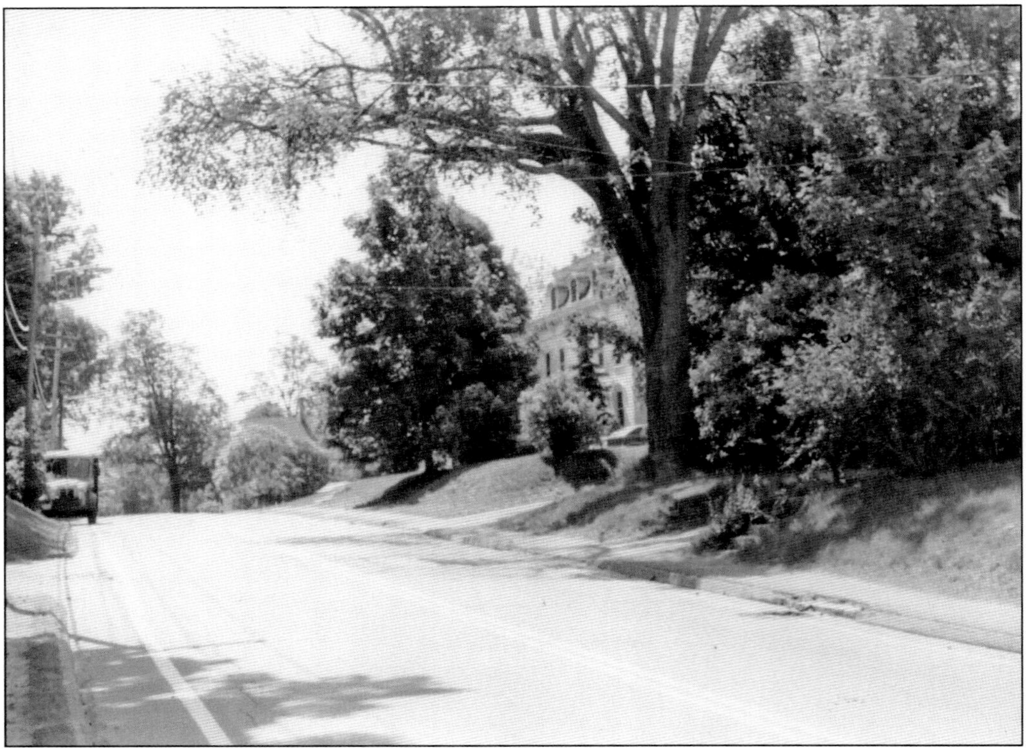

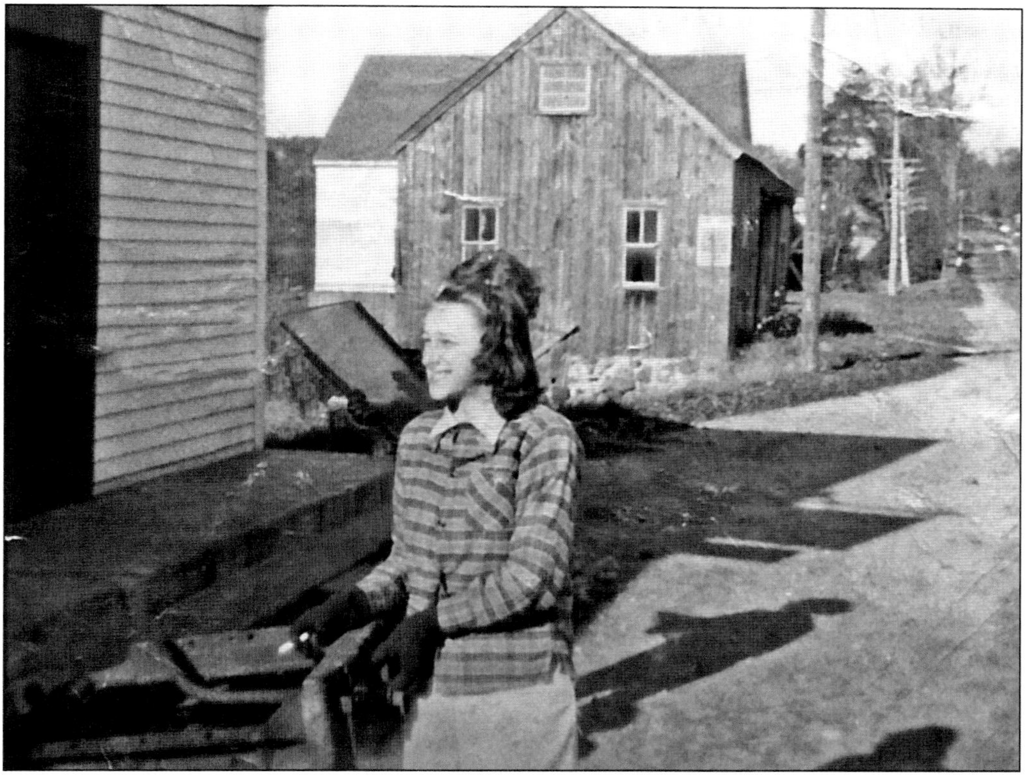

Renice Bennett collects scrap metal for the World War II war effort along upper Main Street in front of Burnap's Store. Ashby residents contributed to the war effort by collecting metal, sending letters and packages to soldiers, and raising vegetables in victory gardens. (Courtesy of Carol Bennett Lielasus.)

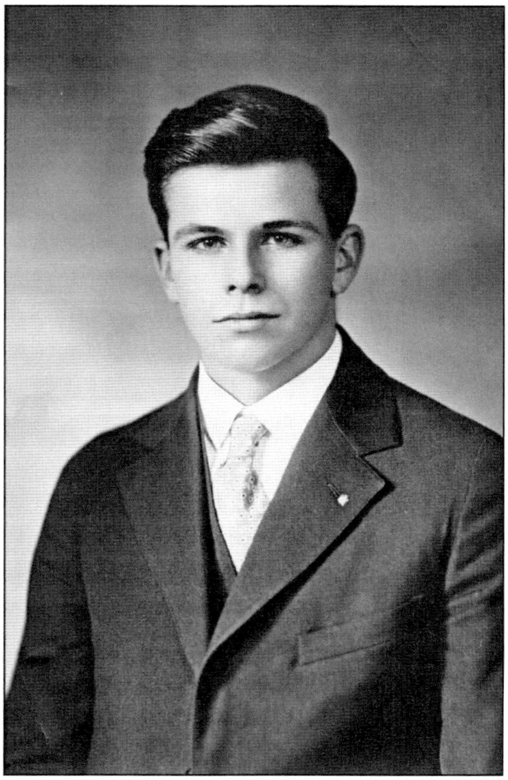

Louis Sears, seen here in 1925, became a fixture in town. He worked on Crocker's farm as an equipment operator. When the snow became so deep the town plow could not get through, Sears would be called to get Crocker's bulldozer and open up the road. He served as tax collector for many years, working from a rolltop desk in his home.

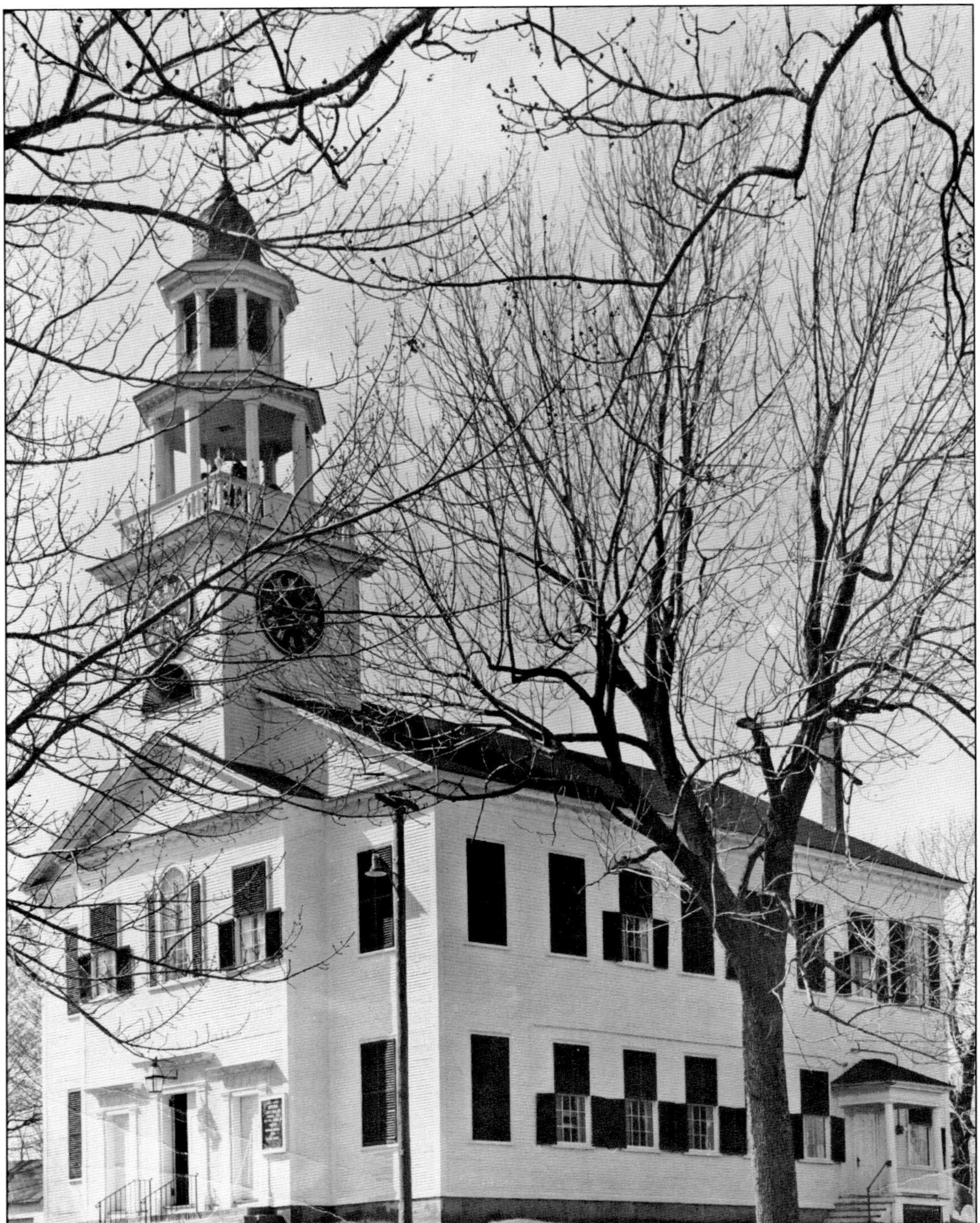

The First Parish (Unitarian Universalist) Church, originally Ashby's town meetinghouse, was built in 1809 to a pattern by architect Asher Benjamin. It houses both a Whitney and a Hammond organ, a bell in the belfry purchased from the Paul Revere foundry, and the Lewis Gould town clock. (Courtesy of Bill Arnold.)

John H. Willard was one of seven Ashby boys who organized the Ashby Band in 1887. The band grew from seven to 25 members over the next few years. Donations from residents allowed them to buy instruments and uniforms for the men in the band.

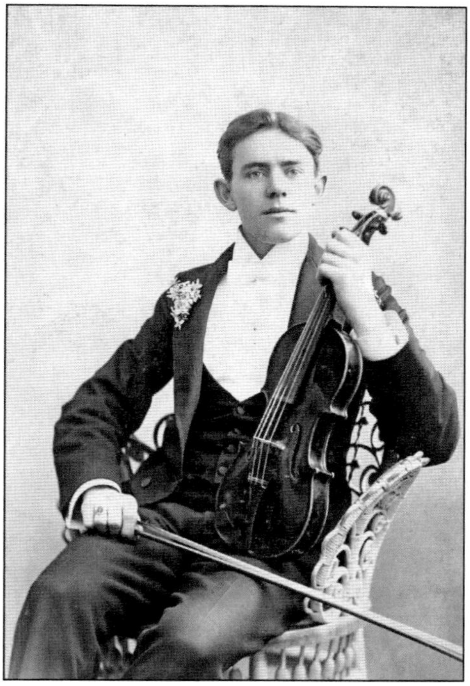

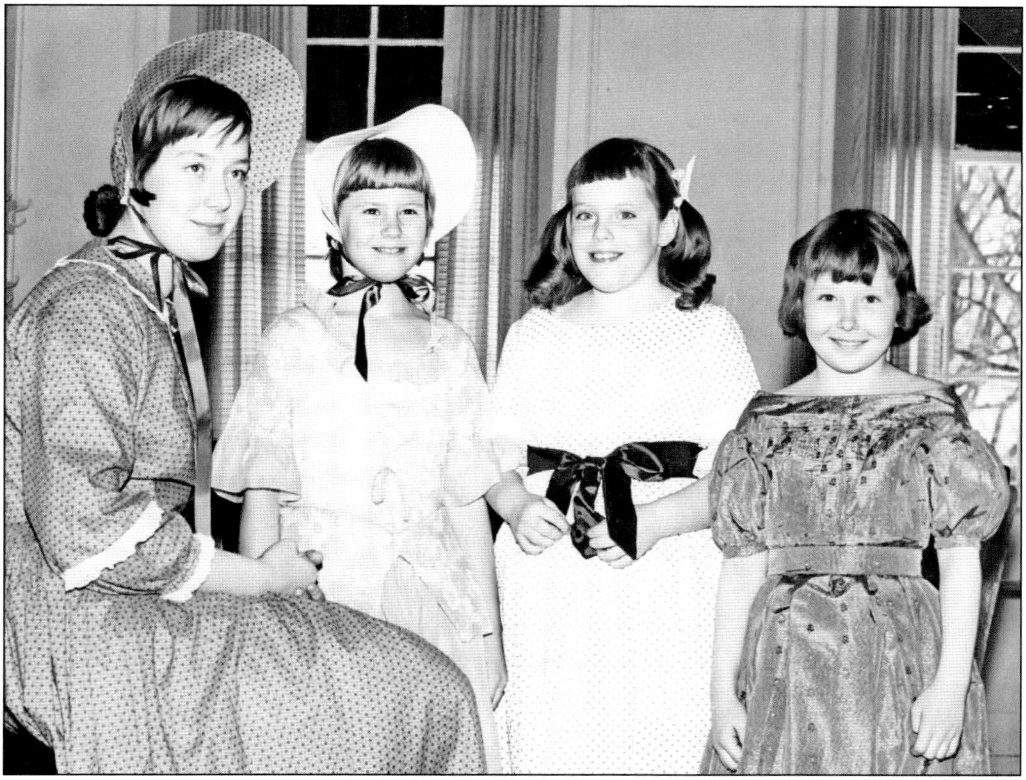

From left to right, Paula Varney, Beth Ann Lundberg, Susan Welch, and Deborah Seymour dress in colonial costumes to celebrate the many year-long events planned for Ashby's 1967 bicentennial. (Courtesy of Ashby Free Public Library.)

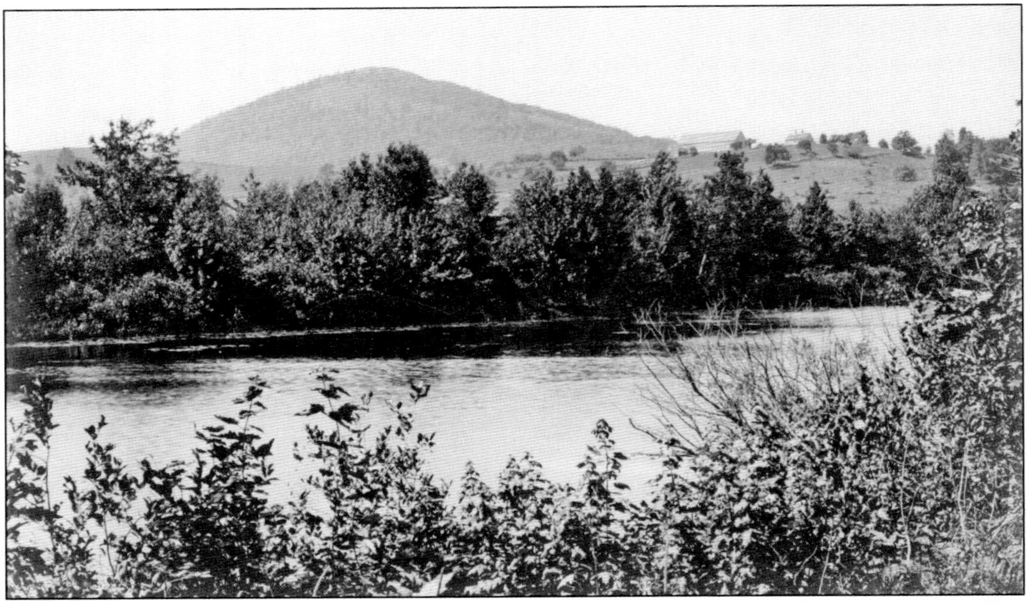

Mount Watatic has always been a prime destination for visitors to Ashby. Its summit offers panoramic views of surrounding countryside. It continues to be a popular hiking destination to this day. This 1930s photograph was taken from Watatic Pond.

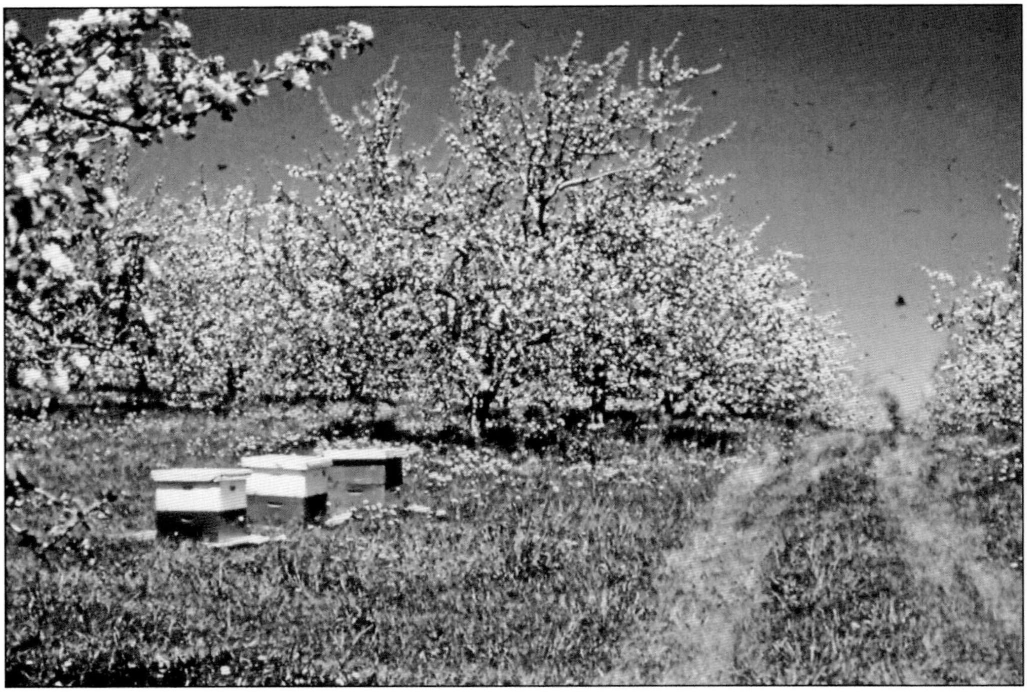

Beehives were kept at the Saari orchards to help pollinate the apple blossoms in the spring. The honey that was produced was an added bonus. (Courtesy of George Saari.)

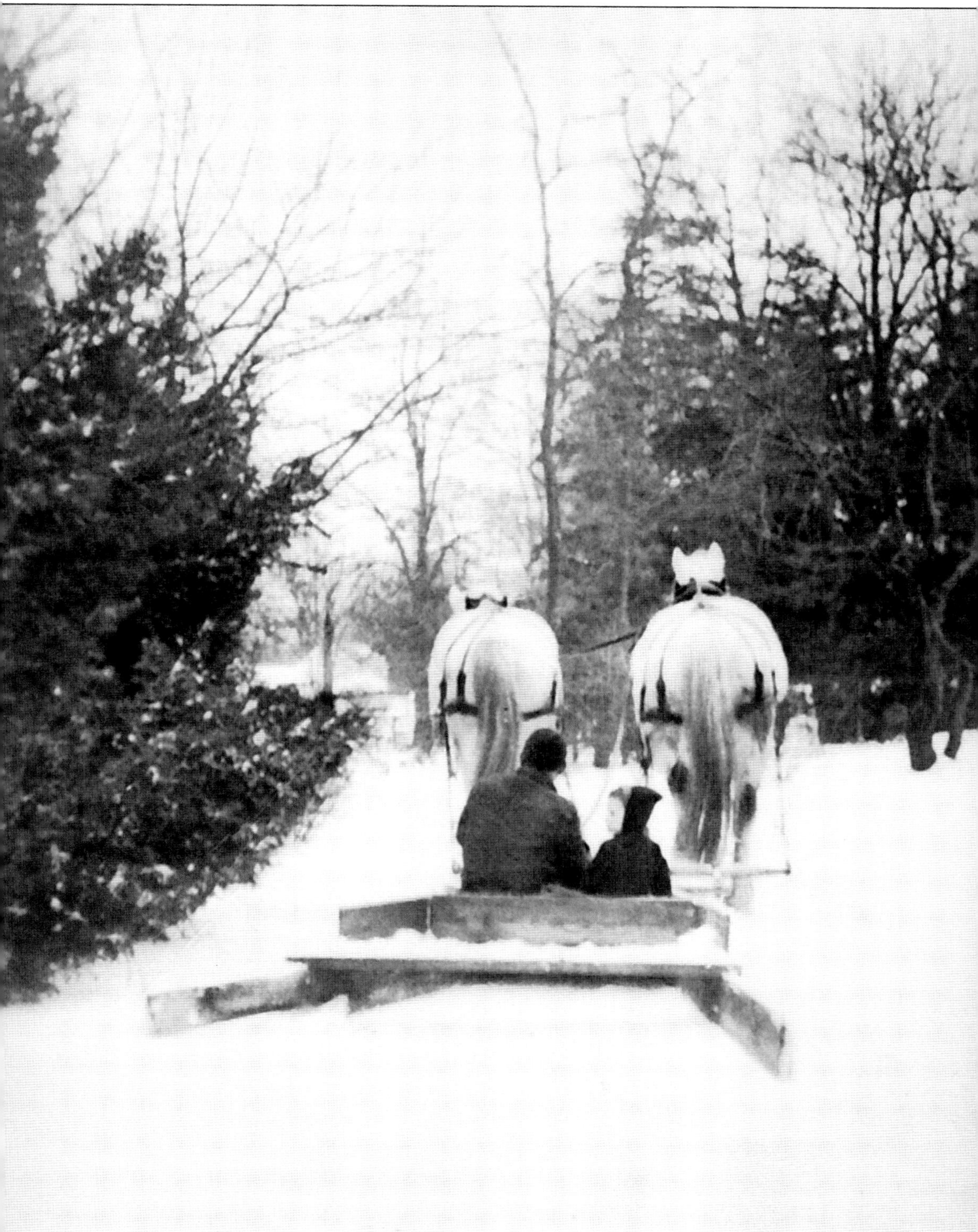

An Ashby citizen and his young friend are traveling home by horse-drawn plow, used to compact the snow for ease of traveling. (Courtesy of the Stacy family.)